"*Leading Healthcare IT: Managing to Succeed* provides a practical framework for understanding critical skills and concepts needed to be an effective healthcare IT leader."

Cara Babachicos
CIO Community Hospitals and Post Acute
Partners Healthcare

"Susan has done an excellent job of expressing and exploring the details of modern healthcare technology in our complex industry. This book is written for all audiences whether non-tech savvy senior leaders to the front-line health IT professional. Her work on consolidating difficult concepts into understandable and digestible information should be lauded. It has earned a place on my HIT resource shelf!!!"

Russell P. Branzell, FCHIME, CHCIO
President and CEO, CHIME

"Susan Snedaker has created a powerful guide to healthcare IT leadership. This book covers the fundamentals in a very approachable and actionable way. This should be required reading for everyone in healthcare IT today. Healthcare leaders who want to understand the IT environment would also benefit from reading this book. Snedaker distills and translates leadership concepts and applies them to healthcare IT. A much needed book in today's increasingly complex IT environment."

Geoffrey "Geoff" Brown, FCHIME
Chief Information Officer
Piedmont Healthcare

"*Leading Healthcare IT: Managing to Succeed* is a comprehensive guide to healthcare IT leadership. Susan Snedaker relies on her wide experience in IT to relay complex topics in a clear and understandable manner. Her recommendations provide readers with powerful, actionable tools. A recommended read for IT leaders and leaders to be!"

Leila Shehab, MA, MPA, PMP
HealthCare IT Professional

"In *Leading Healthcare IT: Managing to Succeed*, Susan Snedaker shows you how to *dramatically* increase the value you bring to your organization as an IT professional. Susan systematically demonstrates how to succeed as a CIO or IT manager, through specific business alignment and risk management activities. She seamlessly guides you through defining and communicating the true and complete business value of your IT organization in moving the organization forward. Susan shows you how to get your staff to perform at their best and deliver the most value to your organization. In fact, *every* IT professional should read this book; it certainly isn't just for healthcare IT!"

Chris Rima, MS, BS
IT Infrastructure
UNS Energy Corporation

"If genius is the ability to reduce the complicated to the simple, then Susan Snedaker needs to be commended boiling the complexities of healthcare information technology down to brilliant simplicity. Susan, in this book, has achieved a remarkable task of creating a powerful guide that covers the essentials of healthcare IT in bite-sized chunks of appetizing insights and fundamentals, in a manner that's easy to read, comprehend, with takeaways that are actionable. The well-curated references at the end of each chapter offer additional insights and opportunities to dig even deeper into specific areas of healthcare IT.

Susan provides a well thought through and laid out roadmap to navigate through the many facets of healthcare leadership and delivery. She outlines the specific new skills needed for healthcare IT leaders and shows that there is a method to the madness of melding together care delivery and information technology. *Leading Healthcare IT: Managing to Succeed* should be a staple for anyone looking to navigate the current and ever evolving intricacies of the healthcare IT landscape."

Rasu Shrestha, MD, MBA
Chief Innovation Officer, UPMC
EVP UPMC Enterprises
@RasuShrestha

Leading Healthcare IT

Managing to Succeed

Leading Healthcare IT

Managing to Succeed

Susan T. Snedaker, MBA, CISM, CPHIMS, CHCIO

CRC Press is an imprint of the
Taylor & Francis Group, an **informa** business
A PRODUCTIVITY PRESS BOOK

CRC Press
Taylor & Francis Group
6000 Broken Sound Parkway NW, Suite 300
Boca Raton, FL 33487-2742

© 2017 by Taylor & Francis Group, LLC
CRC Press is an imprint of Taylor & Francis Group, an Informa business

No claim to original U.S. Government works

Printed on acid-free paper
Version Date: 20160819

International Standard Book Number-13: 978-1-4987-7409-3 (Hardback)

Library of Congress Cataloging-in-Publication Data

Names: Snedaker, Susan, author.
Title: Leading healthcare IT : managing to succeed / Susan T. Snedaker.
Description: Boca Raton : Taylor & Francis, 2017. | Includes bibliographical references.
Identifiers: LCCN 2016032830 | ISBN 9781498774093 (hardback : alk. paper)
Subjects: LCSH: Medical informatics--Management. | Information storage and retrieval systems--Medicine--Management.
Classification: LCC R858 .S57 2017 | DDC 610.285--dc23
LC record available at https://lccn.loc.gov/2016032830

Visit the Taylor & Francis Web site at
http://www.taylorandfrancis.com

and the CRC Press Web site at
http://www.crcpress.com

This book is dedicated to my colleagues, past and present,
who have helped me become a better leader.

Contents

Acknowledgments

The following people contributed to the creation of this book by reviewing material and providing feedback or by contributing commentary (attributed to contributor in chapter).

A very special thank you to Chris Rima. Not only are you a respected information technology (IT) leader and one of the smartest people I know, but also you're a talented IT leader. I learn a lot from you every time we collaborate. Thank you for contributing to this book in all the ways you did.

To my reviewers—This book is infinitely better for having each of your unique perspectives and insightful comments. You made me look at things from different angles. You challenged me to clarify and condense my thoughts. Thanks to each of you.

Chris Rima. Chris was my technical editor in this book, though in an unofficial capacity, he fulfilled the role superbly. I incorporated his recommendations and I know the book is more focused and fine-tuned as a result. Chris is also my long-time collaborator and technical sounding board. His work experience and mine seem to run on a parallel path, and we often face the same challenges, though we work in different industries. Chris's input and perspectives are woven into the entire book. I owe Chris a debt of gratitude for all of his work on this book.

Chris is a senior IT leader at a major utility company. He has over 18 years of experience in IT operations management and has coauthored three books on IT operations and security. Chris has a BS degree in aerospace engineering from the University of Virginia and an MS degree in computer information systems from the University of Phoenix. He taught mathematics and IT courses at both the undergraduate and graduate levels from 1999 to 2007, and has previously worked as a program analyst for the Department of Defense.

Lisa Mainz. Lisa is a serial entrepreneur. She recently sold a company she built and ran successfully for 8 years. Lisa has some of the best management skills of anyone I know, so her insights, comments, questions, and corrections improved every chapter. She also suggested I use QR codes in the References section. I thought that was a great idea and incorporated it into the book. Lisa has an uncanny ability to take an idea and make it better. Thanks for all your support throughout this project.

Renee Paul. Renee is an experienced nurse and clinical leader whose career has spanned years in the military as a combat flight nurse to leadership positions overseeing large perioperative (surgical) departments. I was humbled by having witnessed her care and compassion for patients in a hospital setting and learned a lot from her simply by observing. Through Renee, I made the connection between healthcare IT and the clinical environment. Her perspectives regarding use of the electronic medical record (EMR) (Chapter 10) are a must-read for healthcare IT leaders. Thanks for reviewing the material as well as for lending your clinical perspective to the book.

Ron Bercaw. Ron is a Shingo Prize–winning author and Lean sensei. He is the president of the management consulting firm Breakthrough Horizons, LTD, which specializes in improving enterprises through the application of the Toyota Production System, commonly referred to as

Lean. Ron has over 20 years of experience consulting with healthcare, manufacturing, and military organizations in applying Lean principles. Thanks for your clarifying comments for Chapter 9.

Leila Shehab. Leila is a healthcare IT leader with impressive credentials. Leila has worked in various healthcare settings and held leadership positions in managed care, healthcare IT vendor space, and hospitals. She has extensive experience in project management, quality improvement, and implementation. She holds a license in International Economics from the University of Paris, an MS degree in economics from the University of Virginia, and an MS degree in public administration from the University of Arizona. She has been a certified project management professional with the Project Management Institute since 2003. Leila's review of each of the chapters provided excellent feedback, comments, suggestions, and industry insights that truly helped me tremendously. Thanks for your excellent guidance.

Preface

I tell friends and colleagues that I often write the book I want to read. It usually starts with a fairly exhaustive Internet search for a book on the topic I'm interested in. When my search fails to yield a suitable result, I begin thinking more deeply about what I need to know and how I might go about getting that information. That leads me down the path of reading and researching, which then becomes the foundation for the book I end up writing.

This particular book has been percolating in my mind for several years. As I have grown in my own IT leadership skills, I have continually wanted a "playbook" to turn to—something I could reference when I hit a tough problem, something I could review when I wanted to reenergize my team or my professional development, something I could turn to when situations were murky and confusing. This book is the playbook I've wanted to read for years. I hope it serves the same purpose for you as well.

One of the questions I'm often asked about books I've written, is whether I do all these things perfectly all the time. The answer is no, I don't. This book defines an almost perfect state. It provides best practices, tips, and suggestions for improvement. No one does all these things perfectly all the time.

This book is intended to provide straightforward, actionable information and guidance to help you navigate the complex and sometimes stressful world of healthcare IT; to remind you of core principles and fundamentals that will help you get back on track if you get stuck or sidetracked. Perhaps more than anything, it is an acknowledgment to everyone who works in healthcare IT that this is a challenging but vitally important profession. What we do matters.

Susan T. Snedaker

Author

Susan T. Snedaker, MBA, CISM, CPHIMS, CHCIO, is an experienced healthcare IT leader. She is currently an IT director of a large community hospital in Southern Arizona. Ms. Snedaker is also the organization's information security officer. She has worked in IT in a variety of roles from engineer to vice president for firms including Microsoft, Keane, and Honeywell prior to moving into healthcare. As a consultant, she worked with companies to develop and implement strategy, business plans, and operational improvements. Ms. Snedaker is a noted speaker and author of numerous books on topics including business continuity and disaster recovery, IT project management, and information security. For more about Ms. Snedaker, visit http://www.susansnedaker.com.

About the References Sections

At the end of each chapter is a References section where you will find citations for material mentioned in the chapter. You'll also find additional resources that are not specifically cited in the chapter. These are additional materials related to the topics in the chapter that you might want to read. They are provided for your convenience.

The QR codes for the items in the References section are included for items with lengthy URLs.

About.QR1

These QR codes were generated using https://forqrcode.com/ and can be read by any generic QR reader software. You can download a free QR reader app for your smartphone or tablet from your usual app store location.

For those of you who are security minded, these QR codes are safe to use.

Chapter 1

Healthcare Information Technology Overview

Overview

Healthcare information technology (HIT) has quickly become the center of many healthcare organization's operations. No longer relegated to the backroom or the data center, HIT is now front and center. Being a HIT leader has grown to be an increasingly pivotal role. The challenges we face are new, evolving, and accelerating. This book covers a variety of technology topics related to HIT, but it's not a technology management book. It also covers topics all managers need to know, but it's not a management book. Instead, we're focusing on skills, behaviors, and traits you'll need to succeed as a *leader* in HIT. We're going to review frameworks, structures, tools, and techniques leaders in this field are using today, as well as ideas that are beginning to gain critical mass. We'll also discuss behaviors and traits that drive success as a leader in IT, particularly in healthcare today. References at the end of each chapter will steer you toward additional resources if you want to take a deeper dive into a particular topic. Ultimately, this is intended to be a reference book, a playbook, filled with highly actionable information and advice that you can use when things get chaotic, when you get stuck, or when the path forward is unclear.

We begin by looking at the current state of HIT. We're going to briefly discuss current trends to set the context for why we need new leadership skills.

Background

A few decades ago, most healthcare organizations were using paper charts and had rooms full of files—charts, x-ray films, lab results, release of information forms, etc. Some early adopter organizations were using electronic systems for stand-alone functions, but there was no integrated electronic medical record (EMR, sometimes referred to as electronic health record or EHR) nor were there integrated systems delivering data across the organization. Fast-forward to today, most healthcare organizations are running some form of an EMR, many have integrated systems such as radiology information systems (RIS) and laboratory information systems (LIS), and some have secure mobile solutions for their organizations that provide patients access to their own health records and that allow care providers anytime, anywhere access to the EMR and other electronic systems.

From an industry perspective, HIT is still a bit behind the curve compared to other industries like finance or retail (e-commerce, specifically), but the complexity and criticality are unlike just about any other industry. This complexity inhibits rapid change and the sometimes risky adoption of new technologies—whether software, hardware, or infrastructure. When keeping patients safe and enhancing patient care are the ultimate objectives (vs. maximizing profits or selling more products), HIT work needs to be very well thought-out, well reviewed, and well implemented. Unfortunately, that often translates into a slower, more measured pace that lags other industries.

That does not mean, however, that rapid change is impossible. In fact, change accelerators, innovative HIT leaders and their collaborators, are found in many forward-thinking healthcare delivery organizations. These companies are partnering with technology vendors, researchers, data scientists, and other thought leaders to rethink and re-envision the way we provide care. This is widely referred to as *transforming* healthcare, and we'll discuss that in detail in Chapter 10.

In today's healthcare environment, there are many factors that impact healthcare delivery organizations of all types. Consider that a healthcare organization today must

- Meet federal, state, and local regulations
- Meet financial objectives to remain viable
- Be responsive to the health needs of its population
- Implement medical devices/systems that are often 10 or more years behind from a technology and security perspective
- Meet meaningful use (MU) requirements
- Evolve toward a value-based delivery and reimbursement system
- Interface or interoperate with community providers, state agencies, and federal entities
- Remain compliant for Joint Commission standards (or other accrediting organizations)
- Address the technology needs of a wide range of users (BYOD, mobile, cloud)
- Improve care while reducing length-of-stay (or similar metrics for non-acute care facilities)
- Prepare for personal medical technology advances
- Address the needs of an Internet-educated patient population (self-help, self-diagnosis, better informed)
- Deliver excellent customer service in a variety of areas including clinical care (physicians, nurses, physician assistants, patient care technicians, environmental/janitorial services, food services, facilities services), business office functions, scheduling, communication, social media and more
- Keep the patient safe and provide quality, compassionate care
- Stay competitive in a rapidly changing market

That's a long and varied list of requirements for any organization, and it's not exhaustive by any means. Each of these requirements typically involves HIT in one form or another.

In talking with managers and directors from a variety of healthcare organizations from around the globe, it is clear there are still many large technology hurdles to overcome. These include the reliance on legacy systems running obsolete operating systems, applications that can barely be supported anymore, managing mobility and data security, and leveraging new technology in innovative ways. These are all challenges facing HIT leaders today. While the pressure is immense, the opportunity to make a positive impact on the way care is delivered and on the lives of the patients we serve is exciting. For these reasons, there's probably no better place to work in IT today than in healthcare.

The Current State of U.S. Healthcare

It's important to stay up-to-date on the latest news and trends in healthcare because almost all of them impact your organization. As an IT leader, you need to be aware of the larger environment in which your company operates, and the pressures and drivers that cause the organization to make the decisions it does. Many of these developments end up impacting the work of the IT department.

For the past several years, healthcare providers have been working toward meeting the U.S. government's MU requirements. Beginning in 2011, the Medicare and Medicaid EHR incentive programs were created to encourage providers to adopt and demonstrate "meaningful use" of certified EHR technology. These incentive programs provided financial payments for organizations who successfully demonstrated MU. This also meant that HIT organizations needed to review MU requirements with clinical leaders to determine the best path forward. (For more on MU, visit the Centers for Medicaid & Medicare website, QR1.3.)

At the same time as working to meet MU standards, organizations also have to figure out how to begin moving from *volume-based to value-based reimbursement*. Examples of value or quality programs include reducing hospital-acquired conditions, reducing hospital readmissions, and implementing value-based purchasing programs. According to the U.S. government, by 2018, 90% of Medicare payments will be tied directly to quality programs and outcomes (Burwell, 2015, QR1.2). The challenge today is that we're in a transition state so providers and payers are having to straddle both payment models.

In addition to downward pressure on hospitals and other provider revenues, healthcare purchasers are also looking for ways to reduce costs. The government programs of Medicare and Medicaid are pushing down reimbursements and increasing requirements around outcomes. Many companies across all industries have implemented wellness programs in hopes of simultaneously improving their employees' health and reducing their costs for healthcare insurance for those employees. Finally, individual consumers are increasingly price-sensitive for insurance premiums through government, employers, or public exchanges. As consumers continue to become more informed about healthcare options, they continue to press for higher quality at a lower cost as well.

This is by no means a comprehensive look at the business of healthcare, but gives you some key data points that should spark some questions. As a HIT leader, are you paying attention to the larger picture? This is the new reality for your organization and its future. It's what your Board of Directors and your executive team are focusing on and responding to. So, it's important to be engaged and aware so you can participate in a significant way. These changes have significant IT implications. As a leader, you can rise up to meet the challenge if you're well informed.

Changing How Healthcare Is Delivered

We just explored the changing landscape of the business of healthcare. Now, let's look at another dimension, healthcare delivery, which in most cases is disjointed and fragmented. Just about anyone who has had a direct experience with the healthcare system has experienced some form of disconnect somewhere along the continuum of care. From lengthy waits in emergency departments to lack of coordination of care during a hospital stay to confusing discharge summaries to lack of follow-up after an acute care stay, these kinds of gaps and disconnects happen every day to millions of patients. This happens despite most healthcare organizations' serious commitment to delivering excellent patient care. There is increasing emphasis being placed on continuity of care and population health. If there is such a strong commitment, why do these gaps in care exist? There is a long list of interconnected reasons, but most experts in the industry point to

- A legacy model of care
- Increasing acuity (patients are sicker)
- Complexity of medical device and IT systems
- Regulations/requirements by payors (including the government) regarding reimbursement policies
- Changing demographics and social structures (elder parents no longer live with their families, children are more mobile and no longer live near elder relatives, etc.)
- Aging population

These are just some of the reasons why care is not always smoothly or consistently delivered despite best intentions.

Many organizations are implementing rigorous standards and protocols of work to improve patient care. Many are looking to workflows and standard practices such as Lean to provide a framework for sustainable change (for more on Lean IT, see Chapter 9). Many are also looking to information systems and technologies to assist in the consistent delivery of high-quality care. These efforts thus far have yielded varying levels of success, but they continue to evolve.

The Expanding Scope of HIT

There is an accelerating rate of change in the development and deployment of healthcare-related technologies. The list here is just a sampling of current topics being discussed in this industry. We'll pick up some of these threads again in Chapter 10.

1. EMR optimization
2. Interoperability
3. Mobility/Internet of Things/personal health devices
4. Medical device management and security
5. Information security and privacy beyond the data center
6. Business intelligence/big data/data analytics/quality reporting
7. Population health management
8. Telemedicine
9. Patient engagement
10. Cloud computing, technology, and security
11. Disruptive technologies (3D printing, for example)

The list is long and growing, and it's by no means exhaustive. While it's an incredibly exciting time to be in HIT, it can also be a bit overwhelming. Some describe the general environment as "drinking from a fire hose" and that's an apt description on some days. Though the rate of change is accelerating, there are things you can do as a HIT leader to bring order to the chaos (or at least tame it a bit) and achieve success. We'll discuss these topics throughout this book.

New Skills for HIT Leaders

With all the change HIT is undergoing, it only makes sense that we also need to significantly transform our leadership skills. In this section, we'll mention some of the prominent skills needed by new IT leaders, and we'll discuss these in more detail throughout the book.

Strategy

It wasn't long ago that discussions of strategy were confined to the boardroom. However, the reality today is that every leader of an organization needs to understand what strategy is and how strategy ties to organizational objectives. Some HIT leaders will be deeply involved in formulating the organization's strategies, while others will be responsible for translating strategy into operations. It's important to understand how your organization formulates its strategy and what that means in terms of the work you'll need to do in the IT department. You already know it's no longer acceptable to strive to "just keep the lights on." We need to be active collaborators and contributors to the overall transformation of the organization through the intelligent use of technology. We'll discuss strategy in more depth in Chapter 2.

Strategy Deployment

The term *strategy deployment* has a very specific meaning in the world of Lean. (Lean is based on the Toyota Production System [TPS] and is being used increasingly in healthcare. For more on Lean, refer to Chapter 9.) However, it can also be more generally used to describe the steps an organization must take to tie strategy to operations. It's not helpful to have brilliant strategies if no one can figure out how to run operations in a way that supports, enables, and ultimately delivers on those strategies. This is particularly true for HIT, which is at the center of so many strategic initiatives. As a HIT leader, you're the pivot point. Your departmental strategies and daily operational work must align with, and support, the larger organizational strategies.

Alignment

Alignment is a concept that might be new to you, but it goes hand in hand with *strategy* and *strategy deployment*. Alignment in HIT is the process of ensuring that all activities—from daily standard work to departmental initiatives to organizational projects—are aligned with the vision, mission, values, and strategy of the organization. For some HIT leaders, it's part of their daily work. They look at the assigned tasks of the team on a daily, weekly, and monthly basis to help ensure those activities are aligned. Perhaps the biggest challenge to alignment is that some HIT organizations run in a rather chaotic manner. There is lack of process, lack of standardization, and lack of time to thoughtfully plan activities. These are problems we'll discuss throughout the book and provide ideas and suggestions for addressing these. We'll discuss more about strategy, vision, and organizational alignment in Chapter 2.

IT Governance

Strategy and alignment are important for organizations and for IT, and these efforts need to be coordinated across the environment. Alignment needs to be systemic to be successful. It must be supported by strong and methodical IT governance. IT governance is the set of formalized processes to review, analyze, prioritize, and approve IT projects that have the potential to bring the highest value to the organization. Capabilities of healthcare organizations with respect to IT governance vary greatly. Some organizations have a very well-developed, consistent, and clear IT governance process. Others have the usual chaos and confusion that exists in organizations where just about anyone's "good idea" can become an IT project without any controls.

Ideally, an organization's IT governance councils would include executives, clinical and business leaders, and IT leaders setting the course for HIT. The problem facing most HIT organizations today is seemingly unlimited demand coupled with finite (or constrained) IT resources. This trend of expecting more from IT while containing (or reducing) IT costs is not going away any time soon. Clearly, one of the causes of stress for HIT leaders is managing this supply-and-demand challenge. One of the best antidotes is to have a clear, concise, and systematic process for managing IT demand. We'll cover IT governance in Chapter 3.

Value Generation

In an article entitled "What Is Value in Health Care" in a 2010 issue of *The New England Journal of Medicine*, Michael Porter, Harvard Business School professor and author, wrote

> Value should always be defined around the customer, and in a well-functioning healthcare system, the creation of value for patients should determine the rewards for all other actors in the system. Since value depends on results, not inputs, value in healthcare is measured by the outcomes achieved, not the volume of services delivered, and shifting focus from volume to value is a central challenge. (Porter, 2010, QR1.4)

Porter provides a very clear and succinct message around the fundamental shift in healthcare from volume- to value-based reimbursements. What does that mean for HIT? How should HIT leaders translate that into the work our teams do? How do we create value in IT?

If value depends on results and is measured by outcomes rather than processes, then we have a logical starting point for looking at how HIT value is created. Value is defined by the customer. An easy way to think about it is, would my end user be willing to pay for this service? If the answer is yes, you are delivering something of value. If the answer is no, you probably need to take a closer look. Ultimately, if you're not generating value for your organization, you're contributing to the problem, not the solution. In order to succeed in transforming healthcare, we need to find new and better ways to deliver value. We'll explore the concept of defining and delivering IT value in Chapter 4.

Marketing HIT

Yes, you read that right. Your IT leadership job includes marketing. Your team might be doing all the right things—you might be creating IT strategies that align with those of the organization; you might be delivering services that provide value; you might even be improving processes and reducing costs or eliminating risk through standardization—but if you do all that and no one knows about it, you've done a disservice to all you've achieved. Ensuring your efforts and accomplishments are seen, understood, and valued by the organization takes thought and planning. Many IT activities are not easily seen or understood, sometimes even by others in the department. Developing skills that will help educate the organization about the value you and your teams have delivered is key to long-term success. We'll discuss marketing IT in Chapter 5 and provide insights and ideas on how to approach this topic.

Inform, Involve, and Influence

Informing, involving, and influencing are all aspects of communication. As a HIT leader, you will need to fine-tune your communication skills across the board: face-to-face, phone, email, text, documents, and social media. Your success as a team member and as a leader is in large part dependent upon your ability to effectively communicate at all levels of the organization and in different contexts. We'll take a deep dive into communication skills for IT leaders in Chapter 6.

HIT Risk Management

Risk management is the area of practice related to ensuring the organization is prepared for all the bad things that might happen and has a plan for avoiding or addressing those things. IT activities, as we know, carry a certain inherent risk. Changes to systems, such as patches or new scripts, can cause unintended consequences. There are many other types of risk, though, that may not immediately come to mind. There are the financial risks of deploying a new IT system. There are organizational risks that you don't have the right skills or the right people on your teams to deliver in today's demanding environment. We'll discuss risk management further in Chapter 7.

Manage, Direct, and Lead

In this book, we're focused on skills IT leaders need to be successful. While basic management skills are fundamental to success as a manager, we don't go over these. There are thousands of great books and websites that will help you learn management fundamentals. Instead, we focus on the behaviors and traits needed to be a great manager, director, or leader. For our purposes, managers oversee the activities of teams of frontline staff. Directors typically manage managers, though there are some exceptions. Directing managers is a different skillset than managing frontline staff. We discuss some of the similarities and some of the differences. We also provide a roadmap to learning how to successfully direct the activities of multiple teams through managers. Finally, we'll look at leadership. Leaders are not leaders because their job title says manager or director. Leaders rise up within organizations because they see opportunities to make a positive difference. Whether that's an opportunity to unite a team of peers to solve a difficult problem or to take on a professional challenge with a positive attitude, leaders always emerge naturally. Certainly, leadership skills can, and should, be learned, but the leadership mindset is the required starting point. We'll discuss managing, directing, and leading in depth in Chapter 8.

Lean in HIT

Lean has been increasingly deployed in healthcare because it focuses on standardizing work, reducing waste, improving quality, and solving problems permanently. Lean is derived from the

Toyota Production System (TPS), which instilled a strong process in automotive production. As we face the heightened demands to move from volume- to value-based care, we need to really hone in on generating value at all levels of the organization. To grossly simplify it, Lean is a way of approaching work. It includes a management system as well as tools and methods. This is important because many newcomers to Lean grab a hold of some of the easy-to-use tools and believe they are implementing Lean. While these tools may help improve quality or reduce waste, for example, the changes are usually not sustainable without a mindset and a leadership behavior set (Lean management system) to support them. We'll discuss Lean and, in particular, Lean in HIT in Chapter 9.

Fast Forward

We've taken a quick run through the chapters of this book to give you some insight into what lies ahead. At the end of the book, in Chapter 10, we tie all of these concepts together. We look more deeply at the changes and initiatives that are happening in HIT today. We look at how we, as IT leaders, can help drive transformative change in the industry. The story really just begins when Chapter 10 ends. Putting to use the information and skills presented is where the next chapter begins. We'll leave you with a great starting point as well as a playbook full of tips, suggestions, and information you can refer back to as you head into the next big challenge.

Summary

HIT is a dynamic, complex, and challenging field. It's what draws most of us to HIT. The opportunity to solve difficult problems, to implement new systems, and to have a positive and potentially transformative impact on patient care is exciting. It's also daunting. Without any guidance or support, some HIT professionals get lost or get burned out. This book is intended to counteract that by providing actionable information in each chapter to help you grow as a leader. Throughout this chapter, we've highlighted some of the new trends and new fields emerging within HIT. No doubt these topics and trends will change over time, but some of the enduring truths will remain constant. HIT departments need to be closely aligned with their organizations; they need to deliver more value faster and at a lower cost than ever before. HIT leaders need to have strong business, marketing, communication, and management skills. We'll explore these concepts in the remaining chapters of this book.

References

For more on this topic, visit http://susansnedaker.com/leading-hit.

QR1.1

Burwell, Sylvia Mathews, Secretary of the U.S. Department of Health and Human Services, "Progress Towards Achieving Better Care, Smarter Spending, Healthier People," January 26, 2015, http://www.hhs.gov/blog/2015/01/26/progress-towards-better-care-smarter-spending-healthier-people.html#.

QR1.2

Centers for Medicare & Medicaid, "Electronic Health Records (EHR) Incentive Programs," Last updated April 14, 2016, https://www.cms.gov/Regulations-and-Guidance/Legislation/EHRIncentivePrograms/index.html.

QR1.3

Porter, Michael E., Ph.D., "What Is Value in Health Care?" *New England Journal of Medicine*, 2010; 363:2477–2481, December 23, 2010. doi: 10.1056/NEJMp1011024, http://www.nejm.org/doi/full/10.1056/NEJMp1011024.

QR1.4

TEKSystems, "2016 Annual IT Forecast: Executive Summary," https://www.teksystems.com/-/media/teksystems_com/Files/Research/Executive%20Summaries/TEKsystems-2016-IT-Forecast-Executive-Summary.pdf?la=en.

QR1.5

Chapter 2

Strategy, Vision, and Alignment

Overview

Strategy, vision, and alignment are three key aspects of successfully leading a healthcare IT (HIT) department. Strategy development is one of the most important activities an organization can undertake because it sets the future direction of the business. Peter Drucker, the renowned management expert, said this: "Strategic planning is not a box of tricks, a bundle of techniques. It is analytical thinking and commitment of resources to action." Drucker describes the process as a systematic set of decisions that should answer the question, "What should we do today to be well positioned for success tomorrow?" (Drucker, 2004, p. 342). This is the essence of strategic planning. It sounds relatively simple, but it's often a challenging task. This is especially true in healthcare, where the landscape is influenced by so many factors and where change is constant. Most healthcare organizations have well-developed mission statements that are used to drive strategy. Vision statements are forward-thinking, aspirational statements. Mission, vision, and strategy must all align in order to drive the organization forward in a coherent manner. These all directly impact the work of the IT department.

Organizational Strategy

Let's start with what organizational strategy is *not*. Strategy is *not* doing the same things as your competitors only slightly better. That's operational effectiveness, which is certainly important, but it's not strategy. Strategy involves choosing different activities or doing things differently from your competitors. An often used business school example is Southwest Airlines. Certainly, their boarding process was different from other airlines when they introduced it; but it wasn't a strategy, it was an operational improvement. Over the years, other airlines have copied that boarding model. Southwest was also known for its very friendly and helpful staff—from gate agents to flight attendants. Those are operational efficiencies or activities that can be copied. However, Southwest Airlines also introduced short hop flights and low-cost airfares—those became the foundation of its competitive advantages and reflected the company's strategy. The internal email may have read something like "let's grab the short hop flights the other guys don't want and let's find ways to develop extraordinarily loyal customers." Those form the foundation of Southwest's competitive advantage in the airline industry.

According to Michael Porter, Harvard Business School professor and a leading authority on business strategy development, strategy is the process of choosing a "unique and valuable position rooted in systems of activities" that are more difficult to copy or match than operational effectiveness. Strategy involves deciding what to do, and what not to do, and how to turn these decisions into competitive advantages (Porter, 2011, p. 61).

Healthcare organizations operate within an interesting set of requirements. First and foremost, they must provide competent patient care within regulatory requirements and guidelines. However, they must also provide those services in a sustainable manner, whether for-profit or nonprofit. For-profit organizations must generate revenue and bottom-line profits to the corporate entity and, by extension, to their shareholders. Nonprofit organizations must generate enough revenue and net operating income to maintain operations and fund future endeavors. In all cases, financial health is a requirement for remaining competitive. Healthcare competition is sometimes local to a geographic region, as is the case for primary care physicians, ambulatory surgery centers, or community hospitals. Competition is sometimes broader such as when we start looking at regional providers, specialists who may see patients from around the country, and healthcare systems that operate in large geographic areas. Regardless of the size and financial model of your organization, it must find and maintain a competitive advantage to differentiate itself from other organizations.

Healthcare organizations today are faced with regulatory and reimbursement requirements that are driving some of the strategic decisions of the organization. For example, the imperative to move to value-based reimbursement is causing many organizations to reexamine how healthcare is delivered in a very fundamental way. Each organization responds to these outside pressures differently, but each must respond to the same pressures. Strategic direction must include responses to these environmental changes, yet they cannot be simply reactionary. Some of the strongest healthcare organizations take a long view and set direction. They're the organizations most point to as leaders in the field. The trends discussed in Chapter 1 are impacting all healthcare organizations, and those that develop strategies incorporating these trends will likely find the greatest success. Rather than lamenting changes being "forced" on them, these leading organizations embrace those changes as opportunities for innovation and transformation as the foundation of competitive advantage and long-term viability.

To those outside, it sometimes seems these organizations have some way of forecasting the future. In fact, they spend time analyzing the regulatory and competitive horizon, and they make smart decisions that shape their future. This is the essence of effective strategic planning.

In your role as a HIT leader, you may not be involved at the organization's highest level of strategic planning. Hopefully your executive team includes a CIO (or equivalent role) who participates in the development of the organizational strategy. In whatever manner that may occur, once strategy is set and communicated, your job within IT is to analyze the strategy in terms of IT and develop a vision and strategy that are aligned with the organizational direction.

HIT Vision

Our focus in this chapter is not organizational strategy, but HIT strategy. However, before we delve into IT strategy, we will start with IT *vision* because it really drives strategy. The vision

Figure 2.1 Organizational and department vision and strategy.

should be "a clear and compelling point of view, for how IT can take their enterprise to the next level. ... It must fully align with the goals and vision of the enterprise as a whole" (Broadbent, 2005, p. 23). As you can see in Figure 2.1, you can develop a vision for IT based on the vision and strategy of the organization. Using these as starting points ensures that your IT vision and strategy are aligned with the larger organization.

Once you've developed vision and strategy, you need to review the organizational strategies to confirm you remain aligned. It's easy to get so wrapped up in developing IT strategies that you lose sight of the specific strategies of the organization. Once you're sure your IT strategies align with those of the organization, you can continue your planning processes. If they're not aligned, this is the perfect time to step back and revise your strategies.

Developing Your IT Vision with Organizational Direction

Let's assume your organization has a strategy and it's been well defined and communicated. (We'll address the lack of organizational strategy and vision in the section Developing Your IT Vision without Organizational Direction.) Your starting point is to look at where the organization is headed and what key inputs and drivers have been considered, and to develop your IT vision and strategies from there. By looking at your IT capabilities, you can determine how they can be leveraged to drive organizational strategies. If a vision for IT has been previously created, you don't need to start from scratch. Instead, review the vision to see if it is still relevant. Strategies will change from time to time, but they shouldn't change weekly. You can look at prior IT strategies, if they exist, to see if they are still aligned with organizational strategies.

In developing your IT strategies, you'll need to look externally and internally. For example, sometimes IT is a major part of a larger initiative such as when the organization plans to acquire 20 new clinics in a five-state region within the next three years. Clearly, there are many IT aspects to a plan like that, and your IT vision and strategy will need to align. For example, your vision might then be "to fully leverage IT resources to seamlessly integrate new and existing systems, providing an outstanding end-user experience and ensuring the best service at the lowest cost." That is certainly aligned with an acquisition strategy.

However, there are also times that you may want to lead your organization with technology. Your vision might be "to provide anytime, anywhere IT services to seamlessly meet the needs of the organization." That probably means you don't care whether your data live in your data center or a cloud provider's data center. It means you will look for strategies that align with that vision and support the organization's strategy, say, for connected care (telemedicine, telehealth, etc.).

Developing Your IT Vision without Organizational Direction

Not all companies develop a vision of their ideal future state. Not all are good at developing or communicating strategy. Sometimes, they don't want to discuss strategy too widely because they are operating in a very competitive market. For these reasons, you might be working in an organization that has not clearly communicated strategy. That leaves you at a disadvantage when trying to align IT work with the organization.

Broadbent and Kitzis (2005) in *The New CIO Leader* point to "strategy artifacts" as a clue. These are things like statements made in meetings, conversations with executives, press releases, and emails that point to strategy. It's like astronomers who can determine that a planet or object exists in space because of the changes in the gravitational pull around those objects. They can't see those objects, but they can see the impact those objects have in space. Similarly, you can look for the "gravitational pull" of strategic objects in your environment. For example, take a look at the operational projects, tasks, and work being done across the organization. You may be in meetings or hear about meetings that involve new physician practices, new locations, new service lines, new acquisitions, or new cost-cutting initiatives. You can assume these reflect the organization's wishes even if they are not identified as strategies. Is there a theme? Are there common elements you can build upon? Are there technology platforms that would impact all or many of these initiatives? From there, you can develop your IT vision and strategy to align with those activities you know are underway or are planned in the future. It's imperfect at best, but it is better than having no strategy and no direction. Operating without a vision and strategy may not have an immediate negative impact, but it will certainly lead to less organized work in the IT department and more frustration on the part of your staff who are struggling to connect the dots between what they do and what the organization is doing.

In a worst-case scenario where there is simply a lack of any clear direction, you may choose to spend the upcoming year reducing costs through consolidating technology platforms and applications, work to fully leverage the assets currently in place, and develop a technology roadmap looking three to five years out that incorporates cloud and mobile technologies to increase efficiency, reliability, and availability while reducing cost. These are all operational initiatives driven by an implied vision that could be stated as "Become the most efficient IT department possible by fully leveraging assets and removing those costs that are not specifically adding value to the organization." This is certainly not ideal, but it's a starting point.

Defining Your IT Vision

Thus far, we've discussed how to proceed with and without an organizational vision and strategy. Now, we'll turn our attention to developing our IT vision and strategy. A *vision* is an aspirational statement. That is, it points to where you ideally would like to be, how you would like to operate, how you would like to contribute to the overall mission of the organization. For clarity, a *mission statement* explains the purpose of the organization, the reason it exists. A *vision* statement is what your company (or your department) wants to become in the future. So, when crafting your vision statement, think future state. The following are vision statements from a variety of organizations to give you ideas about what your vision statement might look like.

Cleveland Clinic's Vision Statement
Striving to be the world's leader in patient experience, clinical outcomes, research, and education.
(https://my.clevelandclinic.org/about-cleveland-clinic/overview/who-we-are/mission-vision
-values, viewed November 27, 2015)

Kaiser Permanente Vision Statement
Our vision at Kaiser Permanente is to be a leader in total health by making lives better. (https://healthy
.kaiserpermanente.org/health/poc?uri=center:quality-safety, viewed November 27, 2015)

Tucson Medical Center Vision Statement
Our vision is to enhance the quality of life and overall health for the people of Southern Arizona.
(http://www.tmcaz.com/mission-vision-values, viewed November 29, 2015)

Now, let's look at a few vision statements specific to IT departments.

Boston College Information Technology Services Department Vision Statement
*Information Technology Services will be recognized as a high-performance team providing technol-
ogy excellence that advances learning, teaching, research, and student formation in alignment
with Boston College's mission and goals.* (http://www.bc.edu/offices/its/mission.html, viewed
November 27, 2015)

University of Idaho Information Technology Services Department Vision Statement
*Information Technology Services is committed to its leadership role of fostering the University's goals
through being the partner of choice for technology advancement and innovation.* (http://www
.uidaho.edu/its/strategic-plan/purpose, viewed November 27, 2015)

**University of Washington Academic Medical Centers Information Technology Vision
Statement**
We will be known as a national leader in healthcare information technology. (https://home.mcis
.washington.edu/amcis/documents/amcis_vision.asp, viewed November 29, 2015)

Health Resources and Services Administration (HRSA) Vision for Healthcare IT
*A health care delivery system that uses Health Information Technology and Continuous Quality
Improvement to empower all patients and health care providers for optimal health outcomes.*
(http://www.hrsa.gov/healthit/toolbox/oralhealthittoolbox/introduction/vision.html, viewed
November 27, 2015)

As you can see, the IT vision statements are clearly aspirational and they also speak to alignment
with organizational objectives. Your vision statement should clearly articulate what you want the
department to look like in three to five years and (possibly) how it will be different from what it is today.

Here are four generic examples that might also help you formulate yours. If you'd like to use
one of these (or a version of one of these), feel free to do so. The point is not necessarily to craft
an entirely new, innovative vision, but to create one that resonates with *your* vision for your team
within your organization.

1. We will provide reliable technology and world-class services that support and transform the
   care of our patients.
2. We will improve the health of our community by deploying the right technologies and services at the right time in the right way for our providers, our staff, and our patients.
3. We will strive to become the leading healthcare provider in the community through the
   thoughtful, intelligent, and timely implementation of technology and service.
4. We will be the most innovative, aligned, and reliable information technology services
   department in healthcare today.

Develop Your IT Vision Statement

Before you read further, take a moment to try crafting a quick vision statement for your department. It doesn't need to be the one you ultimately use, but it will give you a sense of what your vision statement might look like. As a leader, you should develop a vision and be able to share that vision with your team. As a leader, you paint the picture of the desired future state and engage the team in developing the strategies and tactics that will deliver that future. As you read through this book, you may want to start a notebook (electronic or paper) and capture some key thoughts you have so you begin developing your playbook. You could start with this vision statement.

You may develop the vision on your own or with your team—it will depend on how your organization runs best. Regardless of the source of the vision, the next step is crucial—socializing the vision and gaining buy-in. If the team helped develop the vision, they already feel some ownership. If they did not participate in this aspect, begin discussing the vision statement, getting input and feedback, and perhaps modifying it somewhat based on that input. If the connection to vision is weak, it will be more challenging to work with the team to develop strategies that are aligned and compelling for the organization.

Develop Your IT Strategy

Now, let's turn our attention to developing an IT strategy aligned with the organization and the supporting IT vision. If you've never developed a strategy before, it can seem daunting. There are major consulting companies that make millions of dollars advising companies on strategy development, but many companies do just fine developing strategy on their own. There are thousands of books and online articles you can read about strategy, but one of the best modern-day primers on strategy comes from Michael Porter. He's a renowned professor, lecturer, and thought leader at Harvard Business School. He specializes in strategy, and a lot of his material is available online. Of course, he's published scores of books, so you can search for one of his books on strategy as well. If you want to really understand strategy, a good all-in-one primer is *HBR's 10 Must Reads on Strategy: Featuring "What Is Strategy" by Michael E. Porter*. This is a compilation of 10 articles on strategy, and it will give you a solid foundation for developing your IT strategy. The full citation is listed in the References section at the end of this chapter.

To develop your IT strategy, you'll need to set aside some time to think and plan. Whether you do this with your executive team, your IT team, or a small group of strategic thinkers is up to you. The key question you'll need to ask and answer is this: what systematic set of activities can we undertake that will support the organization's strategies? There is no one-size-fits-all answer, but HIT departments are all facing the same kinds of challenges, so you can look to your industry peers for ideas and input if you're having trouble identifying your strategy.

Table 2.1 shows some examples of organizational strategies and possible IT strategies to help you begin thinking about your strategy.

In all cases, you can see that strategy describes what you are trying to accomplish, and sometimes it describes how you'll accomplish this at a high level. It is not detailed or tactical. For example, you might want to improve revenue cycle capabilities as a tactic to meet a strategy to improve financial stability of the company. This describes what you're going to do (improve revenue cycle), but it doesn't describe any detail beyond that. There are many ways you could improve your revenue cycle activities from an IT perspective. You could do a survey of existing applications to analyze usability, number of clicks, application speed, etc., to determine how well the applications perform

Table 2.1 Mapping Organizational and IT Strategies

Organizational Strategy/Plans	*IT Strategy*
Strategy: Increase financial resources for future growth opportunities. *Tactic*: Reduce payables backlog by hiring third party vendor.	Improve electronic medical record (EMR) usability. Improve revenue cycle capabilities.
Strategy: Improve financial performance to position company for acquisition. *Tactic*: Delay non-essential projects for 6 months.	Reduce IT infrastructure and application cost by 25%.
Strategy: Expand regional presence to increase market share by 20% over 5 years. *Tactic*: Expand physician group by 50 practitioners.	Enable EMR modules to support new provider types. Enable secure, mobile technologies.
Strategy: Strengthen long-term viability and expand market share by merging with ABC Healthcare System. *Tactic*: Merge two hospitals into one system.	Implement single EMR to replace many stand-alone applications. Streamline infrastructure to improve throughput for both locations.

today. You could survey your customers to find out their pain points. You could look for ways to streamline workflows in the applications or create interfaces to automate data transfer. These are some of the tasks you could undertake to improve revenue cycle within the IT department.

Let's look at another example. Your organization wants to merge with another organization as a growth strategy. What would an effective IT strategy be? One possibility would be to implement a single EMR (rather than support two) or perhaps to streamline infrastructure to reduce cost and eliminate redundancy. Again, these IT strategies are informed by the organization's direction.

Though the example in Table 2.1 shows organizational and *potential* IT strategies, what's missing are specifics in the IT strategies. It's important to quantify your strategic initiatives so you know that you're hitting the target. This may include specific metrics (reduce by $X, increase by Y%, etc.), or it may include specific success statements. You will need to be clear on what success looks like.

Whether or not your organization has a clear and well-defined strategy, you can formulate IT strategies based on several fundamental drivers in healthcare. You can choose to develop a strategy around reducing costs (such as moving from capital investments to cloud-based services). You can develop technical capabilities strategies (such as becoming the leader in mobile HIT). You can develop a strategy around hiring and retaining the talent you'll need for the next three to five years based on how technology is evolving. You can develop a mobile strategy or a patient engagement strategy based on existing or needed technologies. You can choose to work solely on streamlining IT services to reduce cost, reduce variation, and improve service levels. While that may sound rather mundane or tactical, a strategy to streamline operations is almost always appropriate. In other words, you won't lose your job or find yourself horribly off track regardless of whether the organization has a strategy or not.

Finally, if your organization does not have IT governance or you are often required to change direction (weekly or monthly), choosing a simple strategy that is not directly impacted by frequent change is likely to yield the greatest success. We'll address ways to improve IT governance in Chapter 3 and that may help you reduce chaos and develop a more effective strategy.

Strategic direction typically focuses on *people* (employees, customers), *process* (customers, services), *technology*, and *financials*. You may want to focus your strategies on these defined areas and select only two or three. If your vision statement is "Become the best place to work in healthcare IT," then a strategy such as "Improve employee retention to reduce turnover by 50%" can be effective even without clear organizational guidance. Due to the cost of turnover, this would certainly support a company's financial goals. If your vision is "Become a highly efficient and effective IT organization," then "reduce hardware and software contract costs by at least 15%" is a strong, measurable strategy that can drive specific operational tasks.

As you can see, tying these statements to your vision is crucial. Your strategy should provide high-level statements about how you will achieve your vision. If there's a disconnect between your vision and your strategy, you'll simply stall out. To summarize, your vision should provide the *emotional* connection and your strategy should provide the *practical* connection.

HIT Strategy Deployment

Once you have developed your vision and strategy and have checked to ensure you are aligned with organizational goals, you can begin defining the tasks and actions needed to achieve your objectives. Figure 2.2 shows the flow of defining these steps. Each IT strategy task may have numerous steps, tasks, or subprojects associated with it. A strategy task could be a project such as "Reduce legacy applications in the environment by 80%." The tasks or steps under that could be "Inventory all legacy applications," "Define application dependencies," "Review application replacement options," etc.

Defining Strategy Deployment

Strategy deployment is a term often used in Lean environments. It's typically defined as a systematic process of developing work plans and daily activities that achieve the strategic directives. In essence, it's the plan you put in place to ensure the work done every day drives the organization toward its strategic objectives. Even if your organization is not using the Lean framework, the concept of strategy deployment is very useful in keeping activities aligned with strategic objectives.

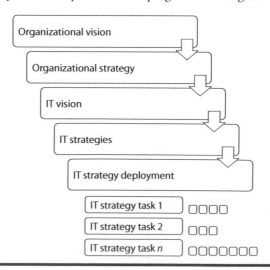

Figure 2.2   Strategy drives action.

How is strategy deployment different from a work plan? A work plan, or even a project plan, defines tasks that must be achieved to reach some end point or objective. In HIT, it could be to patch servers every month or update the EMR software on a quarterly release schedule. However, those don't necessarily drive the strategic objectives of the organization. Some work is necessary to keep the organization running, but it does not drive the organization toward achieving strategic objectives. Of course, *not* doing these tasks sets you back and, therefore, puts all organizational strategies at risk. They are vital to long-term success, but these tasks are not strategic activities on their own. It's easy to lose sight of the larger goals when you're busy providing routine and operational services. Your job as an IT leader is to keep your eye on both the strategic *and* the operational objectives and to strike a balance between the two. This is a topic that will recur throughout this book because it's one of the fundamental skills of a successful HIT leader.

If your strategy is a multiyear strategy or has outside dependencies (capital funding, for example), your work plan will need to address that. As is true with any plan, it is important to be specific in defining the task, the expected outcome, the timeline, the budget (if applicable), the dependencies, the risks, and the stakeholders. That, in essence, is a project plan. Developing a project plan using standard project management processes for each of your strategic objectives will help you clearly define the work you need to achieve to accomplish your goals.

However, before you can create a plan and deploy your strategy, you may need to do some analysis of your team, your IT infrastructure, your applications, and your organization. You may do these before you set strategic direction, or you may do these with specific strategic initiatives in mind.

Internal Capabilities Assessment

Once you've identified your strategic objectives, you can begin to create a plan to achieve those objectives. Often, a good starting point is to perform (or update) an internal assessment of capabilities. If you don't know what skills and expertise your team has, you won't know whether the plans you're creating can be accomplished with existing staff. You and your team will need to be realistic about the skills you have versus the skills needed to accomplish strategic objectives. This is a collaborative exercise where trust and honesty are absolutely crucial to a positive outcome. If you sit in your office and make these assessments and decisions on your own, there's about a 99% chance you'll get it wrong. Worse, you will lack the valuable input and perspective of your team, and they will miss out on the opportunity to craft this plan with you. Of course, if the team sees this as a threatening exercise—if they believe their jobs or status will be compromised or at risk, then you won't get a positive outcome either. Often the most effective approach is to indicate that if needed skills are lacking, you'll train existing staff, hire consultants for a specific set of skills for a period of time, or add staff with needed skills.

Ultimately, your job as a leader is to make very realistic assessments and then look at all aspects of the situation to determine the best course forward. We discuss this topic in Chapter 7 (IT Risk Management) as well as in Chapter 8 (Managing, Directing, and Leading).

Strengths, Weaknesses, Opportunities, and Threats

You may also choose to perform an analysis of the team or the department using the SWOT model—identifying strengths, weaknesses, opportunities, and threats with the strategic objectives in mind. This keeps the exercise focused on achieving required outcomes and focuses the SWOT analysis to those elements needed to achieve the objectives. Contrast that to a general SWOT analysis of your IT department, which may not surface specific information to help drive strategy.

For example, a general SWOT analysis might find that you lack enough technical talent on your infrastructure team to continue to manage the increasingly complex environment. A focused SWOT might find that you lack the technical talent to assess and architect a move to cloud-based solutions, which might be a key element of your IT strategy. The plan you put in place to address these weaknesses could be very different in each instance.

Roadmaps and Visuals

One of the most useful tools for documenting strategic objectives and work plans to support achieving those objectives are roadmaps. Roadmaps can also be similar to master project lists or schedules so that at a high level, you are sequencing projects in an orderly manner based on priorities and natural groupings. Ultimately, you need to tie strategy to operations, and this is one method for doing so.

For example, several projects may be related to a mobile strategy and should be viewed holistically. By grouping by strategy and priority, you gain a much clearer view of what's in front of you. Seeing the whole can often be very illuminating as well, surfacing potential problems long before you're in project planning mode. Visually representing the high-level steps needed to achieve objectives can help not only keep the objectives clearly visible but also tell the story in a very clear, understandable way.

A roadmap, whether in text or in visuals, can help identify priorities. If you have three strategic objectives for your IT department, you may be able to make progress on all three simultaneously. For example, you have objectives surrounding reducing cost, improving process efficiency, and reducing complexity of systems for end users. You may have three directors each focused on one of the objectives, or you may work sequentially through these. Figure 2.3 shows a project roadmap example with dependencies and project manager listed along with the target calendar quarter for project work.

This is a good starting point for ensuring that not only all projects are listed and mapped out for a given time period but also these projects tie to organizational strategies. In this example, you might look at a new analytics program scheduled for Q4 and ask what organizational strategy is driving this request. Upon further review, you may discover that it doesn't add value nor is it really needed to support organizational strategies, and the project may be canceled. This is *not* an IT decision alone. As an IT leader, you need to keep a critical eye on IT projects and monitor continuously for strategic alignment. If something appears to miss the mark, you should raise this with the appropriate groups, which might include an IT governance council or committee. We'll discuss IT governance in Chapter 3 and provide guidance on how to address these types of project concerns. For now, it's important to note that part of your role as a leader in HIT is to ensure projects don't just automatically move forward without thoughtful review.

On a related note, you may be looking at the first and last projects here and wonder how they align with strategic initiatives. In this case, these are required to maintain basic operations for the

Project ID	Description	PM	Dependency	Q1	Q2	Q3	Q4
2016-001	Server Memory Upgrade	Valenzuela		▓			
2016-002	EMR Upgrade	Larsen	2016-001	▓	▓		
2016-003	New EMR Module	Yee	2016-002			▓	
2016-004	ERP Upgrade	McGregor		▓			
2016-005	New Medical Office Building	Salusky	2016-004		▓		
2016-006	New Analytics Program	Larsen					▓
2016-007	Upgrade Wireless APs	Valenzuela			▓		

Figure 2.3 Project roadmap.

organization. They may not be strategic in nature, but are required to keep systems functional for current and future operational needs. However, upgrading the wireless infrastructure could be a task required to support the strategic implementation of mobile workforce technologies. These types of projects need to be listed and managed along with other projects because they typically require the same or overlapping resources, even if they are not specifically strategic in nature.

Using a roadmap can help keep your vision and strategy top of mind on a day-to-day basis. A generic roadmap example is provided to get you started. There is no right or wrong way to develop your roadmap as long as it helps you achieve your goals. In this example, shown in Figure 2.4, we've assumed that a mobile solution is one of the strategic objectives.

If you start with the high-level tasks you know are needed to achieve a strategic objective, it becomes easier to keep track of these items for IT leaders. Of course, each of these needs to be broken down into their subtasks and be assigned with owners and deadlines—all the usual activities associated with creating an effective project plan. However, for an IT leader, you don't (typically) need to track all the details—you need to keep the road ahead in your sights so you can help the team make adjustments and ensure each step is progressing as expected.

You can see an example of an expanded roadmap in Figure 2.5. Clearly, it's starting to look like a project plan, and you may choose to begin developing the plan in a project management

TASK	Q1/Jan	Q1/Feb	Q1/Mar	Q2/Apr	Q2/May
Gather end user requirements	▓				
Survey current mobile capabilities	▓	▓			
Develop functional and technical requirements		▓	▓		
Assess mobile solutions/vendors		▓	▓		
Develop business case, use case, project plan			▓		
Select, pilot, deploy mobile solution				▓	▓
Develop training, policies, procedures					▓
Develop support model					▓
Transition to operational support					▓

Figure 2.4   Roadmap example.

TASK	1-Jan	8-Jan	15-Jan	22-Jan	Q1/Jan	Q1/Feb	Q1/Mar	Q2/Apr	Q2/May
1. Gather end user requirements	▓				▓				
1.1 Create list of users to participate	▓	▓							
1.2 Develop list of questions to guide meetings	▓	▓							
1.3 Assign project manager or coordinator		▓							
1.4 Develop meeting agenda and send invites		▓							
1.5 Conduct meetings, document results		▓	▓						
1.6 Analyze results, develop draft results doc			▓						
1.7 Distribute document to attendees for input				▓					
1.7.1 Send document asking for input				▓					
1.7.2 If needed, set up follow up meetings				▓					
1.8 Finalize requirements document				▓					
Survey current mobile capabilities					▓				
Develop functional and technical requirements						▓			
Assess mobile solutions/vendors						▓	▓		
Develop business case, use case, project plan							▓		
Select, pilot, deploy mobile solution								▓	▓
Develop training, policies, procedures								▓	
Develop support model									▓
Transition to operational support									▓

Figure 2.5   Expanded roadmap example.

tool instead of in Microsoft Excel. However, for visual management purposes, it might be helpful for you to keep a high-level roadmap visible in your office so you can quickly remind yourself of strategic priorities every day. We'll explore Lean IT concepts and visual management in Chapter 9.

Having detailed plans helps break down tasks into actionable blocks of work, which can then be scoped, assigned, worked, tracked, and completed as with any project plan. As an IT leader, you need to keep your eye on numerous projects simultaneously.

Strategies to Roadmaps to Results

In this chapter, we laid out the foundation of working with organizational vision and strategy to develop your IT vision and strategy. In many cases, these are key activities leaders undertake, but they can involve teams at the right times and in the right context. It's not helpful to start with a blank page with a team. Instead, it is more productive to set the context, set the vision for the department, and engage the team in helping formulate strategic and operational plans. If your organization is one that sets strategy at the executive or director level, you can engage your team during the creation of the roadmaps and operational plans that will ultimately deliver those strategic objectives.

As a leader in HIT, this is one of the most challenging but effective areas to focus on. However, experience shows that it can be almost impossible to get to these tasks if you are fighting fires and dealing with chaos on a daily basis. If you're in that position, it's good to try to step back and focus on the direction you want to head. Doing so can bring clarity of purpose and help to organize the work of the department in such a way as to actually reduce the fires and the overload.

References

For more on this topic, visit http://susansnedaker.com/leading-hit.

QR2.1

Bell, Steven C. and Michael A. Orzen, *Lean IT: Enabling and Sustaining Your Lean Transformation*, New York: Productivity Press, 2011.

Broadbent, Marianne and Ellen S. Kitzis, *The New CIO Leader: Setting the Agenda and Delivering Results*, Boston: Harvard Business School Press, 2005.

Bruce, Andy and Ken Langdon, *Strategic Thinking*, London: Dorling Kindersley, 2000.

Drucker, Peter F., *The Daily Drucker*, New York: HarperBusiness, 2004.

Johnson, John E. and Anne Marie Smith, *60 Minute Strategic Plan: 2 Stages, 12 Steps, 300 Words...*, 4th Ed., Gold River, CA: 60 Minute Strategic Plan, Inc., April 2010.

Porter, Michael E., "What Is Strategy?" *HBR's 10 Must Reads: On Strategy*, pp. 1–37, Boston: Harvard Business Review Press, 2011.

Snedaker, Susan T., Nels Hoenig, Tech. Ed., *How to Cheat at IT Project Management*, Boston: Syngress Press, 2005.

Chapter 3

IT Governance

Overview

In Chapter 2, we touched briefly on the challenges healthcare IT leaders face when they work in organizations that lack discipline and process. Many different factors can cause these chaotic environments, but they all have the same impact—less than optimal results at best, massive waste, and failure at worst. One very effective way of helping to instill discipline and process into the organization, at least with respect to IT efforts, is to implement (or strengthen) IT governance functions.

According to Broadbent and Kitzis in *The New CIO Leader*, establishing IT governance is one of the most important tasks a healthcare CIO can undertake—whether that CIO is new to the role or new to the organization. It is vital to ensure the work of the IT department maps directly and closely to the work of the organization. IT governance is the mechanism that weaves these together. But what do you do if you are not the CIO, and you don't directly control this in your organization? We'll discuss strategies for implementing IT governance and demand management when you don't control these functions.

Let's start by defining what IT governance is and then we'll discuss ways to implement or augment it in your organization.

IT Governance Defined

There are many varying definitions of IT governance, but one that captures many of the nuances of IT governance is provided by Gartner, a leading IT research and advisory company.

> **IT governance (ITG)** is defined as the processes that ensure the effective and efficient use of IT in enabling an organization to achieve its goals. IT *demand* governance (ITDG—what IT should work on) is the process by which organizations ensure the effective evaluation, selection, prioritization, and funding of *competing IT investments*; oversee their implementation; and extract (measurable) business benefits. ITDG is a business investment decision-making and oversight process, and it is a business management responsibility. IT supply-side governance (ITSG—how IT should do what

it does) is concerned with ensuring that the IT organization operates in an effective, efficient and compliant fashion, and it is primarily a CIO responsibility. (Gartner, n.d., emphasis added.)

In this definition, IT governance is used to decide among competing IT investments. That's important to remember. The organization is investing in IT projects with time, money, and resources. There needs to be a mechanism in place to prioritize and review those investments. IT governance is the process by which the organization decides what IT should do. Typically, the organization decides *what* IT should work on; IT decides *how* the work should be done.

IT governance is also the mechanism used to *increase* IT value to the organization and *reduce* IT-related risk. IT governance typically focuses on IT project work rather than day-to-day break/fix or maintain/operate kinds of tasks. IT project work typically consumes a significant portion of IT resource's time. Some estimates indicate that project work consumes up to 60%–80% of the IT teams' time. Of course, this varies greatly by organization. The point is that a large portion of time is expended on project work, and much of that project work originates outside of the IT department. Without an effective mechanism in place to manage this demand, you will have one of two things happen. The IT department will work on things that are not driving strategic initiatives forward, or the IT department will attempt to work on so many projects that productivity and effectiveness will be severely challenged. In either case, the IT value decreases and the IT-related risk increases. Figure 3.1 shows the biggest challenges forecast for IT for 2016 (all IT, not just healthcare IT). You can see how this reflects the same concerns we face in healthcare IT. Organizational alignment, governance, and skills account for 73% of the top challenges, and these are directly related to IT governance.

Gartner defines demand-side governance separately from supply-side governance (or simply demand and supply) for good reason. Demand governance is organizationally based. It involves all stakeholders from the organization who use or require IT services (everyone). It entails developing a process by which organizational IT needs are assessed and prioritized recognizing there

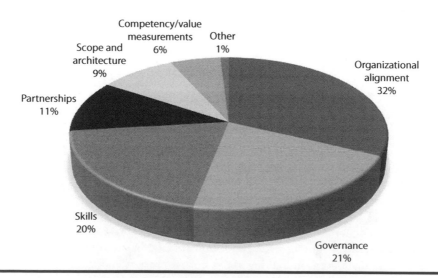

Figure 3.1 Biggest IT Challenges for 2016. (Adapted from TEKSystems "2016 Annual IT Forecast: Executive Summary," QR3.5.)

will always be competing elements. This is key to understanding what successful IT governance looks like.

Supply governance is really how IT departments deliver the services required in the most effective manner possible. In this book, we'll be referencing the Information Technology Infrastructure Library (ITIL) framework along with Lean IT concepts to discuss how IT leaders can improve and streamline operations.

Common IT Governance Elements

IT governance has been well defined, and there are many resources available to those who would like to take a deeper dive into this topic. References at the end of this chapter will get you started. These common elements include strategic IT alignment, value delivery, risk management, resource management, and performance management.

1. Strategic IT Alignment

We discussed strategy and vision in Chapter 2 along with how to ensure you have alignment between the organization and the IT department. IT governance is the mechanism by which you can continually check alignment. Projects requiring IT resources spring up from all different areas of the organization. As technology continues to move to the center stage in healthcare, this will only become more common. Without a mechanism for handling requests in a consistent and methodical manner, you'll end up thrashing. If you're in an organization that currently lacks IT governance, thrashing is probably considered normal. Once an IT governance process is defined and implemented, all project work should be funneled through the process. The process includes ensuring projects have been reviewed by the right stakeholders and developed (business case) for approval. This way, half-baked ideas don't make it onto the IT project list. This is one of the biggest benefits to a solid IT governance process—it brings critical thinking, consensus, and prioritization to projects that are competing for the same limited resources. Projects that do make it onto the project list will be fairly well thought-out, making IT estimates and project planning possible.

[…more…]

If your organization does not have any formal IT governance process, you're probably spending quite a bit of time trying to chase down project details like charter (or scope document), priority, budget, operational sponsor, and more. Worse, you probably find that you have competing demands for the same IT resources, and you don't have a clear path forward for managing this demand. The likely outcomes are failed projects and delayed projects. Neither is an acceptable steady state. The way to change this is to begin to manage the demand inside the IT department first. Develop a clear, concise, and consistent process for analyzing and planning all projects. You can use a standard project management methodology to ensure each project is properly defined before it is started. You can then begin to manage projects as part of an IT portfolio, even if you cannot get your larger IT governance function up and running. Once the discipline of managing projects and IT resources internally is working smoothly, you can then begin to instill this discipline in other areas. For example, you could work with appropriate counterparts to develop governance groups (a clinical project steering committee, for example); you could ask your finance or supply chain stakeholders to vet the projects related to those areas of the business. From there, you can roll the outcomes of these various subcommittees up to executives for review. Initially, they may not engage with the process, but if they begin to see that the most important work of the organization is being completed on time, on budget, and in scope more often, they may begin reinforcing the process. (Also see IT Governance Framework later in this chapter.)

2. IT Value Delivery

IT value is created when IT meets the needs of the end user or customer and when costs are efficiently managed and communicated. How IT delivers value is first defined by the organization. This occurs through the IT governance process. For example, there may be four different requests for changes to the electronic medical record or the enterprise resource planning system. Of those four, two work at cross-purposes, one is not at all feasible given time and cost constraints of the organization, and one is a great idea that will enhance the use of the system. These four projects should be reviewed by the appropriate IT governance group (see IT Governance Framework later in this chapter) and prioritized for IT review. Using this example, we would expect the group to decline or deny one of the two projects that work at cross-purposes and the one project that is not feasible. That means that potentially two projects are put forward for IT review. After IT review, it might be decided that they should both be scheduled sequentially. Assuming these projects are completed on time, on budget, and with the agreed upon scope, this IT work would be considered value-added because it addressed end-user needs in the manner required.

Conversely, were the IT department to decide on its own the projects to be done and the prioritization of those projects, the results would likely miss the mark. More important, the end users would lack the buy-in and insight that comes from having to properly analyze a request and have it vetted through this process.

Delivering value and reducing risk go hand in hand. Value is not achieved if risk is unnecessarily increased (or unmanaged). Increases to risk reduce the value of the deliverable. It is somewhat unusual to find projects that simultaneously increase value and risk in equal measure; though these are often potentially transformational projects. Statements such as "if successful, it has the potential to completely transform the way we deliver care today" reflect both high risk and high *potential* value. As we'll see in Chapter 4, when we discuss IT value, these types of projects are few in number for this reason.

3. IT Risk Management

IT risk management involves managing the likelihood of occurrence and impact of negative events. IT risk involves the planning, implementation, use, and modification of IT systems, and each of these introduces risk to the business. Project management involves identifying risks to the project and establishing countermeasures or mitigating controls for those risks. In fact, one of the primary benefits of formal project management is managing risk since every project injects new risk into the organization. This is another aspect of IT-related risk management that is addressed in a formalized IT governance process. Reducing risk to the organization for IT-related work is the counterpart to value. Risk is reduced for projects when the intent, scope, timeline, deliverables, and dependencies are identified by the stakeholders and are addressed through the IT governance process. We'll discuss IT risk management more thoroughly in Chapter 7.

4. IT Resource Management

The IT governance process helps IT managers effectively manage resources with respect to maintaining and operating the department, and assigning staff to project work. Without a strong governance function, it's virtually impossible to determine whether you have enough staff or the right staff to deliver work needed. With an IT governance process in place, you can develop more accurate estimates of department capacity and ensure you can deliver on IT commitments. Some organizations utilize software to manage IT resources in order to estimate and track capacity and demand. Other organizations use a 90-day look back at capacity and demand to project 90 days forward. Regardless of how you manage capacity, IT governance will help you manage and estimate demand more effectively.

5. IT Performance Measurement

IT performance measurement is something you do every day as an IT manager or leader. Your job is to ensure your team or your department accomplishes its objectives as defined by strategies and goals. You have probably implemented some sort of framework or system to ensure you can measure your results, either quantitatively (using numbers) or qualitatively (using descriptions). Performance measurement links back to the IT governance process. The committees that approve IT work should also be the committees who evaluate the effectiveness and value delivered from the projects approved. This is not specifically an IT measurement. Most IT projects involve a variety of stakeholders, so not all outcomes are the direct responsibility of IT. However, the effectiveness of IT projects should be measured against their intended outcomes, the original project charter, scope, objectives, costs, and timelines.

This aspect of IT governance helps close the loop with stakeholders, and ensures responsibility for outcomes is shared and initiatives that are going off-course can be corrected in a collaborative and timely manner. While it's usually not worth bringing every project back through a review process, large, complex, and/or expensive projects should certainly be reviewed with stakeholders to ensure the benefits expected have been delivered. In addition to ensuring original expectations are met, projects should be reviewed with all stakeholders for lessons learned. These lessons learned should be captured, and a process for reviewing lessons learned during the project planning phase of new projects should be implemented. This will improve the delivery of future projects. These five aspects of IT governance lay the groundwork for developing an IT governance framework in your organization.

IT Governance Framework

There are as many ways to approach healthcare IT governance as there are healthcare systems. There is no one-size fits-all formula, and more importantly, there is no simple recipe for corralling the various stakeholders and decision-makers into a clear, simple process. However, there are several concepts that are important to understand so you can create or modify your IT governance process to fit the needs of the organization.

[…more…]

Be careful not to become so overwhelmed by the challenge in front of you that you simply stall out. Create a plan for implementing or improving your IT governance process and start with the first step. If it takes you 6 weeks or 6 months to accomplish that one task, you're still better off than not having started in the first place. Slow, steady progress is often the most sustainable, so take measured steps and make sure they stick before moving on.

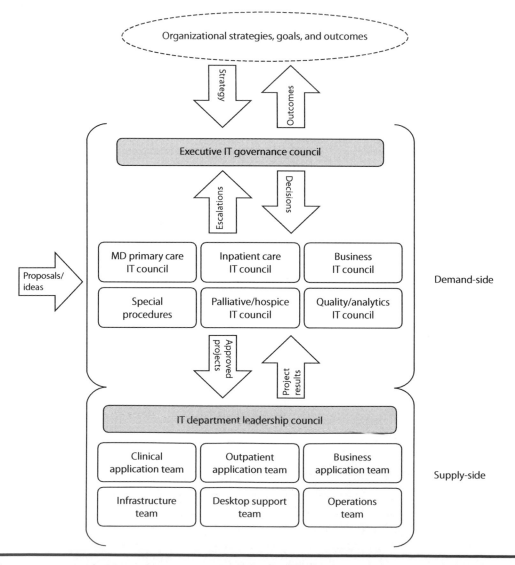

Figure 3.2   Sample IT governance framework for healthcare.

You do not need to be the CIO to create, remediate, or greatly influence IT governance. By understanding what IT governance is (and is not), by understanding the building blocks, and by looking holistically at your organization, you can have a very positive impact on the process— and perhaps actually be the one who finally puts forward a plan to address IT governance.

Figure 3.2 shows an example of how this can work in a healthcare organization. Each of the major functions in the diagram is described here. You can modify this approach to better mirror your organizational structure, but this gives you a starting point for the logical flow of governance activities.

Executive IT Governance Council

The organization's strategies need to inform the executive-level IT governance function. This team is usually composed of vice presidents who oversee large segments of the hospital or organization's operations. This might include CIO, COO, CMO, CNO, CFO, VP of Facilities, and others such as CMIO, CNIO, or area directors. The key function of this team is *to ensure major IT project alignment with organizational strategies and goals*. The executive IT governance team should define how it believes the organization should utilize IT resources at an organizational level. This is not a detailed, blow-by-blow description but more of a vision statement. It should reflect the organization's desired state for IT.

This team also handles escalations, such as when two important projects require the same resources at the same time, or when a project sponsor feels their project has not gotten adequate consideration. Decisions from this team are provided to the various area IT councils.

Area IT Councils

These can be called *area councils* or *practice area councils* or whatever term works for your company. These groups include the key vice presidents and/or directors of the organizational areas. For a hospital, the clinical areas might be inpatient, outpatient, and procedural areas (OR, cath lab, radiology, etc.). For some, it might include primary care physicians, specialists, and lab. On the nonclinical side, it might include finance, HR, supply chain, and facilities functions, either combined or each in their own group.

Each of these councils is responsible for reviewing requests for IT resources, including projects, changes, and enhancements. These teams are not responsible for requests related to "break/fix" or "maintaining operations." Each council ensures that requests make sense, that they are aligned with organizational goals and strategies, that they add value and are not counter to other requests and/or initiatives. This team reviews each proposal, makes sure the business case is clear and complete, that the required elements (as defined by the IT governance process) are included, and that the request is ready for review. The team reviews, approves (or declines), and prioritizes requests. For projects that do not cross over to other teams, the work can be scheduled and completed. Any project that requires a larger number of people and/or teams to be completed may be escalated to the executive IT governance council for review, approval, and prioritization.

Each area council will require IT leadership participation and presence so that projects can be discussed in the proper context. The ideal state is when projects are approved and prioritized by area councils after the input from IT has already occurred. This means that there may be some back-and-forth between the area councils and the IT leadership team so that projects can be clearly scoped prior to being approved and prioritized. In some organizations, the area council ensures the business case, scope, and charter are prepared, and then a prioritized list of projects is given to the IT leadership council so they can develop IT-related scope, timelines, and estimates.

This can then be provided back to the area council for final review and adjustment to prioritization, if needed.

Once project work is complete, the council reviews project results, ensures the outcomes are aligned with the project objectives, that charter, scope, objectives, budget, and timeline were met. If needed, the team can perform after-project reviews to gather lessons learned to improve their process for reviewing and approving project work.

IT Department Leadership Council

This team is composed of IT leaders in each of the IT disciplines. The purpose of this council (or group of teams) is to review approved projects that have been provided by the area councils and to ensure that the project can be delivered as requested. Though Figure 3.2 shows approved projects being handed down to IT leadership and project results being delivered up from IT leadership, the process is more iterative, as described. While minimizing the number of handoffs is crucial, there will be some projects that require offline meetings of subject matter experts to fully understand and vet the project or to create a solution where none exists. As long as the iterative process helps improve outcomes and adds value to the final product, then some back-and-forth makes sense. A document detailing how this process should work should be developed so all parties are informed and needless meetings and discussions can be avoided.

IT Teams

Every healthcare IT department is configured slightly differently. Often it's seen as having "silos," but these functional divisions make sense for how work needs to be done internal to the department. The department's function may be divided into logical work groups, but it's the lack of communication and coordination across these groups that actually creates the silos. In Figure 3.2, some potential team types are shown for illustrative purposes; your teams may be completely different. The key takeaway here is that sometimes the IT leadership team will need to convene a meeting of cross-team IT members to review potential projects from the area councils. In some cases, projects that are small or only impact one IT team may not need a cross-team review; most projects in healthcare IT these days do impact multiple teams and therefore require cross-team review. A well-functioning IT leadership council can effectively function as the gatekeeper for the department in the best sense of the word. Ensuring all requests for changes, new functionality, optimization, and new projects (i.e., excluding break/fix and maintenance/operations) go through this channel will prevent politics, lack of process, and playing favorites from interrupting the approval process.

Not All Ideas Are Worth Pursuing

Not all ideas are good ideas, though some organizations seem to have few filters in how they process ideas for IT work. We've all had moments where we've thought we had a great idea, but when we think it over, we realize it's not nearly as good as it first appeared. If there is no mechanism in the organization that requires critical thinking and analysis before the idea hits the IT radar as a task or an assigned project, there is a high risk of wasting time and effort on ideas that are not properly thought-through or vetted. When this is the case, it often looks like the *anarchy* method of governance described by Broadbent and Kitzis (2005, p. 82). In this model, there is no formal process for reviewing requests for IT time and resources. This is the worst possible model for so many reasons, and still, it is not unheard of in healthcare. The solution is to implement standard business case or request justification processes (with templates to address key data points) to help users submit well-formed ideas.

[...more...]

A business case template can be created for (required) use for all IT project requests. This template can include the essential information for evaluating the project. There are a wide variety of data elements that could be included, and it will vary by organization. However, some typical items to require are as follows:

a. Name of requestor, department, and contact information.
b. Description of request and desired outcome (how will this idea make the business better?).
c. Proposed solution (what is the idea?).
d. Alignment with strategic goals/initiatives (how does this fit into the business objectives?).
e. Financial—return on investment, benefits, savings (how much will this cost or save?).
f. Areas impacted (is this a departmental request or an organization-wide request?).
g. Constraints and risks (what are the issues that can be foreseen that will need to be addressed?).
h. Timeline—hard deadlines (such as regulatory), soft deadlines, or desired timelines (what is driving the timing?).
i. Executive review (which executives should review and who have reviewed and approved?).

It's worth noting that one of the major sources of disconnects in healthcare IT projects is that the right people are not informed or involved early enough. Numerous projects fail because the executive is not aware and, once informed, he or she sees that the project is not aligned or is in contradiction with desired objectives. Requiring a business case to be submitted and reviewed by appropriate people will help reduce the number of wayward project ideas and requests that IT needs to process.

Managing the Mayhem

If everyone can have direct input and can make project requests, the work of the IT department becomes fragmented and chaotic. The clinical application team may be working on something that is at direct odds to something the revenue cycle team may be working on. Without a coordinated look at all requests for IT resources, it is likely that this type of waste is occurring. While looking across the department at all IT requests may be helpful and may be occurring, it does not look at the larger picture at all. This approach does not look at all the hundreds (or thousands) of requests and tie them to strategic objectives, organizational goals, or key metrics. So, while the work may serve a purpose, it might not be the best use of resources. For example, how many times in your own work have you found yourself working on something relatively small and simple just so you could feel a sense of accomplishment or because you could "complete it quickly?" There's nothing wrong with knocking out easy work, but how do we know if that work is more or less important than other work? Without IT governance and guidelines on who can make requests (input), there is no way to know the merit and priority of a request.

Deciding Who Decides

It's true that most IT work is the work of the organization. Applications are not configured and reports are not built just for the sake of it. This work is done to meet stated, defined organizational needs. Once the inputs have been reviewed, who should decide what work should and should not be done? This is the work of your established IT governance councils.

In many organizations, decisions are divided by category so that the most appropriate people can make the decisions. For example, in most healthcare organizations, infrastructure and architecture questions are decided solely within the IT department itself. (Gartner refers to this as the supply-side.) Application decisions are typically made in conjunction with end users. How this decision-making is structured is up to each organization, but there are some guidelines that will help ensure you have the most informed and knowledgeable people making the decisions.

Figure 3.3 expands upon the structure shown in Figure 3.2. It articulates which decisions are made by which groups. Creating this type of diagram for your governance process can be helpful in seeing exactly how decisions are to be made. In addition, you can develop a more detailed description of each group or committee so that roles, responsibilities, and level of decision-making (strategic, business line, IT operations) are clearly defined and understood by all parties.

You can see that the IT Leadership Council has several key functions related to managing the inputs and requests from the strategic and area councils. Each IT department will manage this in

A. Strategic Councils
1. Executive IT Governance Council

2. Technology Architecture Council

Strategic councils ensure alignment with organization goals and set high-level direction. Strategic Councils help manage the demand-side of IT governance.

B. Area Councils
1. Physician Primary Care IT Council

2. Business Systems IT Council

3. Inpatient Care IT Council

4. Interfaces Council

5. Palliative Care/Hospice IT Council

6. Quality/Analytics IT Council

7. Special Procedures IT Council

Organizational councils ensure requests for IT resources are properly prepared, reviewed, and prioritized within the council best able to evaluate requests. Conflict among priorities of these groups is often addressed by the Executive IT Governance Council or a similar high-level, cross-functional committee. Organizational or area councils help manage the demand-side of IT governance.

C. IT Leadership Council
1. IT Teams
Review proposals, prepare work estimates, work on approved projects.

2. Change Management Team
Ensures adherence to change management processes.

3. ITSM Service and Process Management Team
Ensures continued alignment with IT Service Management and ITIL processes.

The IT Leadership Council ensures requests coming from Strategic and Organizational Councils are managed appropriately within the IT department. The council ensures projects are reviewed, and approved internally and that proposals, projects, and work adhere to IT standards and guidelines (architecture, security, etc.)

Figure 3.3 IT governance decision-making groups.

a unique way, but what usually works is to have an IT leadership team that reviews all requests. This helps provide transparency throughout the department and helps ensure standards are maintained. Once proposals/projects have been reviewed and approved, they will flow to the other teams for processing and work. What's not shown here is a project management office (PMO) function. If your organization has a PMO, it should be part of the IT governance team, and all approved projects would be scheduled and planned through the PMO in conjunction with the IT leadership team's input.

Your IT governance process may not be this complex if you work in a smaller organization or one that is less diverse. Regardless of size, your organization's IT governance process should be well defined and documented. The ultimate goal is to funnel all requests for IT services through these gates so that nothing slips in through a side channel and nothing is initiated in IT without having been approved by one of these governing bodies.

There are many effective IT governance models available, both inside and outside of healthcare. Here's a quick list if you're interested in researching any of these models further.

1. ISACA COBIT (Control Objects for Information and related Technology)
2. ISO/IEC 38500 and ISO/IEC 38501 (IT governance)
3. ISO 20000 (IT service management)
4. ITIL (Information Technology Infrastructure Library)
5. ITSM (Information Technology Service Management)

IT Governance Value and Impact

IT governance activities require time, commitment, and effort on the part of the IT leaders and more notably organizational leaders. It can be challenging to pull time from operations to focus on making decisions about IT work. So, it's important if you're going to make that investment that there be a benefit from doing so. There are many reasons why *effective* IT governance should be in place. Regardless of whether you are in a position to create or foster IT governance, understanding the value and the impact will help you find the right people and processes for your organization to develop effective IT governance. As we discussed, IT governance helps ensure strategic alignment with business objectives. It also helps IT managers more effectively manage resources. When project work is planned through a consistent process, it's easier to project staffing needs and meet demand more effectively.

1. *Strategic alignment.* As we've discussed, the most important aspect of effective IT governance is that it helps ensure the work of the IT department is focused on the things the organization has deemed strategic and important. This also assumes executive leadership is genuinely engaged in the process and appreciates the value this process brings to the organization. Typically, part of the CIO's role is to foster this engagement and help educate peers in the executive suite about the importance of this process.

2. *Resource management.* Managing IT resources is challenging in most organizations because there is always dynamic tension between the work the organization requests and the IT resources available to fulfill those requests. IT governance helps everyone understand what resources are available at any given time so that the most important work can be prioritized and scheduled accordingly. IT resources can more efficiently deliver the work needed when waste from switching back and forth among numerous unregulated projects ceases.

3. *Value generation.* Projects that are reviewed, selected, and prioritized by the organization through an effective IT governance process are much more likely to generate value than those that come in through the side doors. When post-Go Live project reviews are part of the governance process, you also have an opportunity to review the value generated by the project as well as lessons learned for future projects.

4. *Financial efficiency.* When projects are properly vetted, there is a higher chance of success. When projects are initiated without proper review, they never get off to a good start. This typically costs organizations more time, more money, and more resources. For more on project success (and failure), refer to The Standish Group's CHAOS report (2013, QR3.7) in the References section.

Success Factors

Let's define what success looks like when you've got a fully functional, mature IT governance process in place. Knowing that you can't go from zero to fully mature in one leap, you can use success factors as a way of monitoring progress toward your desired end state. As a leader in your department, you may not have complete (or any) control over these factors. However, the more you know about the process, the more effectively you can lead through influence. If you can help guide your leadership and your organization toward a more functional IT governance process, you'll be making your job just a bit easier.

1. Define the Desired Outcomes for IT Governance

When starting out, it's important to look forward and determine what success looks like, what outcomes you are expecting. Ask yourself what problems you expect to avoid or minimize through this process. Clearly defining required and desirable outcomes as you begin will help guide your efforts. It may be stated as "Required Outcomes" and "Evidence of Success" or "Required Outcomes," "Baseline," "Measure of Success." You can organize it in whatever manner suits you, but results should be measurable. This could be as simple as "100% of IT projects initiated outside of IT are reviewed by an area council." If desired, you could begin by writing a charter document as you would for any project and use this as the beginning of a "Create IT Governance" project plan.

2. Define Roles and Responsibilities

Define roles and responsibilities, and ensure all stakeholders are educated about these IT governance functions. Since stakeholders change over time, it's important to have a plan for continuously educating new members to reinforce the importance of the IT governance function and the processes that have been established.

3. Develop and Deliver Continuous Education on IT Governance

Continuous education (meaning quarterly or semiannual) on what IT governance is and why it matters is important. Topics should include the items listed here, as well as any organization-specific topics that are important for stakeholders to understand as they review proposals for IT resources.

a. How IT governance drives business value through IT
b. Risks associated with implementing new or maintaining existing IT capabilities
c. How IT governance fits with organizational governance
d. The framework, roles, and responsibilities of stakeholders
e. The governance process—responsibility, delegation, accountability, inputs, and decisions
f. Periodic review of the effectiveness of the IT governance process and revisions made accordingly

By educating the organization and refreshing that knowledge periodically, you reinforce why the IT governance process is important to the organization. When everyone understands that a process is in place for a reason and that process is driving the desired results, they are more likely to participate in the process. If, on the other hand, the IT governance process simply becomes "more hoops to jump through," then you will have a hard time maintaining the needed discipline for effective IT governance.

4. Understand the Internal and External Environment

Everyone involved in the IT governance process, from end users to executives, needs to understand what's going on in the organization and how that effects IT proposals and projects. For example, high turnover in nursing staff or high vacancies in key leadership positions will impact the environment and may cause different decisions to be made. Unusual conditions that impact physicians, nurses, or other care providers will impact the environment. New clinical initiatives or service lines will impact the organization as a whole. These organizational influences also have a significant impact on the operational side of projects. As we'll discuss in Chapter 4, projects typically have a very large impact on operations. If the operational leaders (clinical, business) are not ready or able to effectively manage the operational impact of a project, the overall success of that project will be at significant risk.

In addition, participants in the governance process must also understand the external environment including regulatory requirements, technology advances, industry trends, social trends, generational trends, and competitive aspects of the local or regional market, to name a few. Often, IT leaders keep a close eye on these external factors because they so greatly impact IT work. Holding briefing sessions with key organizational leaders (or open sessions for everyone to attend) to educate them on these topics can be a useful way to educate and engage stakeholders.

5. Develop an Expedited Process for Smaller Requests

We've all been involved at one time or another in putting something small through an onerously complex or cumbersome process. This is one of the primary reasons people bypass established processes. (People will "work the system" when the system doesn't work.) Most successful IT governance processes have a fast track for small projects that are easily understood, scoped, and implemented. Be sure to take a look at the existing body of work to determine which projects should go through the full process and which could reasonably go through the fast-track process. Define guidelines and boundaries and refine those over time as you determine how successful this method is. For example, some teams can look at a request and pretty quickly know what's needed and how much effort it will take and what risk is involved. They might consider the project a "just do it" project.

Of course, this can be a slippery slope. For example, one organization was faced with a problem of larger projects being broken out into smaller projects so these could go through the expedited process. Unfortunately, because the larger project and its objectives were never openly revealed, the smaller projects were not well aligned, and major problems surfaced about midway through this covert process. Keep an eye out for this potential problem and put controls in place to prevent this behavior.

6. Develop a Decision-Making Matrix (Criteria for Evaluation and Prioritization)

You can develop a decision matrix like the one shown here in Table 3.1 to rank a proposal in a semiquantitative manner. Granted, this is a very simplistic decision matrix, and there are more sophisticated and comprehensive models available. However, if you have nothing in place today, it's best to start with something simple and build it out over time. Once you've run a few existing projects or new proposals through this screening method, you can potentially determine what score threshold you should set for small projects that are not required to go through the full proposal process. This will help streamline efforts and ensure that the process effort doesn't outweigh the project or the result.

The proposed numeric values are included with the label. These are arbitrarily selected values to help quantify your assessment. So, if the effort of a proposal is high, you would place a 5 in that box; if the effort is medium, you would place a 3 in the appropriate box.

Let's run two different projects through this quickly to get a feel for how this could work. Based on these rankings, you might conclude that the first project is a small project and could be fast-tracked. Let's also say that you review the second project and determine that this project is more complex and that it should go through the standard process. It's important to define whatever rating system and labels you use. In this case, it would be wise to define what "high," "medium," and "low" mean as well as what "effort," "size," "risk," and "benefit" mean within your organization. Create some brief descriptions and fine-tune them as you go. For example, some organizations might consider high effort to be any project that is estimated to require more than 200 hours of labor. Size might mean any project that requires a project team larger than 12. Without clear definitions, people will make varying assumptions and you'll have a less consistent review process. Tables 3.2 and 3.3 are examples of how you can use this method.

Using this method, the secure text project has a score of 8. The blood bank project has a score of 18. The secure text project may qualify as a fast track project, while the blood bank project may qualify as a large project that is required to go through the full process. You'll need to determine the appropriate values for your project processes.

Table 3.1 Decision Matrix Example

[Insert Proposal # and Brief Proposal Description Here]				
	Effort	Size	Risk	Benefit
High (5)				
Medium (3)				
Low (1)				

Table 3.2 Decision Matrix Example 1

Implement Secure Text Solution for MD-MD and MD-RN Communication				
	Effort	*Size*	*Risk*	*Benefit*
High (5)				
Medium (3)	3			3
Low (1)		1	1	

Table 3.3 Decision Matrix Example 2

Implement Bar Codes for Blood Bank Products				
	Effort	*Size*	*Risk*	*Benefit*
High (5)	5		5	5
Medium (3)		3		
Low (1)				

7. Develop an Evaluation Process for Your IT Governance Function

It's important to have a review function at both Executive and IT Leadership levels. This will help confirm the process is delivering value and not just adding another layer of bureaucracy to the organization. Questions to ask include the following:

a. Is the process yielding the stated objectives and outcomes?
   i. If yes, how can it be improved?
   ii. If no, how can it be fixed?
b. Is the work of the IT department more focused and predictable than before?
c. Are deliverables being met according to stakeholder expectations?
d. Have we achieved the gains via IT projects and initiatives that we expected to?
e. Have we streamlined the request process?
f. Are there problems with the process that need to be addressed?
g. Are stakeholders (including requesters) better informed throughout the project/request life cycle?
h. Are stakeholders more (or less) satisfied with IT deliverables than [insert timeframe]?

Final Thoughts on IT Governance

Regardless of industry, most organizations today struggle with IT governance. It's difficult to maintain the organizational discipline to manage requests through this formal process because things are moving quickly, priorities change, and just about every project in any company involves IT in some way or another.

Don't become discouraged by setbacks or by constant challenges maintaining this discipline. Here are a few tips to remember:

- Continue to keep reinforcing the established processes that are working.
- Fix any parts of the process that are broken.
- Start with very small improvements and get those to stick.
- Don't over-engineer the process—adding process "drag" to an already challenging area of work will slow things down to a crawl or will cause people to actively circumvent the process.
- Document the process both visually and verbally (pictures, words) to help reinforce the defined and accepted processes.

This may well be one of the most challenging aspects of being a healthcare (or any) IT leader, so be sure to set realistic goals. Remember the adage, "Perfect is the enemy of good." You don't have to have a perfect process; you need to have a process that works reasonably well and one you can improve over time.

Summary

IT governance is a very critical component to success in today's challenging healthcare IT environment. As a healthcare IT leader, you will need to be involved with IT governance in some way. Whether you are working with your organizational leadership to create an IT governance function or participating in the IT leadership aspect of IT governance, you need to be well informed about IT governance. As a leader, you'll need to help develop, manage, and maintain the process so that it meets the needs of the organization and helps contain the ever-increasing demand for IT services in healthcare. You should keep the end in mind as you develop your program to understand what success looks like and to understand that incremental improvement can be achieved. Even if you are not currently in a position to drive these changes, you are likely in a position to influence them. You can achieve remarkable improvements in relationships with end users, with transparency of the work (and results) of the IT department, and in the focusing of IT work on what matters most—the organizational objectives.

References

For more on this topic, visit http://susansnedaker.com/leading-hit.

QR3.1

Broadbent, Marianne and Ellen S. Kitzis, *The New CIO Leader*, Boston: Harvard Business School Press, 2005.

Gartner, Inc. http://www.gartner.com/it-glossary/it-governance/, viewed February 01, 2016.

Gerrard, Michael, "IT Governance—Key Initiative Overview," Gartner, Inc., http://www .gartner.com/it/initiatives/pdf/KeyInitiativeOverview_ITGovernance.pdf, viewed February 27, 2016.

QR3.2

Hastie, Shane and Stephane Wojewoda, "Standish Group 2015 Chaos Report—Q&A with Jennifer Lynch," October 4, 2015, https://www.infoq.com/articles/standish-chaos-2015, viewed June 28, 2016.

QR3.3

International Standards Organization (ISO), ISO/IEC 38500, International Standard, *Information Technology—Governance of IT for the Organization*, Second edition 2015-02-15, Reference number ISO/IEC 38500:2015[E], ISO, Geneva, Switzerland, 2015.

International Standards Organization (ISO), ISO/IEC 38502, Technical Specification, *Information Technology—Governance of IT—Implementation Guide*, First edition 2015-04-01, Reference number ISO/IEC TS 38501:2015[E], Geneva, Switzerland, 2015.

Kropf, Roger and Guy Scalzi, *IT Governance in Hospital and Health Systems*, Chicago: Health Information Management Systems Society, 2012.

Nunno, Tina, "IT Governance Key Initiative Overview," Gartner, Inc., https://www.gartner.com/doc/2714817/it-governance-key-initiative-overview, viewed February 27, 2016.

QR3.4

TEKSystems, "2016 Annual IT Forecast: Executive Summary," https://www.teksystems.com/-/media/teksystems_com/Files/Research/Executive%20Summaries/TEKsystems-2016-IT-Forecast-Executive-Summary.pdf?la=en, viewed June 28, 2016.

QR3.5

The Joint Commission, Sentinel Event Alert, "Safe use of information health technology," Issue 54, March 31, 2015. http://www.jointcommission.org/assets/1/18/SEA_54.pdf, viewed February 27, 2016.

QR3.6

The Standish Group, "2013 CHAOS Report," https://www.versionone.com/assets/img/files/CHAOSManifesto2013.pdf, viewed June 28, 2016.

QR3.7

Yale University Information Technology Services website, http://its.yale.edu/about/collaboration-and-governance/yale-its-committees, viewed February 27, 2016.

QR3.8

Chapter 4

Defining and Delivering IT Value

Overview

We are in the midst of a significant change in the way healthcare is delivered and paid for in the United States. The old model of fee-for-service is being replaced by value-based reimbursement. In the fee-for-service model, providers were reimbursed for each service they provided. Value-based reimbursement focuses on quality, not quantity, of service. It's changing the way healthcare operates.

As healthcare organizations focus more on defining and delivering value, the conversation will certainly turn to include all of the support systems—from IT to supply chain, facilities to environmental services, and so on. Every service provided in support of the healthcare organization will need to provide value. So, it will become increasingly important for IT leaders to be able to define, demonstrate, and deliver value in the coming years. As an IT leader, you'll be expected to understand and deliver value.

The total cost of IT services for healthcare organizations continues to increase as a percentage of the operating and capital budgets. We are being asked to define and measure the value IT adds to the organization to ensure that increasing cost is not simply a required investment, but one worth making. In *The Journey Never Ends*, authors Joslyn and Malec state the case very clearly: "IT leaders will have as many opportunities as challenges in the years ahead. Greater value will be sought from IT investments. IT leaders will need to strongly link their recommendations to value propositions, and in business terms" (Garets, p. 170).

In Chapter 3, we discussed the importance of IT governance and of aligning IT efforts with business objectives. That is one of the drivers of value in IT. In this chapter, we'll go into more detail about what IT value is and how you can create it for your organization.

IT Value Defined

Value is defined as *usefulness* or *importance*. The value of a product or service is defined by whether or not your customer would pay for it. The key element is that value is defined by the consumer, not the producer. When you go to your physician's office for a checkup, you'd be willing to pay the physician or nurse practitioner for their services; you'd probably be willing to pay for the services of the person who takes your height, weight, blood pressure, and temperature. These activities are all things you expect and value when you made the appointment, so you clearly would see them as being of value to you.

Would you be willing to pay for the person who booked your appointment or sends you the bill? Would you be willing to pay for the cost of resubmitting your insurance claim for services because an error was made the first time? Probably not. These may be a necessary part of the process, but they do not add value to you or worse, they detract from your experience (as in the case of having to deal with errors or delays).

In Lean terms, there are *value-added* activities, *nonvalued-added* activities, and *necessary-but-nonvalued-added* activities. Value-added activities are those you would recognize and pay for. Necessary-but-nonvalue-added activities are those things like billing or cleaning the office that need to occur even though you, yourself, don't find direct value in them. They are required to sustain operations in order to provide the product or service you pay for. You may expect those things to be done as part of the overall service being provided to you, but you don't want to pay a separate line item for "cleaning the office" or "disinfecting medical equipment after use." Clearly, nonvalued-added activities are just waste. Rebilling, rescheduling, confusion, convoluted work-flows, etc. all add up to waste. These are all helpful concepts in understanding how we define and recognize value. (We discuss Lean IT in detail in Chapter 9.)

Many IT activities fall in the *necessary-but-nonvalued-added* activities category if you look at it purely from your customer's perspective. As depicted in Figure 4.1, those steady-state activities are needed to keep things running, but do not inherently add value to your customer. Those value-loss activities (waste) are things like unexpected downtimes, problems, or process issues that lead to delays or rework—in other words, waste.

In healthcare IT (HIT), value must be defined by the organization and, optimally, by the end users. The organization will look at IT cost as a percentage of operating revenue and expense, but end users will look at IT as how easy the department and the technology are to work with. Value will be determined by whether the IT department is simply keeping things running or contributing to substantially *improving* the operations of the organization. As an IT leader, you know that "simply keeping operations running" is no small task and that it adds value to the organization, though perhaps not in the strict sense of the word in Lean terms.

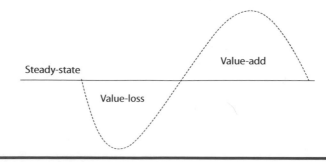

Figure 4.1 Value-add and value-loss.

One way of assessing value is to ask how things would look if this service or this technology did *not* exist or did *not* work at all. When the network is down, when an application is not working as needed, when images are not available in a patient record, the organization is negatively impacted. The organization receives value in the absence of a problem, though it's a bit of shadow chasing. Your users don't *actively* appreciate the absence of a problem, but if you were to shortchange your patching, maintenance, upgrades, expansions in any way, there would be a negative impact (slowness, unscheduled downtimes, etc.) eventually. This is similar to the doctor's office visit we discussed earlier. You wouldn't directly pay to have the exam room cleaned; you'd just expect it to be cleaned as part of the work the provider has to do in order to see patients. However, if it wasn't clean, it would certainly detract from the value of the visit.

The challenge as a HIT leader is *how* to define value for these mission critical services. If you're using the Information Technology Infrastructure Library (ITIL) framework, you could start with defining your services via a service catalog. These service catalog items define scope and functions of IT services and help define even the mundane operational services in a way end users can appreciate. These are not value-add activities, but they will detract from value if not effectively managed. Baseline services are expected and required, so the value comes from the absence of problems. Figure 4.1 depicts the conceptual difference between *value-add* and *value-loss* activities. Value-add is the area where you are finding ways to increase the value of IT through process improvement, projects, and innovation. Of course, that's the sweet spot we aim for, but the challenge is to balance the need to keep operations running smoothly (to avoid the value-loss region) and to find ways to pop into the value-add region, whether for individual initiatives or as your new steady state.

Beyond the day-to-day functions of the IT department, value lies in helping operations optimize and improve their work and workflows; in finding new and better ways to deliver services to end users and ultimately to patients. This IT activity is often divided into *operations* (sustain) and *projects* (change). These two aspects function separately and add value in distinctly different ways.

IT Value Creation

Let's define ways in which IT can create value. We've already determined that while the *run* or *steady-state* (the absence of problems and downtimes) is important, it doesn't *create* value as defined by your end user. However, as we've discussed, the absence of problems is valuable because without uninterrupted IT delivery, the organization suffers. There are generally three types of activities that generate IT value: operations, projects, and innovation, as shown in Figure 4.2. These can be broken down into five types of work that correlate to the three tiers as shown.

1. Tier 1: Standardize and optimize IT operations.
2. Tier 1: Translate operational best practices into IT work.
3. Tier 2: Create and manage strong IT governance to ensure the highest value IT work is being done.
4. Tier 2: Develop data governance to ensure information can be turned into intelligence for the organization.
5. Tier 3: Deliver innovation that delivers not just incremental, but exponential (*transformational*), improvement.

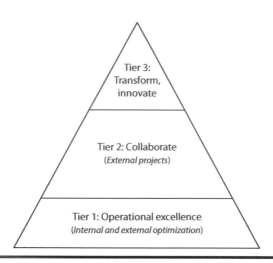

Figure 4.2 IT value pyramid. (Adapted from Ortiz, Darcy et al., 2014.)

We're including steady state in the notion of value because you can't add value to the organization until your systems and applications are running almost flawlessly. So steady state is a prerequisite to value creation. Tier 1 also includes work the IT department undertakes to keep infrastructure and applications up-to-date, highly available, and secure. That may mean project work to replace an aging storage platform or a project to replace a legacy application that no longer meets end-user needs or security requirements, for example. Also in Tier 1 is the work the IT department does in conjunction with operations to find ways to incorporate clinical or business operational best practices into the IT products such as applications, interfaces, automation, or reports.

In Tier 2, we look outside the IT department to projects requested by the organization. This is an active collaboration between IT and the business and is the fundamental driver of IT value. These projects should come through the IT governance process (item #3 in the previous list) to ensure alignment with business objectives. Without this alignment, value is reduced or perhaps absent. Finally, in Tier 2, we also find data governance, which encompasses how an organization manages data and reporting infrastructure in support of activities like business intelligence. We won't go further into data governance other than to say it is similar to IT governance in that it is a formalized process for determining how data are managed in an organization—who can take what actions with data, under what circumstances, and using what methods (The Data Governance Institute, 2015).

The value pyramid shown in Figure 4.2 indicates where most organizations' HIT departments spend their time, resources, and focus.

Business and IT leaders can truly begin to think outside the bounds of operations to look toward new, unique, and compelling ways to move the business forward. The tiers are sequential starting at the bottom because each higher level depends on successful execution at the layer below. Additionally, this also depicts the relative ratio of effort spent in each of these types of activities. IT teams typically expend between 20% and 40% of their efforts on operations and about 60% and 80% of IT resources on collaborative efforts (projects). Transformational initiatives are typically project-based, but they have to be carved out of an already full IT work schedule. Projects in Tiers 2 and 3 typically go through the IT governance process discussed in Chapter 3.

In the next several sections, we'll discuss how value is created in each of these tiers so you can begin to do a review of your own organization and determine where you may have opportunities to improve your value creation.

Tier 1—Standardize and Optimize Operations

As we've discussed, one of the most fundamental ways to deliver value is to avoid losing value. This may sound a bit like wordsmithing, but you're either adding value or detracting from value. You cannot add value to the organization until you achieve a solid steady state, where you don't have random, intermittent, or frequent unexpected issues with applications and infrastructure. The way you achieve this reliable steady state is to standardize and then optimize IT workflows.

Standardization in IT is pretty basic, and we're not going to spend a lot of time on this topic. IT leaders in any sector need to understand the importance of standards and standardization. This includes things like using templates for configuration, requiring applications to integrate with Active Directory or requiring web applications to use HTTPS, for example. These are standards that IT departments develop in order to reduce the complexity (and risk) of implementing and supporting IT applications and services. Standardization simplifies the work and reduces the risk of unexpected results (downtimes, slowdowns, errors, faults, gaps, etc.). You cannot accurately assess value without also assessing the associated risk.

Standardization also applies to *how* work is performed. In many HIT departments, standard work processes are still evolving. If you asked four different analysts or engineers how they do a "standard" task, you would likely get four different answers. Standardization is improving as IT teams find ways to automate more tasks. For example, automating user provisioning reduces risk because it is consistent and less prone to human error. Automation of repetitive tasks is a very effective way to achieve standardization.

Tasks that are not easily automated can be standardized through the use of standard work. *Standard work* is a term used in Lean, but it is also a common practice in many IT departments. Standard work is a documented process that defines exactly what steps should be taken, in what order, and in what manner they should be done. While it's very prescriptive, it's typically created by the people doing the job to document the agreed-upon best way to perform a task. This can include upgrading an application or patching a server. All work that is done frequently is a candidate for standard work. The more these tasks are standardized and performed the same way every time, the less risk your IT department faces. Fewer downtimes, fewer unanticipated interruptions, fewer errors to be corrected all translate into more time and resources for the project work requested by the organization.

Adopting a Framework

It's pretty universally true that adopting a framework will help drive standardization. There are many different frameworks that can be selected and implemented. A framework, such as Information Technology Infrastructure Library (ITIL) or Control Objectives for Information and Related Technology (COBIT), can assist in defining standard work elements and helping to

Table 4.1 IT Frameworks

Framework	Description	Use
ITIL	Widely adopted IT life cycle and service management framework.	Service delivery and process improvement.
COBIT	IT governance framework.	Provides recommendations and best practices for governance and process controls for implementing IT in business.
TOGAF	IT/enterprise architecture.	Provides a framework aimed at maximizing IT value through the coordinated planning of enterprise IT architectural elements.
PMI/Agile/ Scrum	Project management.	Provides a framework for effectively managing projects. Since projects are a significant source of (potential) value, having a project management methodology is a critical element of success.
DevOps	Agile IT life-cycle development.	DevOps is not technically a framework, but rather a mindset or philosophy that advocates for the collaboration between developers and operations to improve the planning and execution of IT work.
Lean/Six Sigma	Process improvement.	Both Lean and Six Sigma are process improvement frameworks. In the past several years, Lean has become widely used in healthcare.

Source: Adapted from Renard, Larent, "Essential Frameworks and Methodologies to Maximize the Value of IT," *ISACA Journal*, Volume 2, 2016, p. 25.

organize work in a standardized manner. Table 4.1 lists some of these and you can also use information in the References section to further explore this topic.

A word of caution about adopting any framework: A framework is intended to be a guide to assist you in managing the work of the department. While there are some frameworks that cover regulatory requirements, most are intended to lay out a structure you can leverage in your work. As such, avoid allowing the framework to become the work itself. Numerous organizations have implemented ITIL only to find layers of bureaucracy or structures they needed to attend to—rather than doing the work of the organization. Let the framework be your guide, allow it to provide a path for you to follow, but don't be held captive by your framework. When the framework becomes the work, you've crossed into dangerous, unproductive territory.

Operational Standardization

Incorporating operational best practices into IT work is another aspect of Tier 1 activity. This means working with end users to determine best practices and optimized workflows, and then finding ways to integrate those improvements into the applications you support. These often come in the form of tasks or IT requests for "enhancements" to an application. Sometimes it's as simple as changing the order of items in a drop-down box to have the most-used item appear as the default. Other times, it's a request to change the structure of a data input screen or add/change data elements. Those types of requests can be deceiving. Work with your teams to learn to identify "projects masquerading as tasks." Sometimes, staff are eager to complete the next request and fail to recognize the task is really a project that hasn't been fully defined. When spotted, those should be escalated to the IT leadership team for review as part of the IT governance process.

Most IT departments worked closely with end users when building, configuring, and implementing the electronic medical record (EMR) software; but that's not universally true. If users did not participate in the design and development of how the EMR is configured, then it's not likely to align with physical workflows and how care is provided. If that happened in your organization, users probably will find odd workarounds and use the EMR in nonstandard ways. That injects risk for patient care and creates a "data mess" (contradictory, inconsistent, unintegrated, unreachable, or unhelpful data) in the EMR that detracts from value. Beyond build/configuration, there's the element of looking at how the EMR is used; that too falls into the optimization category.

Here's a potential pitfall. Optimizing the EMR is a large organizational undertaking, not an IT project. While certain workflows or modules may be able to be optimized, the question of data governance and how the EMR is managed is a larger question your organization must tackle. There's plenty written on this topic, and a few resources are included in the References section at the end of the chapter.

As part of operational standardization, trusted vendors can be helpful in the assessment process. Typically, they see things from an outside perspective, they are not tied to "the way things have always been," and they have seen a lot of other organizations' processes so they can share best practices. Leveraging these partnerships can make sense in the right situations.

[…more…]

Developing Successful Vendor Partnerships

By Leila Shehab, Healthcare IT business and implementation executive.

Organizations that are planning on implementing large projects such as a new EMR or new modules for the EMR often struggle to justify the costs associated with these activities. It is imperative for them to assess and highlight the value that will be generated by these projects.

Pressuring the vendor for best costs is only part of the equation. Successful organizations have enlisted the vendor to assess current workflows and processes, and demonstrate how the new system can improve these and provide value to caregivers and patients. There are clear advantages to having these assessments conducted by a third party who has no vested interest in the current state. However, organizations should tightly manage who and how these assessments are conducted. They should require from the vendor that these activities be performed by experienced healthcare professionals (and not the latest vendor college hire). These professionals should be able to fully understand how and why care is provided to the patients and refrain from thinking "bells and whistles" of the latest version. The vendor team should then look at how the caregivers are using the system in support of patient care. Inefficiencies in the workflow can then be identified and improvements suggested.

Realistic performance indicators can then be identified and signed off as part of the scope of the project.

As Shehab notes, when you have a responsible and capable vendor as a business partner, you can achieve better results. Vendors who understand that providing consulting and advice as part of the product assessment add more value to the organization. Those vendors are more likely to become long-term partners instead of the "end of the quarter" sales promoters. Only those that understand the long game will become trusted partners.

Optimization of IT processes is the starting point that can only begin once standardization has been implemented. Opportunities for these kinds of improvements are everywhere. Of course, sometimes optimization can be bigger than incremental improvement. Sometimes work just needs to be ripped out and reworked in order to improve it. There are times when that is preferable to trying to continually patch and repair something that is fundamentally broken. For example, if an application doesn't meet evolving organizational requirements and it's been patched, updated and reworked, but it's still not meeting needs, the team may conclude that it's better to take that application out and replace it with another application or a new version of the existing application rather than try to continue to work around the limitations.

Optimization, then, provides the opportunity to add value by improving upon what currently exists, whether that's standard work in the IT department or an application workflow or user interface. Optimization efforts should be focused on improving these aspects and adding value (eliminating waste or driving improvement).

While optimization adds value when it improves the end-user experience, optimization of processes internal to IT can also add value through freeing up time and resources to work on more valuable activities. If you can save 1,000 hours per year by improving an internal process, that frees up 1,000 hours to do something that adds *more* value. Looking for these opportunities should be part of the mindset of staff and leaders in HIT.

Best Practices Add Value

Best practices are standardized ways of performing work in the most efficient and effective manner. These are either adopted from industry norms or are developed through honing internal processes. Best practices are essentially the super set of standardized practices. Adopting best practices can quickly move the department toward delivering value to the organization.

For example, most HIT departments have best practices in place (hopefully documented as standards) around how application upgrades are analyzed and performed, how change management functions, how virtualized servers are built (for a consistent, hardened server configuration), etc. These best practices are adopted to drive consistency and excellence in IT operations.

 **Tier 2—Collaboration**

Collaboration is the second tier of IT value. It involves the collaboration of IT with organizational counterparts in the development and deployment of projects that involve IT. These projects should be reviewed and approved through the IT governance process. While IT governance is the mechanism that keeps demand from devolving into chaos, it is also the most primary source for understanding how and where IT adds value to the organization. Therefore, this is very much a collaborative process. Projects that align with organizational objectives and are selected through the IT governance process should, by definition, add the most value to the organization. The process of building a business case, developing potential solutions, assessing options, and implementing a project plan is only successful when it is collaborative.

At a fundamental level, having a strong project management process and discipline is key to your ability to add value through collaborative activities and organizational projects. Value creation and risk management are two hallmarks of IT governance as well as sound project management. If you do not have project management processes in place, that's the first place to start. A discussion of project management is outside the scope of this book, but you can refer to the References section at the end of this chapter for more on project management.

Project work has the potential to add value to the organization in a variety of ways. Most notably, new features and functions needed by the organization to deliver better, safer, more cost-effective patient care are the bulk of projects that fall into Tier 2. The challenge for all HIT departments is managing the demand for projects. If your organization has a program management office (PMO), you may have a very clear, concise, and consistent process for handling incoming IT project requests. You'd likely have your PMO represented in your IT governance function. If you have an IT-based PMO, or it is not involved in the organizational-level IT governance process, you may not have a strong process for managing external demand. If you do not have any formal PMO function at all, there's a good chance projects are running wild in your department.

One of the areas that currently demands a lot of IT project time is optimization of the EMR. According to authors Wager, Lee, and Glaser in *Health Care Information Systems: A Practical Approach for Health Care Management*, "Rarely do organizations re-visit their IT investments to determine if the promised value was actually achieved. … Post implementation audits can be conducted to identify value achievement progress and the steps still needed to achieve maximum gain" (Wager, p. 430). Unfortunately, a post-implementation review is the exception, not the norm, in most organizations. However, it is one of the best ways to determine if value was created and to articulate this value back to the organization. If a project achieves its goals—scope, budget, quality, timeframe—its value should be pretty clear. If it's not, then the pre-project work may be the source of the problem.

For example, if you successfully implement a new module in the EMR but everyone is left wondering why the project was done in the first place, then clearly the IT governance function is broken. A project slipped through, was approved, prioritized, analyzed, planned, and implemented without a clear value statement. Or, it never really went through the formal process in the first place. As an IT leader, you can help prevent these situations by being clear about value early on, before the project gets underway. Ask a lot of questions; be prepared to get some pushback. Politely inquire as to the value, the business case, the return on investment (ROI) expectations. If the answers are misaligned with the proposed project work, speak up. Ask more questions. If every IT leader were empowered (better yet, expected) to speak up and put the brakes on a project that is about to move forward without clear objectives, we would have far fewer of these kinds of projects to contend with after the fact.

[…more…]

As an IT leader, you don't always have the authority to stop a project that makes no sense or that is poorly aligned or unlikely to yield value. Depending on the overall culture and management style of your organization, you may feel completely empowered or completely unable to address this type of disconnect. In many situations, however, you can achieve results by articulating concerns in terms of risks and by providing alternatives or suggestions. If you can remember that someone in your organization is simply trying to solve a problem, you can assist in redirecting the conversation. *Seek first to understand* (to quote Stephen Covey) and then be a solution provider. Understand the problem at hand and find better, more acceptable, more aligned, and value-adding solutions. That's not always easy (or possible), but that is where you can make a positive difference in the organization.

Finally, collaboration can also involve participating in meetings, sitting on committees, and sharing information with colleagues. Though the majority of our discussion on creating IT value has been centered on work delivered by IT staff, there is a huge opportunity to add intellectual or knowledge value through your own activities. By actively participating with peers and colleagues throughout the organization on efforts that are not specifically IT related, you can add value through helping others to understand IT and your perspectives on the business. Though this might be considered a "soft" value, it adds value nonetheless. Collaboration as a value-added activity should not be underestimated. New perspectives and new ideas often come from collaboration, and that leads us into the next tier of IT value—innovation and transformation.

Tier 3—Transform and Innovate

The top tier of IT value is transformation and innovation. This is where a lot of attention is focused in HIT right now and for good reason. Most healthcare organizations have implemented an EMR at this point. By all accounts, results are mixed at best. Some organizations have done an excellent job improving patient care through the deployment of the EMR; others are lagging. Regardless of the reasons for mixed results, the industry collectively is expecting that the next step in using the EMR is to dramatically improve and transform patient care—not just incrementally, but exponentially. According to authors Joslyn and Malec, "Innovation will be an increasing differentiator for organizations. CIOs will need to inspire and foster IT innovations to drive breakthroughs in care coordination, disease management, patient engagement, clinician productivity, and overall organizational effectiveness" (Garets, p. 170).

As an IT leader, how can you best engage in this Tier 3 work? How can you manage the day-to-day operations as well as find ways to innovate? Let's answer that question by starting with how projects can add incremental or exponential value to the organization. Then we'll discuss ideas for how you might find ways to initiate or participate in IT transformation and innovation.

At the top of the IT value pyramid, Tier 3 is still very project-oriented. However, it differs from Tier 2 because projects related to innovation or transformation typically are not "routine" types of projects. And, while these innovative projects certainly have the greatest chance of adding value if they're successful and deliver on the project objectives, they also bring more risk of failure. If a project at this tier fails to meet objectives (or fails altogether), it has a greater chance of detracting from value. Often these types of projects are leading edge, are full of unknowns, and require more organizational resources (time, money, staff, research, analysis, solution development, etc.). With innovation comes the risk of experimentation. So, in order to maximize potential value delivery, managing and reducing risk is key in these types of projects.

A large portion of HIT cost is on pretty basic things such as servers, storage, off-the-shelf applications such as email, monitoring tools, and even financial and human resource systems. Most are pretty fundamental aspects of IT and are needed simply to run the business, as discussed earlier. We mentioned earlier that operations takes between 20% and 40% of a typical HIT department's overall time and resources, but it may be higher for infrastructure teams. Regardless of how you do the math, that leaves roughly 40%–60% of the time left for project work. This also includes new function and new feature requests, Tier 2 projects, and other "external" drivers. That leaves very little time or resources to do something new, something innovative, something that will move your organization out of a linear improvement path and onto an exponential improvement path. Some organizations run large project backlogs. Sometimes that's because the governance process is broken. Other times it's because the IT department is understaffed or lacks the right mix of skills. Still other times it's because the organization is growing rapidly and support departments like IT can't keep up. Regardless of the reasons, it's challenging to get to a place where there's time, resources, and focus on innovation.

Figure 4.3 represents how this plays out in most organizations, and it underscores the opportunity we're missing. Using very simple math just to illustrate this point, you can see the curve of the linear path (dashed line), which represents doing the same thing day-to-day. The solid line represents the curve of the exponential path, where value increases at a steep curve rather than a slow, flat rise. It becomes clear that just delivering on the day-to-day work, even when it's being improved and optimized, is no longer acceptable.

Clearly, the potential for value creation lies between the two lines. Figure 4.4 depicts the same graph with vertical bars showing the location of potential value from innovation. Incremental improvement is expected; exponential improvement is what really drives the organization to another level. It's usually the basis of competitive advantage in a marketplace. In healthcare, that can mean things like introducing and deploying a new technology that is a clear market differentiator such as mobility for physicians, tracking and publicizing ER wait times, or improving patient care through the innovative use of consumer health or mobile technologies.

These are things that matter and these are the types of transformative initiatives that healthcare organizations would love to achieve.

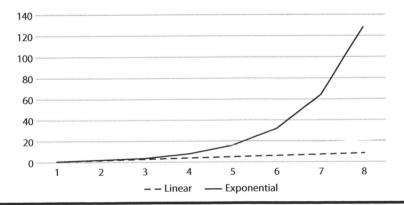

Figure 4.3 Linear versus exponential improvement.

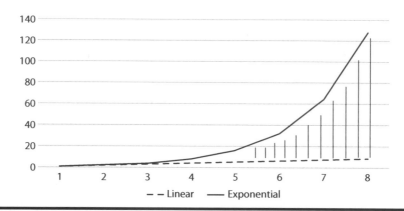

Figure 4.4   Value opportunity.

Making Room for Innovation

More and more healthcare organizations are creating and funding innovation offices, innovation departments, or even innovation organizations. The purpose of these units is to find opportunities to deviate from the standard approach to healthcare and HIT and find ways to truly make a leap forward for patient care.

Granted, these organizations have the vision, the leadership, and the funding to undertake these kinds of initiatives. Many of us work in healthcare organizations that are doing their best to stay one step ahead of the changing healthcare environment by maintaining/improving patient care and remaining fiscally solvent. Those are challenging requirements all on their own. Many organizations don't foster innovation as a separate activity, but try in some measure to incorporate it into the work they do.

If "all" we're doing is keeping things running, we're not adding significant value. So, how do we move toward delivering innovation and how do we carve out time and resources to do so? The key lies in working on the Tier 1 and Tier 2 activities in the IT value pyramid. If you spend time and effort improving operational efficiency (Tier 1), you should be able to reduce the time, resources, and cost associated with maintaining and operating the IT department. Those savings can be translated into time and money available for more innovative work. Likewise, if you improve your project management processes and associated IT governance processes (Tier 2), you may be able to deliver on project work more efficiently. Carving time and cost from both of these tiers of activities can leave you with a small slice of time, resources, and funding to begin innovating. Figure 4.5 depicts a hypothetical breakout of IT expense components over time, showing how efficiencies can be used to move toward innovation.

Clearly, as other costs are contained or reduced, the resources available for innovation can be increased. There is an underlying assumption here—that your organization will understand and appreciate the work you're doing and the value you're delivering. If that critical link is not made, then you will find that your operational and project efficiencies will be absorbed into the organization. In short, if you cannot clearly articulate value to your organization, you'll find yourself fighting harder each year to maintain staff and funding.

There are many different ways to communicate the value IT adds to the organization, but one of the most fundamental is a financial-based approach. Every healthcare CFO wants to understand what value is being delivered for the IT expense. Transparency and clear communication can move the conversation from cost cutting to cost-effectiveness. One effective method is to develop a visual representation of your IT department's costs over time. It's particularly helpful to break out expenses according to categories that make sense to the end user (versus IT). Figure 4.5

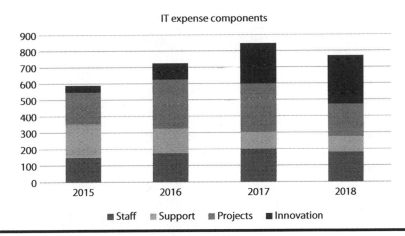

Figure 4.5 Historical and projected IT costs example.

shows an example of how you could potentially break out your historical and projected costs. These costs are broken out into staff, support, projects, and innovation. Where you draw the line between support and projects or projects and innovation is somewhat subjective, but if you define these and use the same parameters consistently, you'll create clarity instead of confusion.

In Figure 4.5, you can see that the cost of staff as a percentage of the entire IT expense is projected to peak in 2017 and may come down a bit in 2018 due perhaps to an increased reliance on cloud or hosted solutions. Support costs in Figure 4.5 gradually reduce as costs for infrastructure are negotiated and/or improved, and standardized processes drive operational excellence. Project expense grows from 2015 through 2017 and then declines in 2018 due to the shift from project work to transformational work. The ratio of projects to innovation (defined here as projects that drive transformation versus projects that drive incremental improvements) changes, and innovation becomes a greater contributor to IT expense (and, presumably, IT value).

This hypothetical model shows one method of how you can report to the organization in financial terms. If you can show that the IT department optimizes costs as part of the standard process and has moved toward adding value through project work and innovation, the conversation shifts from "how much more can you reduce costs" to "how much more value can you add with additional funding." Granted, this change does not happen overnight nor during a single budget cycle. However, as an IT leader, when you begin speaking the language of business and demonstrating, with data and visuals, how you're improving the business, you will gradually change the focus. To paraphrase Edwards Deming, "without data, it's just an opinion." Once we move away from opinion and toward facts and data, we can have a much more productive conversation about IT value.

We can also communicate value through improving our IT governance function (discussed in Chapter 3) and our project management function. Each project is an opportunity to demonstrate IT core competencies in financial management, business alignment, and process improvement. If each IT project is well defined, well run, and well implemented, the business will derive value from those projects. However, delivering a project on time, on budget, and in scope is not enough. There are two key elements that must accompany these successful projects, and those are successfully operationalizing the project (sustained improvement) and clearly articulating that success (marketing). We'll discuss marketing in Chapter 5.

Though statistics around successful project completion vary, the current estimate on project success rates is about 29%. At-risk projects, deemed "challenged," represented 52% of all projects, and failed projects comprised 19%, as shown in Figure 4.6 (Hastie and Wojewoda 2015, QR4.5). While this is specific to software development projects, these data points are a good proxy for the success rate of IT projects overall.

Assuming that only 29% of projects are successful, IT operations has a long way to go in the middle tier of IT value delivery (refer back to Figure 4.2). When IT projects can be delivered successfully on a consistent basis, the value proposition bends upward toward innovation and transformation—or at least, you'll have the option of moving your IT department in that direction.

Communicating project success typically follows project management processes including tracking budget, scope, and timeline. However, in a more mature IT organization, you'd begin with developing a strong business case that includes a proposed ROI. Then, after the project is implemented and operationalized, the ROI can be reviewed as part of the project review and close out process (or later, if more time is needed to realize ROI). This is an IT maturity capability that needs to be consistently demonstrated before you're likely to be asked to undertake more innovative (and potentially, more value-added) projects.

[…more…]

Healthcare Information and Management Systems Society (HIMSS) has developed a program for HIT leaders to benchmark and evaluate their IT value. In 2013, HIMSS unveiled this *Health IT Value Suite*, a set of tools and data intended to help HIT leaders assess IT value. This framework uses the acronym STEPS to categorize areas of IT value in healthcare. It stands for satisfaction, treatment/clinical, electronic information/data, prevention/patient education and savings. At the annual conference in February 2016, HIMSS announced the addition of the Value Score, a numeric score summarizing HIT value. The score is composed of baseline, perceived, recognized, and innovative value scores. This scoring system relies on organizational input and may be a helpful tool to use in assessing and articulating IT value in your organization. (HIMSS 2016, QR4.7)

Enabling Innovation

Certainly, the topic of transformation and innovation in HIT is a new focus. According to a March 2016 blog post by Dr. John Halamka (2016, QR4.4):

> In the next 24 months we'll see an accelerating evolution of fee for service into alternative payment models fueled by MACRA (Medicare Access & CHIP Reauthorization Act of 2015) and MIPS (Merit-Based Incentive Payment System, a physician reimbursement program set to start in 2019). We will no longer be driven by compliance imperatives (Meaningful Use, HIPAA, Affordable Care Act, and ICD10), but instead will need to improve outcomes in order to survive financially. No one is completely sure how to do that, but there are enablers. (Halamka 2016, QR4.4)

This points to the need to move more quickly to improving the state of healthcare through innovative and transformative initiatives, all of which have IT as key enablers.

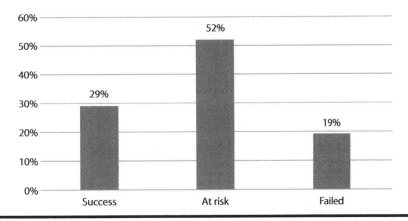

Figure 4.6   Project success and failure rates.

In addition, there are a number of leaders in this field who are forging new ground. HIMSS opened the HIMSS Innovation Center in Cleveland, Ohio, in 2013 as a showcase for innovative new technologies and approaches to HT (HIMSS, "Innovation," QR4.6). Many leading healthcare organizations have created innovation roles (Chief Innovation Officer), departments, or even separate companies to spur transformation in a focused and intentional manner.

Clearly, this is where the future of HIT lies—in leveraging existing systems and processes in new, innovative ways to effect significant change in healthcare delivery. That's the exciting, forward-looking work happening in HIT today, but it's not always easy to find the path forward from where we are today.

Being innovative means first having the fundamental aspects of HIT working well. It also means having a culture that appreciates forward-thinking, an organization that accepts change, and an IT department that can work in two modes simultaneously. That can be challenging for any IT leader, but looking first to deliver operational excellence, then deliver projects on time, in scope, and on budget will provide the foundation for finding and delivering transformative value to your IT organization. No one ever said being a HIT leader would be easy, but the challenge is certainly what drives most of us to keep forging ahead in this complex and compelling field.

Summary

Defining and delivering value in today's HIT environment can be challenging. The tools and techniques we've discussed are very practical and actionable, but that doesn't make the job easy. It should be clear that operational excellence and strong project management processes are the underpinning of value creation and are necessary to drive the conversation away from cost cutting to value creation. As a HIT leader, your efforts to standardize and improve operations (operational excellence), collaborate (deliver IT projects or projects with IT components successfully), and innovate will be the measurement of value. When you are able to articulate the value your team brings to the organization and demonstrate the positive business impact of your work, you'll be leading IT that is making a contribution to the organization and driving transformative change in healthcare delivery. Using data to present the value proposition to your organization will help forge the foundation for making positive gains toward innovation and transformation in HIT.

References

For more on this topic, visit http://susansnedaker.com/leading-hit.

QR4.1

Binder, Leah, "Good News and Bad News About Value Based Healthcare," October 1, 2014, http://www.forbes.com/sites/leahbinder/2014/10/01/good-news-and-bad-news-about -value-based-health-care/#7e6a09a3431d, viewed February 27, 2016.

QR4.2

Broadbent, Marianne and Ellen S. Kitzis, *The New CIO Leader*, Boston: Harvard Business School Press, 2005.

Brown, Bobbi and Jared Crapo, Health Catalyst, Inc., "The Key to Transitioning from Fee-for-Service to Value-Based Reimbursement," 2014, https://www.healthcatalyst.com /wp-content/uploads/2014/08/The-Key-to-Transitioning-from-Fee-for-Service.pdf, viewed June 28, 2016.

QR4.3

Coplan, Scott and David Masuda, *Project Management for Healthcare Information Technology*, New York: McGraw-Hill Companies, Inc., 2011.

Garets, David and Claire McCarthy Garets, Editors, *The Journey Never Ends: Technology's Role in Helping Perfect Health Care Outcomes*, Boca Raton, FL: CRC Press, 2016.

Halamka, John D., MD, "At HIMSS16 buzzwords are dead. It's about innovating at all costs," March 3, 2016, http://medcitynews.com/2016/03/himss16-buzzwords-innovation/?rf=1, viewed April 16, 2016.

QR4.4

Hastie, Shane and Stéphane Wojewoda, "Standish Group 2015 Chaos Report—Q&A with Jennifer Lynch," October 4, 2015, http://www.infoq.com/articles/standish-chaos-2015, viewed June 28, 2016.

QR4.5

Healthcare Information Management and Systems Society (HIMSS), Innovation Center, http://www.himssinnovationcenter.org.

QR4.6

Healthcare Information Management and Systems Society (HIMSS), Value Score framework, 2016, http://www.himss.org/ValueSuite, viewed June 30, 2016.

QR4.7

Institute for Health Technology Transformation, "Lean IT: Making Healthcare More Efficient," New York: Institute for Health Technology Transformation, 2013, http://ihealthtran.com/iHT2LeanHealthIT.pdf, viewed June 29, 2016.

QR4.8

ISACA, "COBIT 4.1: Framework for IT Governance and Control," http://www.isaca.org/Knowledge-Center/COBIT/Pages/Overview.aspx, viewed May 9, 2016.

QR4.9

Kropf, Roger, PhD and Guy Scalzi, MBA, *IT Governance in Hospitals and Health Systems*, Chicago: HIMSS, 2012.

Ortiz, Darcy, Aziz Safa, David Aires, CXO Talk #56, 2014, https://www.cxotalk.com/darcy-ortiz-general-manager-aziz-safavp-david-aires-vp?cat=2014, viewed April 03, 2016.

QR4.10

Porter, Michael E. and Thomas H. Lee, MD, "The Strategy That Will Fix Health Care," *Harvard Business Review*, October 2013, https://hbr.org/2013/10/the-strategy-that-will-fix-health-care, viewed June 27, 2016.

QR4.11

Renard, Larent, "Essential Frameworks and Methodologies to Maximize the Value of IT," *ISACA Journal*, Volume 2, 2016, p. 25.

Snedaker, Susan and Nels Hoenig, Tech. Ed., *How to Cheat at IT Project Management*, Rockland, MA: Syngress, 2005.

The Data Governance Institute, "Definitions of Data Governance," 2015, http://www.datagovernance.com/adg_data_governance_definition/, viewed June 30, 2016.

Wager, Karen A., Frances Wickham Lee, and John P. Glaser, *Health Care Information Systems: A Practical Approach for Health Care Management*, San Francisco: Jossey-Bass, 2009.

Chapter 5

Marketing Healthcare Information Technology

Overview

Most people who work in healthcare IT (HIT) don't really connect with the concept of marketing IT. Why would we need to market a core service like IT and who is the target audience? While this concept of marketing may seem out of place in a book on HIT leadership, it is actually a core competency for IT leaders of the future. In this chapter, we'll explore the elements of successful marketing and provide recommendations on how you can implement this in your HIT organization.

Marketing is defined as the set of activities undertaken to make people aware of your products or services. According to Christian, Kirby, and Bennett in *Make I.T. Known*, "Healthcare IT marketing is a process that defines and satisfies the hospital's IT wants and needs. ... It is also concerned with anticipating hospital departments' future needs and wants, often through market research" (Christian, p. 3). Marketing activities can run the gamut from advertising to promotional events and beyond—but the common element is that they are intended to increase *awareness* and foster a *positive perception* of the organization. Measures of effective marketing include how well consumers can identify your products or services, how desirable they appear, how much value they appear to provide, etc. If you look at HIT projects, deliverables, and even maintaining/operating services as the "product" that needs to be marketed, you can see that driving awareness of these activities might be beneficial. If your customers (clinical, operations) understand what you do and perceive it as being valuable, you will be well on your way to increasing the value (both real and perceived) your department lends to the organization.

In this chapter, we'll explore marketing activities related to HIT including branding, relationship building, project and departmental marketing activities, and public relations (PR). Of course, what we'll cover in this chapter is just a thin slice of marketing information. If you're really interested in learning more about the fundamental concepts and activities of marketing, we've included some resources in the References section at the end of the chapter.

First, Know Your Customers

Before you can undertake any sort of marketing activity, you need to understand who your target market is. We'll refer to this target as "your customers," and for our purposes, we're referring to all the people that use information technology in healthcare today. The reason this is a crucial starting point is because HIT has many customers, and they are quite varied in their needs, wants, and opinions of HIT. It's important to understand these segments so marketing activities and messages can be tailored to these groups. A one-size-fits-all approach will likely mean that your message will fall flat for most of your customers.

You can begin to understand your customer groups by breaking down your organization by role or function. At a high level, you have your executive team. You also have physicians, nurses, other care providers (therapists, patient care techs, etc.), and services such as OR, cath lab, radiology, pharmacy, and lab, each with their array of roles. Within the physician population, of course, you have a wide range of types—from hospitalists to neurosurgeons, cardiologists to primary care physicians and everything in between. Outside of the clinical areas, you have customers in the business areas (finance, HR, payroll, supply chain), facilities, security, and communications, to name a few. Finally, you have other IT staff who are your service providers or your customers or both.

In order to effectively bring your message of IT value to the organization, you will need to engage with your customers to understand what is valuable to them. The value discussion begins with executives and (hopefully) occurs through a formal IT governance process where priorities are set based on value potential. You should have a pretty clear idea of what your executive team wants through this process.

Do you know what your physicians want? Is it even possible to lump them all into one group? If you work at a hospital, you probably have many different service lines, and each group of physicians has their own set of objectives. Do you need to survey every physician that works at your healthcare organization (HCO)? No, but you should be sure you are connecting with the thought leaders in that population. Is there a physician forum you attend (or could attend)? Does your HCO have a chief medical information officer? If so, work with that person to define how, where, and when to best engage with a variety of physician leaders to ensure you understand their needs. Do you have a chief nursing informatics officer or a chief nursing officer? He or she would be another crucial ally in developing your marketing strategies. Physicians and nurses are typically the most challenging audiences to reach, but they are among your most important customers. Therefore, it's important to focus on successful strategies with these two core customer groups.

Stephen Covey (1989) introduced the phrase "seek first to understand, then be understood." This is excellent advice for anyone, especially in HIT. Listening to your customers, understanding their jobs and the role of technology in those jobs, seeing how they interact with technology, and observing the challenges they face in using that technology is a necessary first step. Of course, this is key to everything we do in HIT, not just in marketing our services and successes. Some of what you learn may lead you to fixing IT problems, which is part of the value of this effort. However, in this marketing context, the information you glean from these conversations and observations will help you understand what the customer values, what they need, and what you need to improve upon. From there, you can develop strategies for communicating the IT value.

[...more...]

Listening to your customers, is a repeating theme in healthcare (and all) IT. We've discussed it in all the preceding chapters in this book. As you can see, there are many facets to knowing your customer. Each of these elements informs strategy, vision, value creation, and more. All of these stem from fundamental marketing activities that help you understand what your customer needs, what they want, how you add value, and how best to deliver that value to them. It's not about always saying yes; it's about truly understanding the organization and accurately assessing your team's capabilities to deliver what's needed. It's one of the most challenging and most rewarding aspects of being an IT leader in today's healthcare environment.

Customer Segmentation

Since this is not a marketing book, we're not going to delve into tremendous detail in this section. However, it is useful to understand some basics about customer segmentation so you can develop a marketing plan that will address your customers' unique needs. Typically segmentation involves breaking your customers into groups of individuals who share defined traits. For IT purposes, they're likely large segments such as executives, nursing leaders, physician leaders, special procedure leaders, supply chain leaders, etc. There are many different approaches to customer segmentation, but they all share some fundamentals, which we'll cover here.

1. **Divide your customers into defined segments.**

   Define these segments in writing. What makes a customer belong to this segment, what makes them unique from other segments? Writing this down will help you focus efforts later. If it's helpful you can give formal names for these various segments so you can work with each segment separately. You might look at job function (physicians, nurses, business office), interaction with information technologies, and demographics, to name a few attributes that might be useful in HIT. For example, who are your executives or your practice managers or your nursing leaders? What traits do they share? What do they care about with respect to the business in general and IT specifically?

2. **Determine the opportunity with each segment.**

   In traditional marketing, you would look at the profit potential of each segment and determine which your most valuable segments were. In healthcare, that's less applicable. The goal in these marketing efforts is not to drive sales or profits but to increase awareness of the value and contribution of IT in the organization. So in this respect, the opportunity with each segment could more accurately be defined as understanding how these groups view IT and where you have the most improvement to make (or where having a more positive reputation would be most helpful). If a small, vocal group of physicians grumbles frequently about IT, then that group might be your highest value target. If a large group of nurses routinely complains about the electronic medical record (EMR) workflows they need to go through in caring for a patient during a hospital stay, that group might prove to be a high value marketing target.

3. **Invest time and effort in tailoring a communication/marketing plan, especially to your toughest customers.**

One-size does not fit all and if you get sloppy or lazy in this key step, you'll lose your opportunity. Take time to think about the best approach with these customer groups. Talk with their formal or informal leaders to understand what type of message will get through. Content, timing, frequency, and delivery mechanisms all come into play. For some, it might be providing a dashboard of current status for key projects; for others, it might be a monthly recap of features released into production and the impact on the customer's workflows.

4. **Measure results.**

In a perfect world, you would take a baseline survey or sample then develop a theory as to what will make a difference with the customer segment, create the plan, do the action, and measure the results (standard Plan-Do-Check-Act, to use Lean language). But the world is not perfect, and we have to work with the reality of our organization. Observation and anecdotal information, while qualitative and nonscientific, can be acceptable methods of measurement. You can track and catalog the number of times you get an executive escalation about issues within a customer segment and compare that over time. You can ask participants in a committee, group, or meeting about their perception of IT and ask it again in 90 or 180 days. You may need to get creative in how you measure results, but measurement of some sort needs to be part of the equation or you're just tossing things at the problem without having any supporting data about the impact of those actions.

Understanding your customers and finding ways to tailor your marketing and communication efforts is a very important element to IT marketing, especially in healthcare. It also helps to address one segment at a time rather than try to improve all customer segments at once. We've already discussed that a one-size-fits-all approach actually fits no one and is a waste of time. At the same time, trying to tailor marketing messages to many customer segments at once is likely to fail through lack of time and focus. Instead, choose one or two tough customers to start with and work through those challenges before taking on another segment. It's also important to understand that some higher-level "branding" messages, intended to be somewhat universally applied, can help support your efforts by providing a broader context for your targeted messages. Moving customers from detractors to allies will require you to use a variety of tools and techniques. Let's start by looking at branding.

Branding

Branding is an activity to which we've all been exposed. In its purest form, branding involves activities that are not specifically tied to selling you a product or service. Instead, branding aims to increase your awareness and opinion of a brand (think Nike®, Amazon®, Tesla®, and Liberty Mutual®, to name a few). Branding also includes things like wrappers on city buses, sponsorships of stadiums and athletic events, logo placement (on athletic team jerseys, for example), and other kinds of awareness activities that don't necessarily try to sell you something. What consumers think of a brand is the sum total of their knowledge, awareness and experience of the company, its products and services, reputation, and actions.

So, how does that translate into HIT? If we focus on two key elements of branding—*awareness* and *perception*—we can begin to draw clear lines from branding to an HIT department. What do your customers think of your department? What reputation do you have? What is the perception? Are you seen as a black hole? The department that says NO? Difficult to work with? Impossible to understand? Or are you seen as a valued business partner? An innovator? A "we'll figure it out with you" department?

A common saying in marketing is "own your brand or someone else will." This means that you must actively manage your brand to deliver the message you choose. How do you do that with a HIT department?

If you can develop statements about how you want your team to behave, or be viewed, you can begin to understand how to brand your efforts. Every organization is different; every IT department is different as well. Some organizations may highly value an IT department that is always thorough and analytical, basing decisions on rigorous analysis and data. Other organizations might value responsiveness more. They might need or expect an IT department that is agile and responsive, reacting almost immediately even in the absence of complete data. That is part of your job as an IT leader—to develop a strong understanding of what is needed and expected so you can align your brand with the organization's objectives.

Brand Builder: Service Delivery

In Chapter 4, we discussed developing and refining operational excellence as the foundation of building IT value. Part of operational excellence is service delivery. Providing excellent customer service for every end user is the foundation of building your IT brand. If service requests take weeks when they should take days, if every request for a new computer or a new function of an existing application takes months, if your IT staff make users feel stupid or insulted, then you have some serious work to do before even considering branding. If that is the case with your department, you need to go back to square one. In Chapter 8, we'll go into more detail on managing successful teams.

If you have a customer service mindset already instilled in your team's culture, you might want to engage the team in figuring out how to amp that up further. What would it take to give "ridiculously good" service? Remember, it's rarely about money; it's almost always about people and process.

For example, do you use service level agreements (SLAs)? If you have defined service levels, do you (a) rarely, (b) sometimes, (c) consistently, or (d) always meet them? Defining and delivering on service levels is a great place to find opportunities for service delivery improvements. Perhaps you're consistently or always meeting service levels; you might ask whether those service levels are actually helpful to your customer. For instance, if a high priority break/fix task has a service level of 3 days, your customers are left with broken or unusable technology for 3 days. Is that really acceptable? Review your service levels with your customers, make sure they meet the needs of the organization and are reasonable expectations for your IT teams, then meet them consistently and communicate.

[…more…]

One of the areas I have seen a lot of IT departments fall short on is communication and follow-up. In HIT, it's particularly challenging because the nurse that reported a broken computer on wheels, for example, might not be on shift when the device is repaired and returned to service. The physician who reported a problem with an order set in the EMR may not be easily found for follow-up when the problem is fixed. Engage your team in solving this problem. It might involve sending an email as follow-up, a printed tag that's left at the nursing station, a weekly or monthly email blast (like a newsletter) showing service tickets opened and resolved, etc. If you have monthly or quarterly councils, forums, or meetings, assess whether those might be appropriate venues for communicating responsiveness and results. Get creative in communicating the resolution of a request—it will add to your team's reputation for delivering service excellence.

Great service delivery does not always mean saying yes. However, there is an artful way to say no without that being the first word out of your mouth. Many IT staff have strong analytical skills, and when a new idea is proposed, they immediately begin thinking of all the problems and all the things that could go wrong. While that's a useful set of skills, it's often a brand killer. Some organizational development experts suggest leading with "That's an interesting idea. Tell me more about it" or "We could do that with a few modifications" or "Yes, if. ..." Language is an incredibly powerful tool, and it can support or undermine everything you and your team accomplish. If you need some assistance in this area, do a search for "great customer service phrases," and you'll find a wealth of valuable resources.

Brand Builder: Projects

IT projects come in all shapes and sizes. They are another area of opportunity for building your IT brand. Projects can be IT-centric (i.e., the IT department initiates it) or organization-centric (someone else needs something that involves IT). When a project is IT-centric, you have a huge opportunity to engage customers at the very earliest stages to get input, suggestions, and buy-in. It is through this process you build your brand as a valued business partner. The opposite would be delivering an IT project without proper end-user engagement and developing a reputation as a department who just "jams things in" without due consideration.

Part of a strong project management process includes getting stakeholders involved early in the project process as well as developing communication plans for before, during, and after project implementation. Project activities and project results can build your IT brand—attributes such as "helpful," "organized," "effective," and "collaborative" all can be reinforced during project work. We'll discuss projects more fully later in this chapter.

Brand Builder: Reports and Communication

Publicly traded corporations publish an annual report each year. The obligatory financials are usually printed in microscopic print at the back of the document. The front of the document is usually a long, glossy, well-designed promotion for the company. It touts the amazing results, the wonderful work, the incredible future ahead. These are intended to be aspirational. Reading these reports should leave you with an emotional response the firm wants you to have—joy, excitement, enthusiasm, optimism—there's a whole host of positive emotions firms try to evoke through these documents.

So how is that related to your HIT department? Every document, every report, every communication you distribute is an opportunity to build your brand. "Your brand" here refers both to your professional brand as an IT leader as well as your IT team's reputation. Each communication can add to, or detract from, your brand. Consider the following two examples. The first example, shown in Figure 5.1, is what you'd typically see from most IT departments. It's clear, it's to the point. It's a bit sulky ("already overbooked"), but it states the facts.

By contrast, the example shown in Figure 5.2 has basically all the same information, but it's formatted and worded in a way that is more likely to engage the reader and generate a more positive response.

You may not have realized it in the past, but *how* you present information can be as powerful as *what* you say. Spending a bit of effort to format your reports can dramatically improve how they are perceived. If you need assistance, ask if anyone in the IT department has design skills or ask for help from your communications/marketing department. A minor investment in style can reap big rewards.

Finally, infographics have become very popular for communicating a wealth of information in a visual manner. Though creating an effective infographic is not as simple as it might appear,

Quarterly Results
The Information Technology Services department completed 4 projects this quarter. In addition, we started 3 new projects requested by clinical operations focused on a variety of clinical areas. These projects are intended to improve patient care, reduce hospital length of stay and reduce OR turn-around times. Though the IT project worklist was already over-booked, the team found a way to include these 3 new unplanned projects on the project schedule.

Figure 5.1 Report Example 1.

> ## Quarterly Results
>
> **The Information Technology Services department had an impressive quarter,** completing 4 strategic projects and initiating another 3 new mission-critical projects aligned with:
> > Improving patient care
> > > Reducing hospital length of stay
> > > > Reducing OR turn-around times

Figure 5.2 Report Example 2.

you can leverage some of your more creative folks in the department to help communicate information about achievements, statistics, or general IT topics in a way that is clear, compelling, and engaging. The proliferation of social media sites that rely heavily on visual content is testament to this growing trend. Leverage it for your IT communications—but be sure it's well done. A poorly done infographic (or any visual document) can hurt more than it helps. If you're not familiar with infographics, just type "infographic examples" into your favorite search engine's image section and you'll see thousands of great examples. There are also many ways to simply make existing data more visual so they can be understood at a glance. Figures 5.3 and 5.4 show examples of visual data reports. Of course, they lose a bit in translation from full color to grayscale, but you can see that this type of data reporting is more engaging, is easy to understand, and supports the IT brand.

Brand Killers

Generally, doing the opposite of any of the brand builder activities can detract from, or even kill, your brand. Poor customer service, poor service attitude, poor communication and language, poor project processes, and poor reporting and communication can all reverse the good work you might otherwise be doing in building your brand. As Warren Buffet said, "It takes 20 years to build a reputation and 5 minutes to ruin it. If you think about that, you'll do things differently."

Most IT departments have earned the reputation they have—whether that reputation is good or bad. What you do consistently over time is what will create that reputation, and reputation is a strong component of brand. As an IT leader, you should spend some time thinking about your department's reputation and how you may want to change it. It takes slow, consistent effort to revise a reputation, and as Mr. Buffet notes, it can quickly be ruined by thoughtless action. How do you want your department to be known, and what steps will you take to improve upon your current state?

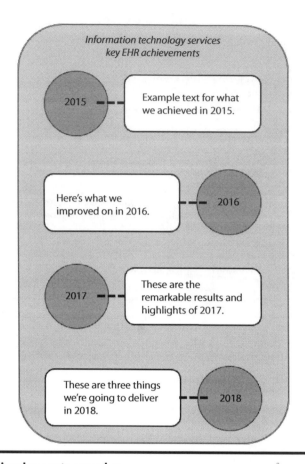

Figure 5.3 Simple visual report examples.

[…more…]

If you want to improve service excellence, improve project processes or even elevate communication, engage your team in a discussion about the problem. If the department has a poor reputation for follow-up, figure out what the problem really is before launching into remediation. Is it because the follow-up communication is not happening or because the follow-up communication is ineffective? Keep asking questions to get to the root cause. Once you believe you have a root cause identified, have the team determine what countermeasures or remediation activities they want to try. Give it a shot and measure results. If it doesn't yield the intended result (or generates undesirable, unintended results), try something else. Use small, short-duration experiments to see if you're heading in the right direction and adjust as necessary. Getting in the habit of asking "what problem are we trying to solve?" and asking questions until you uncover root cause will help you in every aspect of your leadership. It's particularly powerful with "softer" problems such as communication issues because information is often more subjective and harder to quantify.

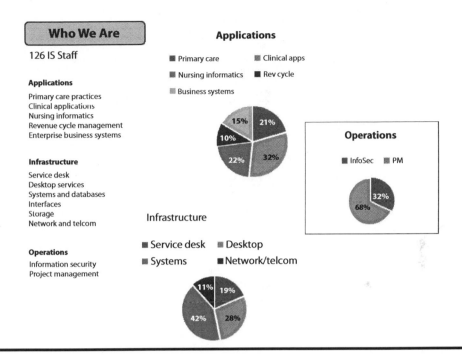

Figure 5.4 Simple visual report examples.

Relationship Building

We'll discuss leadership traits in more detail later in this book, but it's important to discuss relationship building here, as an aspect of branding. Part of marketing your IT department is tied to your professional reputation. How you are perceived is tightly intertwined with the reputation your team develops over time. If you're seen as a roadblock, it's likely your team not only will be seen that way as well, but they are more likely to behave that way—we all tend to follow the leader.

As a HIT leader, this is particularly important to understand. As you move up the ranks from frontline staff to supervisor to manager to director and beyond, your words and actions are given more weight. Whether you see this or not, most people are psychologically inclined to put more weight on words from a VP than they are from a supervisor. What you do and what you say matter—and in that order. Your behavior is the primary driver behind your reputation. Your relationships are an extension of that.

In order to develop a positive reputation and improve your branding for the IT department, you need to cultivate positive relationships. If you and your team are seen as helpful, go-to people, your reputation (and therefore your brand) will improve. The same holds true for your team's behaviors. Most teams have people who naturally want to be helpful and may overextend themselves, which is also a problem when commitments are not kept. Teams also have the naysayers who will immediately find a problem or a roadblock and start with "no." Both responses can be problematic because neither meets the customer's need.

[…more…]

I was fortunate to attend the CHIME* CIO Bootcamp in 2015. It was an extraordinary experience and it was facilitated by a high-powered group of seasoned CIOs. I learned a tremendous amount and developed strong, lasting relationships with peers and mentors from that event. One of the truly transformative concepts discussed was related to relationship building. It's easy to build relationships with people we like; it's another matter to develop relationships with people we don't like. We all have to work with a wide variety of people, so figuring out how to develop good working relationships with people we don't particularly like was a powerful takeaway. You might want to take a moment to think of how you might cultivate more positive relationships with those people who just rub you the wrong way. This will impact your reputation and your brand in positive ways.

Relationships are important in all aspects of life. In the work arena, relationships often determine outcomes. Think of times when you've selected one vendor over another—chances are good the relationship with the vendor influenced your decision. As the authors state in *Make I.T. Known*, "Healthcare IT has little customer turnover and virtually no sources of new customers. In the healthcare IT environment, relationship marketing plays an important role in the day-to-day business…." (Christian, p. 100). Relationships play a key role in how business is conducted and in how your reputation and your brand are perceived.

Project Marketing

We've discussed projects from several different angles throughout the first four chapters of the book. That's indicative of the importance projects have in HIT. Projects are perfect little microcosms of the larger dynamic at play in organizations. As such, each represents an opportunity to improve many different aspects including the department's reputation.

Many HIT leaders would say that they don't get enough credit for all the work their teams do to deliver successful projects for the organization. Many would also say that their department does an excellent job managing projects using a standard project management methodology. Oddly, those two statements are counter to one another. Why? If the team isn't getting credit, then someone is not communicating effectively. An element of strong project management includes effective communication. So, if your team is not getting the credit it deserves for successful project delivery, you need to look at your project communication and your overall marketing of project success.

Reviewing detailed project management processes is outside the scope of this book, but there are many resources available to learn more about communicating about projects. Some key elements are creating a communication plan and understanding that your messaging likely needs to have three or four levels of information and three to four different communication paths.

---

* CHIME is the College of Health Information Management Executives; see References for more on CHIME.

1. *Project staff.* Your first communication plan and process is for frontline staff involved in (or impacted by) the project. This information is most detailed, for obvious reasons.

2. *IT management.* IT managers need relatively frequent communication regarding project status. The cadence and level of detail need to be determined during project analysis and planning. Communication would include slightly less detail than project staff receive, but would still be relatively detailed (such as including which task is currently work-in-progress, risks, constraints, roadblocks, etc.). This helps IT managers assess their team's workload, availability, and resource constraints more effectively. This level of communication can also be distributed to others, such as certain project stakeholders who would benefit from having this level of visibility into the project.

3. *Stakeholders.* Depending on the nature of the project, you may need a less detailed project communication for your stakeholders. In this context, stakeholders are people who are involved with, or affected by, an activity. IT stakeholders are those people involved or impacted by IT—whether that's daily operations or project work. IT management needs details, but stakeholders may not, because IT managers are often called upon to remove roadblocks or adjust other work to address project needs. For stakeholders, the communication often needs to be less detailed and less technical. Instead, it needs to focus on the stakeholder's and the business needs. It should address the elements the stakeholder cares about—is the project on track to deliver the deliverables agreed upon at the outset? If you provide too much detail or too much technical information, your stakeholders will more likely tune out and you'll reinforce the unfortunate reputation many IT departments create of "being a bunch of eggheads that no one can understand." Instead, use nontechnical language, avoid jargon, and communicate on the elements of the project the stakeholders care about. Keep it short and focused; your stakeholders have many other things to deal with besides the status of an IT project, no matter how important it is to them.

4. *Executives.* At the executive level, you should have very little project detail. The communication should be short and concise. It should focus on the overall project deliverables—Is it on time, on budget, in scope? Is it on track to deliver the value promised or expected? Is it aligned with business objectives and organizational strategies? Does it require executive intervention (i.e., is it significantly at risk, does it require executive approval of a large change or additional funding)? These communications are key to developing a reputation as a transparent IT organization. Yet, this is typically the most difficult group to get in front of and get their undivided attention. The more concise the information, the better. The clearer you are about the intent of the communication, the better. Indicating "status update" versus "escalation" can be very helpful in setting the expectation of attention and action required.

If you have an IT governance function, this can be the right forum for both stakeholder and possibly executive communication about project results. Recall that the intent of discussing project communication in this chapter is that it is an opportunity to improve your IT department's brand and reputation. Thinking about project communication as a marketing tool can help you and your project team focus on the right cadence and content for project communication to not only inform about project status but also to market your achievements.

Departmental Marketing

There are several different target audiences for departmental marketing. Your internal staff is one audience; your stakeholders are another audience; your organization, executive team, and Board of Directors may be another audience (those who are not direct stakeholders); and your local community is another. Each of these avenues requires different information and marketing efforts. For now, we'll focus on team and organizational efforts. However, IT leaders can also engage their executives and their marketing/communications departments in assisting with the broader marketing IT efforts.

Internal Marketing

There are many ways to build the brand of the IT department with internal staff. As discussed in Chapter 2, the foundation of just about everything you do is the department's strategy and vision. The vision statement can be a very effective tool for communicating and developing brand. Well-crafted vision statements can be used for all types of communication and marketing efforts, both internally and externally. If you haven't crafted your vision statement yet, you might want to pause here and go back, review Chapter 2, and develop your vision statement. As you can see, it's key to developing internal and external marketing and branding activities. Think about it this way: do you think the NBA® or Facebook® or Barnes & Noble® care about how you view their brand? Of course they do. They spend a lot of time and money ensuring that their brand (perception, awareness, connection) aligns with their customers (and in some cases, causing their customers to align with their brand, but that's outside the scope of this chapter). Every form of communication they undertake reflects that desire to align brand with customers. So it follows that you should spend some effort on this if you want to be more proactive in developing and managing your IT brand.

Other opportunities include hosting events such as Lunch-and-Learn sessions where staff share knowledge or expertise on relevant IT topics such as "How medication pumps interface to the EMR" or "How storage actually works." Another idea is to host CIO or executive roundtables where IT staff have the opportunity to interact in a casual and informative manner with the CIO or organizational leadership. These kinds of activities promote the work of the IT department internally and can be good topics for broader communication as well.

The messaging in team meetings, department meetings, IT blogs or websites, and at all organizational events should be consistent and should build your brand. Have you ever seen one of your IT colleagues get up in front of a meeting with stakeholders and say something brand-bashing like "Well, we rarely get it right, but somehow we managed this time?" Have *you* ever done that? Sometimes there's a fine line between being honest and being self-destructive. Perhaps a better brand-building message might be "This project was really challenging, but we worked closely with clinical, business, and IT staff and we are really pleased with the result."

The same goes for departmental, team meetings, special events, and celebrations. It's important to understand that as an IT leader, your words and actions have weight, whether you want them to or not. Be aware of how your meetings convey your message and build (or destroy) the IT brand. Behave as if this is *your* business and every step forward or back in building your brand impacts your revenues, your bottom line, and your future—because it does. You may not be running an independent small business, but you are running the IT business for the organization. Find opportunities to reinforce the brand in positive, genuine, and congruent ways.

External Marketing

One of the most effective methods available to you as a HIT leader in marketing departmental accomplishments is a quarterly or year-end report. These reports, when produced consistently and professionally, can be powerful communication tools. They can serve the following purposes:

1. Effective recap of financial results with explanations or footnotes
2. Review of project work, project success, and project return on investment
3. Review of support services (can include statistics and/or comparison to agreed-upon service levels)
4. Highlights or excerpts of collaborative outcomes
5. Highlights of innovative or transformational work accomplished
6. Notes (comments, concerns, constraints) regarding future projects or future state

In addition, these reports can reinforce your branding messages, reinforce your vision, and garner broader support for IT. In the clinical world, the saying goes "if it wasn't documented, it didn't happen." The same holds true for IT efforts. If it's not documented in some manner, no one will know. Using reports as a way of capturing successes and promoting IT contributions to the organization can be a powerful tool as well as a great way to archive accomplishments.

If your IT department has a website, a blog, or a newsletter (electronic or paper), these are all excellent vehicles for communicating and building your brand with external stakeholders. If you have one website for internal IT staff and another site for external stakeholders, make sure external communication meets stakeholder needs, not your own. Internal IT sites can be as geeky and technical as you want; external sites need to be engaging, informative, and useful—three traits we've discussed repeatedly throughout this chapter. Remember, it's not about *you*; it's about your *customer*. When you keep that top-of-mind, you'll focus your behaviors and communications the right way.

Finally, find ways to get your IT staff (and management) to fully participate in organizational events and activities to raise visibility for your team. Be a shameless IT promoter—make sure that everyone knows that IT is there and participating. The more your staff actually *does* engage with end users, the more end users will know and appreciate IT work—so leverage every opportunity you can to engage with the organization more fully. Authors Christian, Kirby, and Bennett, in *Make I.T. Known*, offer up to 101 HIT marketing suggestions—you might want to invest in this book and develop a robust marketing and branding plan for your team. It will pay off tenfold in terms of improving the understanding, perception, and awareness of the IT contribution to the business. That leads to fewer conversations about "how much more can you cut from your budget" and far more conversations about "how else you can contribute."

Public Relations

Public relations (PR) is a marketing and branding activity. It is the process of managing information about the company or brand. PR and branding go hand in hand. Branding is often associated with developing the "identity" through visuals (logo) and awareness (sponsoring athletic events). PR influences how branding may be perceived. Just about everyone in the world recognizes the

Apple brand. PR efforts have created a perception of Apple as the sleek, sophisticated choice for electronic devices through well-timed articles, reviews and announcements.

A few ways you can ramp up your PR engine include writing an IT blog on your company's intranet (for internal staff), writing an IT blog on your company's external site (in conjunction with your marketing/communications group), contributing information or articles for your company's newsletter, sponsoring clinical events, developing and delivering IT events like "ask an expert" events, National IT Day, or attending non-IT meetings to share information (and learn), or setting up a table outside the cafeteria once a month to address technical issues on the spot. All of these types of activities provide an opportunity for people to get to know you and your IT team and for you to influence people's perception of the IT team.

Celebrating team success is also another powerful PR tool—both for internal and external marketing. Of course, the primary driver for these events should be to recognize and celebrate success, not to leverage it as a PR event. IT staff tend to be smart and sophisticated and can sniff out ulterior motives in a heartbeat. Be sure you're planning a celebration for your team first; if you can get some good PR out of it, then so much the better.

Of course, if you're like many IT people, you're not good at planning (or even attending) celebrations and attention-getting events. Many IT professionals are far more comfortable at a keyboard than at a social event. IT leaders are often cut from the same cloth. The difference is that you've learned the importance of these kinds of events and you've developed skills in this area. But if you had to give yourself a letter grade for how *well* you celebrate success in your IT department, what would it be? *C*? *D*? Or are you one of those rare IT people who is really good at planning and promoting celebratory events? Regardless of where you fall on the spectrum, it's important to note that celebrating success is essentially a PR event. Perhaps if you think of it as such, you'll find it easier to manage. Internal PR happens when you recognize team (and individual) results. External PR happens when you promote the event or share the story afterward. Either way, celebrating success not only serves to recognize and reward your team for its efforts, but also can be a nice addition to your marketing efforts. If this is really outside your wheelhouse, find someone on your team who is good at this or ask your HR or communications team to assist you in devising these events. Your team deserves the recognition and your department deserves some positive press.

Plan to Succeed

All of the thoughts and ideas in the world won't do you any good if you don't have a plan to put them into action. That's actually the hardest work in all of this—creating and carrying out the plan. In HIT, we have so many things going on every single day that it's hard to weave yet another thing into your day, your week, your year. However, developing and implementing a plan can be managed. If you add this element to your overall departmental planning, you can make this as a goal for yourself. Start small, engage your team in generating ideas and on delivering results. Find ways to systematize these activities so they become ingrained into the very culture of the department. These activities can actually be fun, and you more than likely have a few people on your IT team that would relish the opportunity to get out and spread the message (just make sure they understand the message first). Marketing, branding, and PR activities don't need to be painful—just the opposite. It should be gratifying to share your vision and your successes, knowledge, and IT culture with the rest of the organization. When you begin to see the results of these activities and you hear positive feedback and comments about your department in the broader organization, you'll know these efforts are paying off. If you need help, work with your communications or marketing department to leverage their expertise and organizational insights. Think about creating a marketing plan for your IT department and execute on that plan. Every incremental improvement is a win that you can build upon.

Summary

This chapter is by no means exhaustive with respect to marketing IT within your organization. Instead, it is intended to increase your awareness of the need to undertake these types of marketing activities. If you don't tell your story, if you don't drive understanding, awareness, and appreciation for the great work your department does, you will be short-changing yourself, your department, and your organization. As we discussed in Chapter 4, our mission in the new healthcare world is to drive value; but if we drive value and no one knows it, we've missed a significant opportunity. Tomorrow's world of healthcare will require each department to deliver the highest value to the organization. It's much easier to communicate that value through consistent marketing efforts than to wait until budget time or project time to try to justify and explain your value proposition.

Undertaking these types of activities can engage frontline staff, build organizational awareness, improve your IT department's reputation, and ultimately create an upward spiral of success that you can build on. Moving the conversation from cost cutting to value creation not only involves creating and deploying a vision and strategy, but also requires understanding and awareness of those activities in the larger organization. Seize the opportunity to manage the message and get credit for your IT team's results.

References

For more discussion on this topic, visit http://susansnedaker.com/leading-hit.

QR5.1

Christian, Charles E., Judith A. Kirby, Steven R. Bennett, *Make I.T. Known: Marketing Strategies and Case Studies in the Healthcare Environment*, Chicago: HIMSS, 2010.

College of Health Information Management Executives (CHIME), http://www.chimecentral .org.

QR5.2

Coplan, Scott, David Masuda, *Project Management for Healthcare Information Technology*, New York: McGraw-Hill Companies, Inc., 2011.
Covey, Stephen R., *The 7 Habits of Highly Effective People*, New York: Simon & Schuster, Inc., 1989.
Snedaker, Susan and Nels Hoenig, Tech. Ed., *How to Cheat at IT Project Management*, Rockland, MA: Syngress, Inc., 2005.

Chapter 6

Inform, Involve, and Influence

Overview

Communication is one of the most often cited sources of problems in the workplace. It's ironic that we communicate almost incessantly throughout the day, but we often do so poorly. Clear, concise communication is powerful. It can inspire bold action, it can simplify complex topics, it can coalesce a team that is at odds. To become a strong leader, you need to be a strong communicator. Though you may rise through the ranks for your technical skills in IT, you will stall out in your leadership role if you do not also hone your communication skills. The primary purposes of communication in business are to *inform*, *involve*, and *influence*. In this chapter, we'll explore these aspects of communication. As with other chapters, we are taking a focused approach to this topic. We've provided additional resources at the end of this chapter to facilitate further exploration of this subject.

In each of the preceding chapters, we've covered elements of an IT leader's job—from developing strategy to aligning project work to defining value to marketing IT successes. In some ways, this chapter covers all of those aspects in a more foundational way. In each of those endeavors, influencing, involving, and informing others is key to successfully achieving your objectives. These are essential skills of an IT leader, especially in today's healthcare environment. In subsequent chapters, we'll talk specifically about leadership and management skills and traits, and we'll draw upon the material in this chapter. Having strong communication skills is among the most needed skills for any leader, and the same holds true for IT leadership.

In this chapter, we'll look at some of the elements that impact your effectiveness as a leader with respect to communication, the elements that impact your ability to influence and inform various audiences. We'll look at how your communication style needs to flex with various audiences and how you can develop these skills as you progress in your career. This chapter should help you identify areas for improvement, and the resources in the References section can be used as a starting point in your journey to discovering your strengths and opportunities in effective communication.

Honesty and Trustworthiness

Before we jump into the subject of communication, let's start with something even more fundamental—the foundation of all effective communication: honesty. As leaders, we can't always share everything we know with our teams; sometimes we even need to put a "positive spin" on seemingly negative events or concerning information. We also don't blurt out the first thing that comes to mind—that's not honesty, that's impulsiveness. Honesty is ensuring that your communication is rooted in the truth and that it is presented in a manner relevant to your audience. That might mean preparing one message for executives, one message for your peers, and another message for your team. If the facts are fundamentally the same in each version, modifying your message to meet the needs of the intended audience is honest, effective communication.

Communicating with honesty is core to leadership. Sure, some "leaders" get away with being dishonest and shady, but that's the exception. The way to develop your leadership skills is to work on always being honest. That is not easy in some circumstances, especially if you feel you're being attacked or blamed, but it's the only way to build trust. If your team, your peers, or your manager don't trust you, you might as well go home. Delivering bad news is one of the hardest times to be honest, so it's worth examining your abilities in this area and developing skills. This chapter is about communication, and it is built upon the assumption that you are honest in all you do. If you're not, you may want to pause and reflect on that. Most people are dishonest when they are afraid of looking silly or dumb; or they are afraid of being held accountable or they're under attack. While it's outside the scope of this chapter to address solutions for handling these difficult situations, it's worth doing a quick gut check to see if this applies to you. If so, do some independent work to figure out when you tend to lie or misrepresent the truth, then create a personal action plan to find better, more honest ways of handling those situations.

Inform|Involve|Influence

Let's define these terms in the context of this chapter. *Informing* is the act of providing relevant information to someone. It implies that someone receives information they need. It also implies the relaying of facts. *Involving* is the act of causing others to become engaged with a task, activity, or effort, to include others. Finally, *influencing* is the ability to cause something to change without direct force or action. These are the three cornerstones to successful communication. Figure 6.1 depicts the communication hierarchy of these three types of communication, and we'll discuss each in turn. You may have noticed that these are essentially the same types of communication used when managing staff, participating in planning meetings, or overseeing projects, so you can

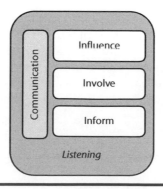

Figure 6.1　Communication hierarchy.

apply everything in this chapter to your work as a leader in your organization. Each of these three communication methods are supported by a foundation of effective listening. If you are not a good listener, you are not a good communicator.

Inform

Informing is basic communication and happens constantly in business. While it seems fairly simple, informing can run the gamut from very effective to completely ineffective. As an IT leader, your first step should be to ensure that you are informing those around you effectively. This includes how you communicate with your direct reports, those you report to, and those higher up or outside of your department. What does "effective" communication at this layer look like? It has to consider these four traits:

1. *Timing*—information must be provided in a timely manner. Depending on the situation, that may mean before, during, or after some action or event. When you receive information with poor timing, it is not helpful, and in many cases, it causes other downstream issues.
2. *Target*—information must be tailored to the audience receiving it. For example, it's rarely appropriate to send a very detailed, technical email to the CFO or to clinical staff. If information is being presented in a meeting, the information needs to be prepared and presented in a way that engages the target audience.
3. *Topic*—it's important to be very clear on the topic of the communication. If it rambles, if it has no clear message, if the reader (or receiver, if it's a verbal message) cannot discern the topic, the message will be ignored.
4. *Tone*—the tone of the message includes the words you choose and the attitude those words express. Tone can be business-like, casual, humorous (on the positive side) or biting, punitive, insulting, or pedantic (on the negative side).

[…more…]

One of the biggest problem areas for IT staff (and leaders) is communicating effectively with non-technical language. For example, the CFO is likely most concerned with these questions:

a. Do we *need* to spend the money?
b. If we must, how little can we spend and still achieve the result?
c. What is the timing of the expense?

None of the "right" answers, from a CFO perspective, involves explaining what a load balancer or a virtual machine is, or how an application uses the latest XML file format for better interoperability. Here's a very specific example. If you need to replace your edge switches because not all of them support Power over Ethernet, then the conversation with your CFO is "we need to replace network switches with newer ones because some of our old ones don't support modern devices that we use." You can have some specific examples available. More effective still might be, "we have 320 network switches, 28 of which are old and need to be replaced to meet current technology standards and reduce our risk of failure. Those 28 are completely depreciated and there is no residual value, though we will try to sell them on the third party market. The cost of 28 new switches is $X and we intend to purchase and replace these during the next 90 days." As you can see, there's very little technical information; it's primarily financial and timing information. If the CFO wants technical information, you can certainly provide that. Often, IT people tend to go into a discussion like this primed with too many reasons why we need this new technology and we then miss the mark. Always think about *who* you are informing, *why* you are informing, and what information you *really* need to provide. If you are informing to get a decision (as in this case), then do your homework to understand what information will the CFO need to make a decision. Using this process for understanding your intended target audience and the desired outcome will help you choose your language more effectively.

Involve

Have you ever been in a meeting where you struggled to stay awake? If you're like most people, the answer is a resounding yes. And if we were to ask why they couldn't focus, most people would cite boredom as the number one factor. So, why are meetings boring? There are many reasons, but one of the most common root cause issues is that while the meeting organizer may be busy *informing*, they are not likely *involving*.

Involving takes a lot of different forms, depending on the nature of the communication. In a meeting, it's about engaging participants to think, to process, to decide. If the meeting is simply about informing, you might want to consider whether an email might suffice. Sometimes informing requires a meeting—such as when you need to inform the team about change to the organization that will likely require a question and answer period. However, if you routinely hold meetings where someone just talks at a group, you may want to rethink that.

[…more…]

Try this: take an inventory of all the meetings that originate from your calendar (aka "your meetings"). Next to each meeting, write down whether the intent is to (a) inform, (b) involve, or (c) influence. Think about the effectiveness of each meeting and try to determine whether or not you are using the right approach. For example, perhaps a better way to inform is to send out a weekly email blast to your team with updates instead of having 12 people sit through an hour meeting just to hear updates. Then, work to cancel unneeded or ineffective meetings. Finally, ask participants if the meeting is fulfilling their needs and how it could be improved. "Death by meetings" is a common problem in many companies. The complex and ever-changing environment in healthcare requires frequent and effective communication. Meetings can serve that purpose, but too often they fall short of the mark.

Involving as a leadership trait means understanding that people need to engage with information in different ways both to process and to act upon that information. Involving can be as simple as using the phrase "does that make sense?" or "what are your thoughts?" during a meeting, during a conversation, and even in email. The old style of "command and control" communication was very directive. "Do this thing in this way." Involving your team was not considered a requirement. The new, more effective way of leading teams revolves around involving the team in the process. From a Lean perspective, frontline staff doing the work know the most about the work, so any conversation or decision around that work should absolutely involve those staff. Involving them in conversations, analysis, and decisions is the primary way to involve staff. Lean IT is discussed in Chapter 9.

Beyond direct reports, a healthcare IT leader needs to learn to involve others through effective communication. How do you get the time and attention of the inpatient nurse managers when they have a hundred things competing for their attention at any given moment? Involving them in decisions that impact their clinical world is key not only to your success but to organizational success as well. There are no "one-size-fits-all" solutions as to how to involve staff, peers, or stakeholders. However, there are a few tips that can be used in almost any situation that will help you get started.

1. *Ask for help.* Admitting you need assistance is a great way to involve others. Of course, you have to do it honestly. If you just use it as a ploy, it will work exactly once. Ask for their help in understanding a topic, understanding a workflow or task, removing a roadblock, or engaging others, etc.
2. *Admit you don't know.* This is similar to asking for help, but when you admit you don't know something, you show vulnerability and allow others to assist. Again, it has to be an honest statement and you need to have an open mind about the solutions provided.
3. *Ask for their input, feedback, or opinion.* Asking people what they think is a very fundamental way of engaging people in a conversation or a solution. Asking people what they would do or how they would approach a problem opens the door to communication and engagement.
4. *Ask why this will or won't work.* If you've put together a plan or you need to bring something that's already pretty well formed to your team, ask why it will or won't work. Don't limit it to just supportive comments—ask them to really "kick the tires" of the concept and help you find any flaws or risks that have not yet been discussed.

[…more…]

Years ago, when I was a new director, I had a direct report, we'll call him Ben, who had been a rising star until he was promoted to manager. Slowly over time, he became less and less effective. I had several conversations with him about my expectations and his performance. I was trying to understand what was going wrong. Unfortunately, we were not communicating well at all. A chance phone call from a woman who is an organizational development consultant prompted me to ask for help. I told her about the problem and said that if Ben wasn't able to improve, I was going to have to take disciplinary action. I indicated I really didn't want to, but I felt I was out of options. She heard me out, then asked me to wait before taking any further action. She asked if she could meet with Ben. After their meeting, she came to my office. She said "would you be willing to change one thing about the way you communicate to help Ben be successful?" I was afraid it was a trick question and replied, "Well, maybe…what is it?" She told me that I tended to simply tell him (*inform*) what I needed and expected him to deliver. She asked if I would be willing to let Ben know what I needed, then *ask* him what he thought (*involve*). I was pretty sure I could do that, so I agreed.

For the next task, I did exactly that. I even gave him a few days to think it over. Ben came back and said "Well, I can do what you asked, but here's what I would suggest we do instead." The solution he proposed was so elegant, so much better than what I'd asked for (and so much less effort), I was literally stunned. At that moment, I realized that over the course of the prior year, I had missed this brilliant side of Ben because I'd been busy handing out assignments. I'd been *informing* instead of *involving*. It was at that moment that I grew leaps and bounds as a leader—because I connected the dots. I realized that I had been the problem all along by not involving him more effectively. From that point on, Ben's performance improved tremendously and he became one of my strongest managers. It was a lesson I'll never forget and it made me a far better leader than I would have otherwise become.

Influence

Influencing is the top tier of communication in our model (refer to Figure 6.1) because it is the least direct method. Influencing is a powerful leadership tool. We influence others in a multitude of ways—through our position (title or role), our knowledge, our words, and our actions (and inaction). Influence comes from many sources, but it's important to understand that influence and power overlap, but they are not the same.

Think of it as the difference between a manager and a consultant. As a manager, you have power because the organization has granted your role certain authority. Now think about a consultant. They don't have power over their clients, but they have influence. They were hired for a reason, usually to provide expertise the person or organization lacks. They can't hire or fire anyone. They can't spend the company's money. However, they *can* influence those decisions.

Power typically comes from role, position, title, or knowledge. It is often used directly. Influence is more indirect. If your CIO tells you to reduce IT security risks using 2-factor authentication, you're going to do that because the role has the power to cause you to do it. Of course, the implication is that if you do not, you could be reprimanded or terminated. On the other hand, if your CIO tells you about this really amazing new 2-factor authentication technology she saw in use at a conference she recently attended, she may have simply influenced you to consider implementing 2-factor authentication as a way of reducing security risk. The first action was direct, the second indirect. Both are likely to have the same effect—that you investigate this product. However, you're more likely to be engaged when you've been influenced to consider something versus when you're directed to do so. You typically feel you have a choice; that you are deciding for yourself. And, in most cases, you are, but that action is prompted by the seed that's been planted by the suggestion.

Sound manipulative? Yes, it does, because when it's used in an underhanded way, it is. (Remember our opening section on honesty?) We've all used influence to achieve objectives more softly than barking orders. Influence can also be wielded through the simple use of words that convey emotion—excited, disappointed, compelling, crushing—these kinds of words connect to us emotionally and bypass the logical brain functions. They sneak in the side door of your brain and cause you to connect to an idea, a concept, a feeling.

So, how is this helpful in healthcare IT? How do you motivate your team to do a great job every day? How do you get them to achieve the day-to-day tasks and find time to innovate? How do you get them to pull together to accomplish a seemingly impossible task because it's crucial to the organization? Most great leaders use influence to coalesce their teams.

Emotional Intelligence

The term *emotional intelligence* (EI) was first used in 1964, but gained widespread use in 1995 after Daniel Goleman published a book with that title. The study of EI has branched out over the past two decades, but the fundamentals remain substantially the same. According to Bradberry and Greaves in *Leadership 2.0*, of the 12 skills that define adaptive leadership, 4 are EI skills. They separate these into personal and social competence. The four elements they identify are self-awareness, self-management, social awareness, and relationship management.

In *On Emotional Intelligence* (a Harvard Business Press compilation), Daniel Goleman describes five traits of EI at work. You can see in comparing Goleman and Bradberry/Greaves, these traits are not categorized exactly the same way. A quick Internet search will yield many different variations, but they all contain the same fundamentals. We'll use Goleman's model (Goleman, 2015) to explore these traits. The five elements, according to Goleman, are

1. Self-awareness
2. Self-regulation
3. Motivation
4. Empathy
5. Social skill

1. Self-Awareness

Self-awareness is the foundation for other EI traits. Self-awareness is having a deep understanding of oneself—one's strengths, weaknesses, emotional triggers, needs, and motivations. People with a high degree of self-awareness recognize how these elements affect their work, their interactions with others, and their emotions. They are neither overly self-critical nor unrealistically optimistic. Obviously, self-awareness is the first element of EI, because if you don't know what's going on internally, you won't be able to interact effectively. For example, if you were overly critical of yourself, you might avoid opportunities to leverage your strengths and grow professionally. If you were overly optimistic and thought you had skills and talents you didn't, you might put yourself (and your organization) at serious risk of failure. There's a big difference between taking a calculated risk and taking on a "stretch" assignment versus being completely delusional about your skills and abilities.

According to Goleman, the three hallmarks of self-awareness are self-confidence, realistic self-assessment, and self-deprecating sense of humor (Goleman, p. 6).

A 1999 study by Cornell University researchers found a very interesting correlation between self-assessment of a skill and actual skill level. Here's the abstract summary:

> Despite the importance of self-awareness for managerial success, many organizational members hold overly optimistic views of their expertise and performance—a phenomenon particularly prevalent among those least skilled in a given domain. We

examined whether this same pattern extends to appraisals of emotional intelligence (EI), a critical managerial competency. We also examined why this over optimism tends to survive explicit feedback about performance. Across 3 studies involving professional students, we found that the least skilled had limited insight into deficits in their performance. Moreover, when given concrete feedback, low performers disparaged either the accuracy or the relevance of that feedback, depending on how expediently they could do so. Consequently, they expressed more reluctance than top performers to pursue various paths to self-improvement, including purchasing a book on EI or paying for professional coaching. Paradoxically, it was top performers who indicated a stronger desire to improve their EI following feedback. (Sheldon et al., 2014, QR6.3)

Take a moment to let that sink in. Then ask yourself if you fit into either of these two categories. Think about feedback you've received, challenges you've faced. Do you tend to give yourself too much or too little credit for your skills? The irony of the question is that, according to research results, whatever your answer, you're likely to be wrong. Those with strong skills see themselves as needing improvement. Those with weak skills see themselves as having strong abilities. Let's assume for just a moment that you are someone who thinks you have really strong skills, but you're willing to entertain the possibility that you're wrong. How can you change?

While it's challenging, you can choose to improve your self-assessment skills by listening to constructive criticism and taking appropriate actions to change, or by working with a coach. It really comes down to a willingness to be wrong and to find ways to improve your self-awareness so you can become the most effective leader possible.

If you have team members who do not self-assess well, this view of the problem may help you develop additional strategies for managing these kinds of people. Think about the really competent manager who is abrupt, harsh, and punitive. They don't self-assess well and this is evidenced by a look of surprise when you provide critical feedback about their behavior. They argue with you, they attack the veracity of the facts, or they become defensive in some other way. This behavior points to someone who has poor self-assessment skills and for whom coaching will be ineffective in many cases. These types of people may be able to develop better skills if they choose to work on this. However, as the study shows, this tends to be a closed-loop problem that is difficult to break. As a manager, you'll need to determine whether the value they bring to the organization outweighs the problems they drag along behind them.

Finally, what do you do if you work for a manager who doesn't self-assess accurately? Clearly, providing feedback is unlikely to change their behavior. It's also not good to remain silent while your manager sends the department off into a massive problem because they just didn't read the situation correctly (they were overly optimistic in their assessment of their skills). This is a very challenging situation to be in because acting or staying on the sidelines both have potential negative consequences. In these situations, your best bet is to try to persuade your manager to take a different path without implying (or overtly stating) that there is a problem with their assessment. Sometimes you can play "devil's advocate" if your manager is a person who is willing to listen to views counter to their own. Finally, you can take a stand if the action is clearly wrong. You run the risk of getting on the wrong side of your manager, but if the issue is important enough, it might be worth taking a risk. There are no right answers, but hopefully this information helps you formulate strategies in dealing with people you work with who simply don't self-assess accurately.

2. Self-Regulation

Self-regulation is the ability to manage ourselves, to acknowledge and control our impulses. Emotions drive our impulses, but what we do *next* is what matters. We will all have emotional responses to the things in our environment—whether we're feeling anger, frustration, excitement, joy, or anything in between. Self-regulation is the ability to feel and acknowledge the emotion and then to make conscious choices about how we respond next.

Have you ever been in a meeting where someone did a terrible job—they weren't prepared, theydidn't present well, they were difficult or confrontational? As a leader, what was your first response? Most likely you were angry, frustrated, or disappointed. How did you behave? If you have good leadership skills, you didn't call them out in the meeting or make a big deal out of the problem at the time, but you got your emotions under control and determined what the most effective way of providing feedback would be. That's self-regulation. You don't just fly off the handle and reprimand someone in a meeting. You don't just criticize someone in front of a group of people and embarrass them. Your behavior is modulated to fit the social and business circumstances.

This isn't always possible to do. We are human and we have strong emotions, especially when things go really well or really poorly. As a leader, it's crucial to develop this skill. As we discussed in Chapter 5, it takes decades to build a brand and 10 minutes to destroy it; the same holds true of your professional reputation, which is *your* brand. How you respond in the minutes immediately after a disruptive event can make or break you professionally, so continue working on developing this skill.

Self-regulation also relates to how you manage conflict. While discussing conflict management and resolution is outside the scope of this chapter, we've included a couple of books in the References section to get you started (Crowley and Elster, 2006; Maravelas, 2005).

Remember, your first response is *emotion*, your second response is *choice*. Develop a short "go-to" list of things you can do for yourself when you are not sure you can self-regulate. Take a walk, close your office door, grab a cup of coffee, take 10 deep breaths—do whatever works for you.

3. Motivation

Motivation is defined as the act or process of having a reason for doing something. Motivation can be external or internal. External motivation can be positive, such as a promotion or raise, or negative, such as avoiding being demoted or terminated. Internal motivation is how we drive ourselves toward goals and outcomes. When people drive themselves because they want to grow, learn, and achieve, they don't need external measures to motivate them. That's not to say they won't strive for a pay increase or a promotion—most people will—but that's not what really drives leaders and those with high EI. And, as a leader, you also know that those external "motivators" only last so long. The raise is forgotten a month or two later; the much-sought-after promotion also brings with it new responsibilities and new challenges.

How do you spot up-and-coming leaders in your organization who have strong EI? Look for those who seem to continually challenge themselves to grow, to learn, to improve because they are demonstrating internal motivation. Look for those who are generally optimistic, who can face uncertainty or even failure with a sense of calm. If they're asking themselves "what went wrong and how can I learn from this?" then they'll learn from the situation instead of collapsing under it. More importantly, what they do next is the real key. Most who are internally motivated will look for ways to turn the failure into a success—whether it's turning around a bad situation or cutting losses and refocusing on something that will succeed. Leaders and those with high EI will continually readjust and look for ways to succeed despite obstacles and setbacks. They'll also know when to stop and redirect their efforts elsewhere.

Strong internal motivation is a trait all great leaders share. Ask yourself how often you give in to a sense of failure. How often do you pause to acknowledge the situation (self-regulation), then assess current state and regroup to find another path forward? These are traits you can work on and that will help you professionally regardless of the work you do.

4. Empathy

Empathy is the ability to share someone else's feelings. As with all communication skills, it starts with really listening. People who work in healthcare, especially those directly involved with patient care, are typically very empathetic. Even people who choose to work in healthcare support services such as Facilities, Human Resources, Finance, Supply Chain, and IT, for example, often seem to have strong empathetic tendencies as well. We choose to work in healthcare because we care about the patient experience and we want to make a difference.

As a leader, we have to make decisions that don't please everyone all the time. We also have to make tough choices and choose among imperfect options. Empathy allows us to view a situation from another person's perspective so we can take their feelings and situation into consideration. It doesn't necessarily mean we change our decision or the outcome. Instead, it means we find the best path forward given all the circumstances and constraints.

Consider the scenario where you've been told your department is going to have to be reorganized due to a shift in the business strategy. You're not yet clear what that means for you or your staff, but you want to communicate this before it hits the grapevine. You call a team meeting. Without empathy, you might say "we're going to have to reorganize this department. That means some of you will not be reporting to me anymore, but I don't yet know who you will report to. It's possible some people will be asked to move into new jobs." With empathy, you might say "we're reorganizing to meet the business's changing needs. I'm not certain at this point what that means to any of us. Like you, it makes me feel a bit uncertain, but I also think there's an opportunity in this change for us to streamline and redefine some roles so we can be more effective in the future. I'll let you know as soon as I know more."

Which message would you rather hear? Why did the empathetic message "feel" better? Did they both convey the same information? They were both honest and factually accurate, but the second message is the one most of us would rather hear.

Another aspect of empathy is coaching and performance management. As a leader, you need to look at the workplace from your employee's perspective and provide guidance to help them be successful. If you can't empathize with the employee, you won't be able to assist them effectively. Consider this scenario: You have a manager who reports to you. He reports that he really isn't on board with a recent process change and he feels that he communicated it very poorly to his team. Without empathy, you might reprimand him—"why did you talk with your team about it if you weren't comfortable with the message? Now we're going to have to undo the damage. I really didn't need this today." With empathy (and coaching) you might say, "Tell me how the meeting went and why you think you didn't handle it well." You might follow up with, "I can see you aren't comfortable with the new process and I'm disappointed that you communicated with the team this way. As you learned, that leads to a suboptimal result. So, let's talk about that so I can understand what's driving your concerns about the process. Then we can figure out how to repair the situation with your team." Again, both messages are honest and factually accurate. The second message is softer, but it still communicates that you believe he made a poor choice. Then, it focuses on moving forward.

As you can see, using empathy to understand what the problem is can help you coach the employee to be more successful in dealing with similar situations in the future. According to Goleman, outstanding leaders know how to read their team and give *effective* feedback. "They know when to push for better performance and when to hold back" (Goleman, p. 18).

5. *Social Skill*

Most of us develop key social skills in grade school and high school. People who are natural extroverts often find social life to be a bit easier than their more introverted peers during those formative years. However, according to Olivia Cabane in *The Charisma Myth*, research also shows that introverts who stay on the social sidelines often become more adept at reading social queues than their extroverted counterparts. The theory is that extroverts are busy *doing*, introverts are busy *observing*. It can be argued that they both end up with the same knowledge, but the skills are different. Since extroverts are often busy interacting, they can miss key social queues. Since introverts are often busy observing, they can struggle with actually behaving in the most socially appropriate manner. Consider the extroverted manager who is so busy greeting the team as they arrive for a meeting that they miss the subtle queues that one teammate gives off through body language—low eye contact, no smile, a subdued manner. Conversely, the introverted manager may observe these clues but be unsure as to the most appropriate way to handle the situation.

There is no inherent "good" or "bad" related to being an extrovert or an introvert. They're just different ways of experiencing the world and processing information, including social queues. According to Cabane, extroverts typically recharge their batteries by being around others. Introverts typically recharge through spending time alone or in a quiet setting. Why does this matter and how does this relate to social skill? If you are an extrovert and you're managing introverts, or the reverse, you will have to make a bit of effort to understand the "other."

Social skill is about your relationship with others and often your ability to influence others. This ties back to our communication stack of *inform*, *involve*, and *influence*. It's about one's ability to manage relationships with others, and it's built upon the dimensions we discussed earlier—self-awareness, self-regulation, motivation, and empathy. Socially adept people are typically very good at managing teams—as Goleman puts it, "that's their empathy at work" (Goleman, p. 19). Whether you're an extrovert or an introvert, you have the basic skills needed to become socially adept, but you'll have to work on different aspects. And for some, becoming socially adept is just that—work. It's a skill set that can be learned and honed.

One aspect of having strong social skills that can be difficult for new managers and leaders is this: sometimes building relationships (social skills) looks like goofing off. How can you tell whether someone is just chatting with everyone that walks by or whether they're purposefully connecting with colleagues? Though it's not always easy to tell the difference, the key is to look at how *respected* and *productive* they are. People who just talk to talk will develop weaker reputations. Those who talk to build relationships also get work done, because that's another way that relationships are fostered and strengthened. We've all worked on teams where someone spent a lot of time flitting around, talking to everyone, and getting little done. The team became resentful because they were picking up the slack. That chatty person's reputation suffers and they likely begin to lose the respect of the team. Conversely, we've all worked with people who were personable, who'd stop in to talk about weekend plans or the latest movie, but they got work done and they were energizing to work with.

As you develop your leadership skills, you'll need to develop your social skills and develop an ability to discern building relationships from goofing off. Of course, things like setting goals, monitoring productivity, establishing key performance metrics, etc., are also important in helping you assess staff effectiveness.

As you can see, developing high EI is a mix of skills that can be learned. Since leadership studies confirm that those with higher EI tend to make better leaders, this is an area worth working on. The higher up in the organization you rise, the less your job becomes about the work you produce and the more it becomes about the influence you wield. Most VP or C-suite executives view their jobs as *causing* work to be done in alignment with the organizational objectives. That's pretty much the definition of *influencing* that we've been discussing. Developing these EI skills can help you in your professional development regardless of what role you hold now or what your aspirations for the future are.

Relationship Building

So far we've discussed the building blocks of communication (inform, involve, influence) and we've also discussed EI. Together, these are the elements that we use to communicate effectively and build strong relationships, both in our personal and professional lives. Leadership success is more often tied to how well we build relationships than any specific subject matter expertise. Certainly, a CIO needs to understand information technology. A CFO needs to understand finance. Yet, at the C-suite level, the skill lies in building trusted relationships in order to drive organizational objectives and successful outcomes.

As we develop healthcare IT leaders for the future, it's vital that these leaders understand the importance of relationships and the mechanics behind establishing and nourishing those relationships.

[…more…]

It's important to note that some relationships are very unhealthy and not all relationships are within your direct control. The focus in this chapter is on those relationships that can, and should, be functional. The information that follows assumes that the relationships, whether strong or weak, are healthy enough to be worked on. If you find yourself in a really toxic (or dangerous) relationship with direct reports, peers, or your manager at work, you'll need to address that separately. You should seek assistance from an HR professional, a trusted peer, a professional therapist, or a friend outside of work who can help you navigate this issue. It's real, it's serious, and you should not remain in an unhealthy situation if at all possible.

Figure 6.2 shows, in a simple manner, that at any given time, you probably have six different *types* of relationships you're managing. That means you likely have 50 or 100 or more *active* relationships. Think about that for a moment. Each of these relationships provides an opportunity (or an obstacle). Each of these relationships requires a bit of care and feeding. These relationships may not be with people you like or respect, but they are relationships, nonetheless.

In a 2012 Fast Company article (QR6.2), author and management expert Ken Blanchard and his son Scott, executive vice president of the Ken Blanchard Companies, said this: "Relationship building is about being a positive factor in someone else's life. Does the person see you as someone

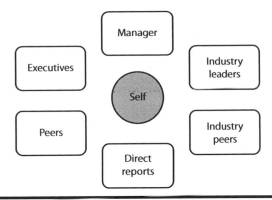

Figure 6.2 Relationship framework.

who is helping them along the way? Are you adding value to that person's life? Or are you actually inhibiting the other person's success?" They point to five mistakes people make. We've taken that list and turned them around to point out five things you can do right to build strong work relationships.

1. Give before you take.

    The art of building relationships is to give as much as you can without expectation of reciprocity. The work environment will create opportunities to develop shared goals and the scales should balance over time. Of course, that doesn't mean you should be doing someone else's job or taking on their responsibilities. Giving also means giving of your time—and that starts with listening. Giving someone your undivided attention while they speak is one of the most powerful things you can give.

2. Build relationships at all levels.

    Figure 6.2 shows that you have at least six different types of relationships to develop and nurture. Effective leaders nurture them all. If you spend more time working on the relationships "above" you and little time on the relationships "below" you (referencing Figure 6.2), your manager may love you but your peers and staff may dislike you. That may work in the short term, but it will not drive long-term success. In the worst case scenario, your peers and direct reports will begin to sabotage you, whether consciously or unconsciously, directly or indirectly. More importantly, it will severely limit your effectiveness. Pay attention to all levels in your relationship building.

3. *Who* you know is more important than *what* you know.

    As IT experts, we've built our career success around what we know—technical abilities, troubleshooting abilities, subject matter expertise. As you move forward in your career, you begin to notice that your technical skills are important, but your relationships are even more so.

[…more…]

Early in my career, I was a field engineer for a large company. My territory was a bit remote from the main office, so most of the time I was on my own to manage my customers, schedule service, and generally keep things running. At that point in my career, I lacked the deep technical expertise that some of my more experienced peers had. I went on vacation one time, and my company sent a very seasoned field engineer, I'll call him James, to cover my region during my absence. When I came back, one customer pulled me aside and said "Don't ever send James back here, he doesn't know what he's doing!" I was very surprised by that and started asking questions. Did James show up on time and start fixing the problem in a timely manner? "Yes, he came right away." Did James fix the equipment? "Yes, he got here within the hour, he was here a short time then left." Was it fixed? "Yes." So, why don't you want James to come back? "He didn't say anything, he just came here then he left." It was a lesson that has stayed with me since then. James was a far better engineer than I was at that point in my career. However, what James didn't do was interact with the customer. He didn't build that relationship. As a result, the customer did not value the work James did, even though I'm sure he fixed the problem in half the time it might have taken me. The lesson I learned was that it's rarely only about *what* you know; it's also about how you manage the relationship.

---

4. Relationships should be about driving results.

The flip side to not building relationships is relying too heavily on relationships instead of driving results. We all have worked with people who are outgoing and spend a lot of time talking with people but deliver few results. If you work with a person like that, it can be challenging because they appear to be nice, personable, engaged—but when it's time to produce results, they're unable to do so. As Ken and Scott Blanchard put it, "It's important to remember that a primary reason to cultivate good work relationships is to better accomplish organizational goals."

5. Develop a wide range of relationships.

It's easy to limit our relationships to people we like and who are similar to us in age, background, ethnicity, etc., because that's what's most comfortable. Strong leaders develop relationships outside their peer groups with people who are not like them. This broadens your view of work, the organization, and the world and will strengthen your skills as a leader.

For those of you who are naturals at this, you may be amused that we are giving pointers on building relationships. For the rest of you, you're probably breathing a small sigh of relief. If this is not your natural strength, you can improve these skills through consciously practicing. Using all the information presented in this chapter, you can create a plan for developing your leadership communication skills as well as your relationship skills. Becoming more self-aware and developing self-regulating strategies, for example, can help you relate better to others. Understanding your natural tendency toward extroversion or introversion helps you understand how you tend to prefer to interact with others.

Following the five tips for building relationships will also give you a good start in fine-tuning your own leadership development plan. Here's an exercise you can do in just a few minutes that will lead you to greater insights into your relationship-building opportunities. This is a tactical exercise you can do on your own. You also don't need to spend much time on it—you can do this in 10 or 15 minutes if you focus.

1. *Perform a relationship audit.* Look at the relationships you currently have and determine where they fit in the broad categories—friends, peers, direct reports, "superiors" (your manager and above), people like me, people not like me, etc.

2. *Identify strong relationships.* What makes the relationship strong? Does it have attributes discussed earlier in this chapter? How do you know the relationship is strong? What are the attributes that you identify in your best relationships?
3. *Identify weak relationships.* What makes the relationship weak? How do you know it's weak? Does it lack the attributes of your strong relationships?
4. *Determine which relationships you want to improve.* Let's face it, some relationships in our personal lives are not healthy and it's wise to move on. At work, however, it's difficult to decide you don't want to have a relationship with someone you have to work with. So, from a work perspective, determine which weak relationships would benefit most from some extra effort and which ones are pretty damaged. You might start by improving the weak ones first. Once you see the results and what techniques work for you, you can then focus on any damaged relationships.
5. *Develop a plan for improving relationships.* What steps will you take to improve relationships? You can try casual get-togethers ("Would you like to grab coffee tomorrow and update me on that project you were working on?"), meetings ("I'd like to schedule time to understand more about how you approached this problem, I'm facing a similar issue and I'd love to learn from what you've done."), even emails ("Hey, just a quick note to let you know I heard your project was going really well, give me an update when you get a minute.").

Two books mentioned earlier and included in the References section can also help you sort out how to manage broken (or toxic) relationships. Maravelas' *How to Reduce Workplace Conflict and Stress* and Crowley and Elster's *Working with You Is Killing Me* are good starting points, but there are thousands of great resources on this topic.

By first identifying what works in your strong relationships and what doesn't work in your weak relationships, you can begin to find ways to build stronger, more positive relationships using all the skills and traits we've discussed in this chapter. Building relationships with people you dislike is perhaps one of the most challenging aspects of relationship building, but it pays the biggest dividend. Imagine what it would be like to feel that every one of your working relationships was positive—or at least neutral. Your ability to lead in all circumstances will be strengthened by your ability to build positive relationships.

One Final Note: Clinical Communication

Throughout this chapter, we've discussed various ways of communicating effectively in healthcare IT, but we'd be remiss if we didn't call out the obvious. One of the key disconnects that happens is between IT and clinical counterparts. It seems we use the same words to mean very different things. For example, what do you think of when you read the word *monitor*? A nurse probably thinks of a device that displays patient heart rhythms, not a computer screen. You have to pay attention and work to be very clear. Avoid the use of technical jargon or even words that can be misunderstood (like "monitor"). Frequently check for understanding, stop and define (or clarify) terms, if needed. Go out and observe the clinical environment to really understand what's going on. You can't possibly have a good grasp of operations if you are not frequently out in the environment. By developing strong relationships with clinical counterparts, you can bridge the gap. You'll know you're making progress in closing the communication gap when you find yourself using clinical terms correctly and your clinical peers are using technical terms correctly. More importantly, you'll see that communication improves, and there are fewer misunderstandings and frustrations in working together on collaborative projects.

Summary

We've covered a lot of ground in this chapter. Communication is always an area for learning and growth. No matter how well we communicate, no matter how much effort we put into it, there's always an opportunity to improve. As a leader in healthcare IT, it will become increasingly important for you to build and maintain strong relationships with your counterparts across the organization. This means understanding the basics of business communication. It means assessing and developing your EI. It means honing your social skills and your ability to develop effective and collaborative working relationships. And it means coming to work every day ready to be as open, honest, and transparent as possible to foster teamwork and success.

References

For more on this topic, visit http://susansnedaker.com/leading-hit.

QR6.1

Bacon, Terry R., PhD, *The Elements of Power: Lessons on Leadership and Influence*, New York: AMACOM, 2011.

Blanchard, Ken and Scott Blanchard, "The 5 Biggest Mistakes You're Making with Work Relationships," April 23, 2012, http://www.fastcompany.com/1834912/5-biggest -mistakes-youre-making-work-relationships, viewed May 01, 2016.

QR6.2

Bradberry, Travis and Jean Greaves, *Leadership 2.0*, San Diego, CA: TalentSmart, 2012.

Cabane, Olivia Fox, *The Charisma Myth*, New York: Portfolio/Penguin, 2012.

Cain, Susan, *Quiet: The Power of Introverts in a World That Can't Stop Talking*, New York: Broadway Books, 2012.

College of Healthcare Information Management Executives (CHIME), http://www.chimecentral.org.

Covey, Stephen R., *The 7 Habits of Highly Effective People*, New York: Simon & Schuster, 1992.

Crowley, Katherine and Kathi Elster, *Working with You Is Killing Me*, New York: Warner Business Books, 2006.

Goleman, Daniel, "What Makes a Leader?" *HBR'S 10 Must Reads: On Emotional Intelligence*, Boston: Harvard Business Review Press, 2015, pp. 1–21.

High, Peter A., *World Class IT*, San Francisco: John Wiley & Sons, Inc., 2009.

Maravelas, Anna, *How to Reduce Workplace Conflict and Stress*, Pompton Plains, NJ: Career, 2005.

Sheldon, Oliver J., Daniel P. Ames, and David Dunning, "Emotionally Unskilled, Unaware, and Uninterested in Learning More: Reactions to Feedback about Deficits in Emotional Intelligence," *Journal of Applied Psychology*, Vol. 99, No. 1, 2014, 125–137, DOI: http:// dx.doi.org/10.1037/a0034138. (Note: Additional references to this study can be found by searching on Dunning-Kruger Effect.)

QR6.3

Chapter 7

IT Risk Management

Overview

As a leader in healthcare IT, an important part of your job is managing risks of various kinds. Risk is part of every IT job and as a leader, you must find ways to identify, manage, and mitigate risk to the greatest extent possible. This is not always easy, given that IT is an ever-changing arena where application and infrastructure modifications can have far-reaching consequences and where change can have unintended outcomes.

In this chapter, we'll discuss sources of risk and strategies for addressing risk. While there is no one-size-fits-all answer to risk management in healthcare IT, there are processes you can put into place that will assist you in this effort. We'll look at methods to assess risk and review some of the common IT risks we face today. Of course, if you are interested in learning more on this topic, there's a wealth of information available on general risk management, healthcare risk management, and IT risk management.

Not surprisingly, if you do a search for books on IT risk management, you're most likely to find hundreds of results related to information security. Risk related to healthcare information security is high. Hackers are interested in infiltrating networks and either gaining access to patient data or locking down data (ransomware) in hopes of a quick, easy payout. We're not going to spend a lot of time on information security, though it's a very important topic. We'll cover it as we would any other risk so you can better understand IT risk management as a process. From there, you can apply it to all IT risks and tune it to your specific role in your organization.

This chapter is not intended to make you an expert on risk management. If you have a risk management department or risk management experts in your organization, you might set up a meeting to learn more about what they do and how they see and manage organizational risk. You'll learn a lot about your organization and you'll see things in an entirely different light afterward.

This chapter is intended to help you understand the types of risk you're likely to face as a healthcare IT leader and provide you suggestions and strategies for addressing those risks. Before we delve into those details, however, we will cover the basics of risk management.

Risk and Mitigation

Throughout this chapter (and this book), we'll use the terms *risk* and *mitigation*. So, let's begin by defining each of these terms. *Risk* is typically defined as the chance or possibility of being exposed to injury or loss. In broader terms, risk is really just uncertainty. Risk is a possibility of loss or harm, not a certainty. However, some risks are clearly more dangerous or more imminent than others, and sometimes evaluating risk is a matter of degree. *Mitigation* is to make something less harmful, to limit the potential negative impact of the risk. Clearly, risk and mitigation go hand in hand.

Elements of Risk Management

The basic steps in any risk management program or effort are shown in Figure 7.1. This is a greatly simplified diagram, but it's a good visual reminder of the key elements.

Healthcare organizations all have risk management functions, though the names, the roles, and responsibilities may differ. Your company's risk management function, regardless of the risk areas it looks at, will use these same basic steps. We'll review them briefly here.

Policies and Standards

Organizations develop policies to establish statements of principle and guiding concepts. They identify what's required, what's permitted, what's not permitted, and so on. Policies related to risk might not specifically be called risk policies. For example, your organization likely has a policy regarding the use of IT assets such as tablets, smartphones, and other mobile assets. That's a risk management policy even if it's called "Mobile Device Policy" because it establishes baseline rules and requirements regarding the safe, appropriate, and permitted (or required) use of these devices.

Standards are established to describe required or desired behaviors and outcomes. Standards are typically established through documentation of processes and procedures. For example, you probably have a standard around change management that describes the processes and procedures required to be used when making changes to systems, applications, or infrastructure.

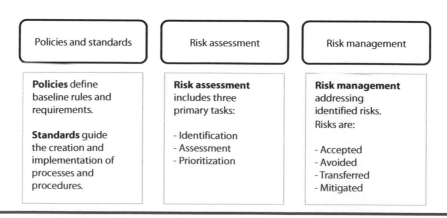

Figure 7.1   Risk management overview.

Risk Assessment

The *risk assessment* is the process of identifying risks and then evaluating them. One of the often overlooked steps is the *identification* process. People will often rattle off a list of risks and assume they're set. Spending time engaging staff to identify risks will yield a much more well-rounded view of risks than if just one person comes up with the list. Risk identification and assessment is a standard part of project management, and it should be a standard part of the work you do in IT whenever anything is changing. There are other times risk assessments should be conducted as well, but change in IT is the most common cause of problems.

Once a thorough review of potential risks (risk inventory) has been conducted, each risk should be evaluated. The most commonly used method is to look at both *likelihood* and *impact*. How likely is it that the risk will occur? High or low? If the risk does occur, what would be the impact? High or low? Figure 7.2 shows a simple likelihood/impact matrix that can be used to review risks. Once these risks are defined, they can be evaluated and prioritized.

Risk Management

Risk management is the process of addressing the prioritized risks. There are essentially four different ways you can address risk: *accept, avoid, transfer,* or *mitigate.* To mitigate is to alleviate or lessen. With respect to risk management, it means finding a way to reduce the potential likelihood or impact of a risk. Risks should be addressed in order of priority so you spend your time dealing with the most important risks first.

Clearly, some risks should be *accepted.* If the impact is low, it may not be worth addressing at all. If the impact is enormous, but the likelihood is low, you might also choose to accept the risk. This is particularly true when the cost to mitigate is higher than the impact of the risk occurring. In this situation, the risk would be accepted and continuously monitored. If the nature of the risk changes, it should be reevaluated.

Avoiding a risk may mean choosing to take a different action or taking an alternate path that will remove the risk from the environment. Typically, the risk assessment will show that this risk has both a high likelihood of occurring and a high impact if it does occur. Some actions are simply not worth the risk, and the organization may choose to go another direction rather than face the potential threat.

Transferring a risk can be done through a service contract, for example. Paying a service provider to repair equipment at a set cost transfers the financial risk of broken equipment to the provider for a fee. Another common risk transference mechanism is insurance. Healthcare organizations these days carry cyber security insurance of some sort. This is a method of transferring the risk. Risk is typically transferred when it has a low likelihood of occurring, but a high (usually financial) impact if it does occur.

Finally, risks that can't be addressed in these other ways can be *mitigated.* If a risk has a medium to high likelihood of occurring but a low to medium impact if it does, it is probably a candidate for mitigation. IT departments typically spend a fair amount of time in this area—looking at potential risks and coming up with back-out plans, testing plans, etc., to reduce the likelihood and/or the impact of the risk. One less often cited method of addressing risk is to *exploit* it, but that's not a common element of a standard risk management plan. An example of exploiting a risk is this. Suppose the risk is that business expansion may drive the need for a significant amount of additional compute or storage capacity. One way to exploit that risk is to use it to develop a cloud strategy that gives you expansion-on-demand. So, rather than trying to avoid the risk, you jump into it and use it to your advantage.

Now that we've reviewed the basics, let's look a bit more closely at how risk can be assessed, since that is at the core of risk management.

Risk Attributes

Risks can be opportunities or threats. Opportunities inject uncertainty on the "upside" while threats inject uncertainty on the "downside." Either way, they both create uncertainty of outcomes. This is important to understand because when we're evaluating an action or a process or a project for risk, we tend only to look on the downside. What can go wrong and how can we limit that? We sometimes forget to look at the risk of opportunities and ask how we can minimize the risk while leveraging the upside of the opportunity.

Risk can be assessed either quantitatively (with numbers) or qualitatively (with attributes) or both. Sometimes risk can be easily measured, such as financial risk. Sometimes risk is more difficult to measure, such as process risk or people risk. You should attempt to quantify your risk, regardless of the difficulty of measurement. For example, in Figure 7.2, we show a risk matrix with the values "low," "medium," "high medium," and "high." If you assign each of these words a numeric value, you can come up with a semiquantitative score for each risk. For instance, if "low" is equal to 1, "medium" is equal to 3, "high medium" is equal to 5, and "high" is equal to 7, you can score a risk. Let's test this out. Let's say you have a risk, Risk A, that you determine has a relatively low likelihood of occurring, but if it occurs, it would be a major event. We'd score 1 for likelihood and 7 for impact, giving this risk the score of 8. A different risk, Risk B, has a medium likelihood of occurring and a medium impact if it does happen. It would be scored with 3 plus 3 yielding a score of 6.

Using these two examples, you can see how you can develop a method for scoring risks. The problem, of course, is that the words low, medium, high medium, and high are all subjective. If you go this route, you should also try to define what those terms mean so you can use them in a consistent manner.

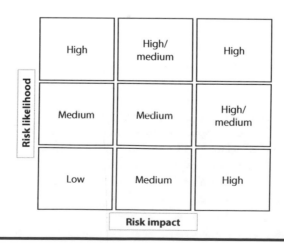

Figure 7.2 Risk assessment grid example.

Strategic Risks

Strategic risk is defined as the risk associated with the unsuccessful pursuit of a business plan or objective. It includes risk from making poor business decisions, substandard analysis or execution, inadequate funding or resource commitment, or failure to respond effectively to changes in the market or business environment.

Your organization faces numerous strategic risks as it tries to navigate the complex world of healthcare. There are federal, state, and local regulations that change, which creates risk. There are changes to the science of healthcare (new specialties, new treatments, new modalities, etc.). There are changes to your community demographics, and there are other healthcare organizations competing for your patients. These are just a few examples of strategic risk your company faces.

When your executive team is developing their strategic plan, they are looking at the horizon and trying to make intelligent decisions about where the market is headed and how the organization needs to grow in order to thrive. Clearly, they don't always get it right despite their best efforts perhaps because they had imperfect data or they made incorrect decisions based on the data. These are the sources of strategic risk for your organization.

As a healthcare IT leader, you have to deal with this reality. The strategic plan might not go exactly to plan. The organization may pivot if it learns of a new factor it had previously not considered. You need to be steadfast enough to execute consistently and yet nimble enough to respond and revise the plan when these changes occur. This is one of the more challenging aspects of being an IT leader today. You are required to consistently deliver, and the absence of problems is the goal (though seldom applauded). Yet, when things change, you also need to guide your team to effectively shift priorities, rework plans, and deliver results.

You can't control events, but you are required to manage them. It's your job to lead your team effectively when uncharted change happens. Here are some suggestions for how you can respond (or even prepare):

1. *Anticipate.* Sometimes IT leaders see trends and changes others miss. If it's significant enough, raise the concern through your manager to leadership.
2. *Plan for change.* For significant projects and tasks, think about alternatives. What could you do if things changed? Would this project be a sunk cost or could you repurpose it? Thinking through this process may surface risks you or your organization may not be willing to accept.
3. *Assess projects for risk.* Part of effective project management is to perform a risk analysis. If you include strategic risk as an element of your assessment, you may spot instances when a project could be jeopardized by larger strategic changes. Once identified, these can be brought to the executive sponsor for discussion. Risk management includes deciding and documenting how risks will be addressed—through accepting, avoiding, transferring, or mitigating. If your major projects include an assessment of strategic risk, you can address them before the project begins.

While no one has perfect insight into the future, we have all experienced times when we saw a problem coming. Inaction is often caused by a lack of understanding about how to respond to risk. Remembering that there are four primary actions (accept, avoid, transfer, mitigate) can help you decide how to address these oncoming issues more effectively.

Operational IT Risks

1. Misaligned expectations
2. Operationalizing technology
3. Service portfolio changes (new applications, new services, etc.)
4. Change management (release and configuration)
5. Process changes

These five types of risk impact IT departments just about every day. Let's look at each of these in more detail.

1. Misaligned Expectations

Much of IT work that is not operational involves project work. Projects can certainly be operational and involve only IT teams, such as a software upgrade or firewall replacements. Most projects, however, are done at the request of the organization. Operational leaders need new applications, new functionality, new interfaces, new systems…the list goes on. Perhaps the biggest risk to these types of projects is *misaligned expectations*. Misalignment occurs when IT views a project one way and operations sees it in a completely different way. All projects contain elements related to people, process, and technology. Interestingly, the view of how large a role each of these plays in a project may differ based on one's organizational perspective.

Figure 7.3a shows a representation of people, process, and technology risks as they might appear to operational owners (clinical, business) outside the IT department. Figure 7.3b shows that same risk represented from an IT perspective.

This is important to understand as a healthcare IT leader. Your constituents see projects as IT projects or as *technology* projects, as shown in Figure 7.3a. But if you have spent enough time in healthcare IT (or any IT, really), you've quickly come to realize that most projects' risk is related to *people* and *process*, and less so with technology, as shown in Figure 7.3b. Understanding this misalignment of perspectives will help you more successfully navigate IT operations and projects.

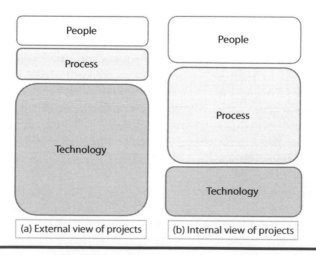

Figure 7.3   Misaligned view of project/IT risks.

When you understand that your end users see projects that involve technology as technology projects, you can immediately see that operational risk comes from lack of end-user (or stakeholder) engagement and lack of development of solid processes to support success. If users think you'll solve all their problems with a new application or a new interface, they're not likely to do the work needed for success. This can include tasks such as analyzing workflow, defining desired future state, or defining changes to policies, procedures, standards, or standard work. Understanding that there may be a tendency to see IT as the simple solution to a complex problem helps you understand where your leadership skills may be best utilized.

The best methods for addressing the risk of misaligned expectations are to *avoid* or *mitigate*. Avoiding this risk occurs when your end users fully understand their roles and responsibilities in a project. They understand their deliverables; they have committed adequate resources and time to the project. They commit to getting their staff trained. They participate in the project planning and implementation as full business partners. When this happens, misalignment can be avoided. However, we know that's describing an idyllic state that most often does not occur. Ensuring all IT projects go through the established IT governance process (refer to Chapter 3) will certainly help increase engagement and reduce the risk of misaligned expectations. The rest of the time, you'll need to work on mitigating the remaining risk.

An assessment of your operational risk from this perspective can be extremely helpful in developing your mitigation plan. This is standard project risk assessment and mitigation process, but with a leadership twist. As the IT leader (assuming you're not also the project manager), you'll need to step up and ensure the communication of expectations as well as roles and responsibilities happens with the right stakeholders at the right time in the right way. Asking a clinical nurse manager, "Hey, are we good with moving forward with this new scheduling module for your staff?" is not going to work. Instead, you'll probably need to be a bit formal—perhaps through a document, a project kick off (with documentation), and a phone call followed by an email at minimum—to ensure expectations are set. If your project has an executive sponsor, the project planning and review meetings, prior to formal project approval and kickoff, would be the perfect time to set these expectations. Gaining commitment at this time helps you document agreed-upon timing, roles, responsibilities, and dependencies. This helps later when the project is underway and things start to go off track.

[…more…]

It can be helpful in these planning meetings to indicate key milestones or deliverables for the operational owners (clinical or business). For example, suppose you're deploying a new application and you've scheduled to have the vendor come in to assist with workflow analysis and application design. This is fully dependent upon the operational owner participating. That means they need to agree on a mutually convenient time/date for the vendor to come in, they need to be available when they say they will be, they need to commit time and resources to meet their obligations and commitments for deliverables that result from this vendor engagement. In the project meeting with executives, you can use phrases like, "Success of this phase is dependent upon these three things: participating in vendor kick off meetings, following up with workflow documentation as requested, and participating in vendor design sessions. These will require two dedicated resources for four full days the week of [insert date]. If those resources are not committed, this phase will be in a hold state and will delay the completion of the project." The point is to be very clear about the implications to the project if commitments are not met.

In addition to setting expectations, your projects will be more successful if you develop a simple, clear, and consistent communication plan. End users and stakeholders need to be kept informed so they can remain involved. It's no wonder many projects are viewed as technology projects (Figure 7.3a), because IT often takes the project and runs with it. Sadly, IT often sees projects as technology projects as well, and this leads to poor user engagement and communication. As an IT leader, you'll need to continually remind yourself and your staff that the project is an operational project that has a technology component (Figure 7.3b). In this way, you can help mitigate the operational risk that comes from misaligned expectations.

2. Operationalizing Technology

We just discussed how projects are seen as technology projects and how that creates risk. There is also risk in how technology is operationalized. It relates to misaligned expectations. To illustrate this, we'll use a real example, which is modified only slightly to ensure the source remains anonymous. This is an example outside of healthcare but is applicable nonetheless.

> An organization with approximately 4,000 employees and an IT department of approximately 200 was working on deploying a mobile solution for its warehouse operations. Warehousing was not a core business, simply a needed function within the organization. The project sponsors came forward with a project request to automate the warehouse with a new mobile technology, much like what Amazon® had deployed (and advertised). This solution was not cutting edge when this company began to explore this option. They believed they could save millions of dollars each year through improving their warehouse management using this technology. This project was so high profile and so important to the company that it leased an off-site location for the project team to work so they would not be interrupted or pulled off this strategic project. The company spent about two years and $2M on this project. The big Go Live day came and within hours, the frontline staff in the warehouse declared the technology was unusable and they reverted to their old methods. The project was scrapped, never to be resurrected.

If you've worked in IT long enough, you recognize this story at its essence—a failed project. As you were reading, you probably were listing possible issues that caused this project to fail so horribly. Without going into the actual root cause from this example, let's walk through possible root causes for this outcome. This will help us identify risk and mitigating strategies for operationalizing technology.

Business Case

If you work in a typical healthcare organization, there's a chance there is an inconsistent process for creating a business case for a new technology project. Some organizations may go all out and require a lengthy business case; others may simply require someone to have a "good" idea. Clearly, a well-developed business case can help define many important elements of the project including desired and required outcomes, costs, return on investment, ongoing operational costs, risk, and organizational expectations, to name a few. It's difficult to deliver a project that meets expectations when no expectations have been set.

Risk mitigation strategy: The best and most consistent cure for this situation is to implement an IT governance process. A basic business case should be required for every significant project or solution. If you don't have a strong IT governance process, you can still back into a business case. *Backing into a business case* means that you may not have all the elements, but you can develop many of the required elements and get your end users to fill in the blanks. The template you use for IT governance serves this purpose. If you have a weak IT governance process, you can create a business case template that can help you instill a standardized process around this aspect. Whatever you do, try your best to avoid launching half-baked projects. They are certain to fail without heroic effort.

Technology Assessment

End users will often go to a conference and hear about a new company, a new technology, or a new solution. They come back all fired up and want to implement right away. However, what they may not realize is that the solution the vendor is proposing (or heavily marketing) may not be the right fit for their problem or for your organization. Performing a technology assessment based on functional and technical requirements is a must.

Risk mitigation strategy: Require that all new proposals include a technology assessment. This will allot time in the proposal cycle to do a deep dive into the technology. When possible, step back and start with this question: What problem are you trying to solve? This will focus your end users on the problem rather than the solution (aka "shiny new object") and help you develop both functional and technical requirements. You may have to respond to the end user with an alternate proposal that will solve their problem. This is often the case when the user brings forward a proposal or request that does not conform to organizational or IT standards such as server, storage, or connectivity needs or information security requirements, for example. And, before you start thinking that your end users are your clinical staff, take a look inside your department. How many times has an engineer or manager proposed a new tool or application without doing a similar assessment? The rules apply equally inside and outside of IT.

If a technical assessment turns up too much technical or operational risk, you should consider a pilot or proof of concept (POC) project before scheduling an implementation project. The benefits of a POC include the ability to test operational assumptions prior to implementation at low or no cost, thereby greatly reducing the technical risk during implementation. Just be sure that the POC doesn't turn into a production system without a formal transition process.

End-User Engagement in Design

In the example, it sounds like the project team went off to its off-site location and simply designed the project based on what they thought was needed. Perhaps they worked with a vendor or consultant who claimed to have vast experience. It sounds like everyone behaved as though the end users were dumb or unnecessary. Let's be clear—even when end users are involved in the design, there is no guarantee things will turn out better. Often end users don't understand technology or understand the implications to workflow or processes. So, while they may be involved, they may not always drive a more successful outcome unless they are guided. It's not that users aren't smart, it's just that their expertise is outside of IT.

Risk mitigation strategy: Work to develop very clear and very basic desired outcomes. If the project involves frontline staff using a technology, as this one did, ensure those staff are involved in discussions up front. Assist them in envisioning new workflows, new technologies. Insist the vendor assist with demos and walk-throughs of the space to simulate what the new work will look like. Just as most people can't envision a completed house by staring at blueprints, most people can't envision how a new technology will change their work. Your responsibility is to meaningfully engage everyone necessary, from frontline staff to executives, to ensure everyone is engaged to the extent necessary.

End-User Testing

Clearly in this example, there was no testing done—or if testing was done, it was completely ineffective. Often IT will configure or install an application, test it from an IT perspective, and deem it "tested." Nothing could be farther from the truth. Regardless of who your ultimate end user is, you need to ensure end users test the product along the way. It helps them begin to visualize the new workflows, and it also helps ensure the product works the way they need and expect it to.

Risk mitigation strategy: Whatever process you have in place today for testing applications, software, interfaces, new technology, etc., be sure you include end users in the design of the test plan and the actual testing. Document this plan as part of your standard project management process, including expected outcomes. Document actual results. When testing is done in a casual *ad hoc* manner, results never live up to expectations.

End-User Training

A knowledge gap is created when users are not trained on the specific solution they will be using. End-user training must simulate, to the greatest extent possible, the final technology solution they'll be working with.

Risk mitigation strategy: Engage with end users to determine optimal times and methods for training. If Revision A is available but it's Revision B that will be used, find a way to defer training to avoid training on the wrong solution or at the wrong time. Schedule the training as close to the Go Live as possible so knowledge is retained. Develop super users who get extensive training so they can assist at Go Live and beyond. If users are not attending training, call a time-out and escalate. If your end users are not properly trained, the project will fail and you'll be left holding the failed project. In clinical areas where census drives staffing, you're doubly challenged. This is part of getting appropriate clinical and/or business unit operational engagement and executive commitment to provide the time and resources needed for success. If possible, develop a competency test that is required after training or before first use to further support training efforts.

Clinical Considerations

Clinical considerations is a short phrase for a big topic. Essentially the risks in operationalizing technology with respect to clinical operations are around workflows (does the configuration support clinical workflows and best practices), interfaces (does the right data flow to the right place at the right time), and information (do we capture the right data). As we know, misconfiguration of the electronic medical record (EMR) can create convoluted workflows, unauthorized workarounds, user errors, and certainly user frustration.

Risk mitigation strategy: The best way to avoid these issues is through using the mitigation strategies discussed. This includes ensuring there is a strong business case (so everyone is on the same page), documenting decisions regarding workflows when involved in end-user design, creating documentation for end-user testing so it is consistent with required outcomes, and ensuring end-user training adequately covers the needed knowledge and skills to successfully use the new technology.

Operationalizing technology is a significant risk to IT and hopefully this section has given you some ideas in terms of risk within your own organization as well as mitigation strategies and techniques you can use to reduce the *likelihood* and/or *impact* of these risks.

3. Service Portfolio Changes

The term *service portfolio* is a term taken from Information Technology Infrastructure Library (ITIL) and it refers to the set of services provided by the IT department. Part of managing operations is to manage demand, including the number of new services (which can be servers, network, applications, interfaces, etc.). These can be divided into planned and unplanned and can be tracked as Key Performance Indicators (% of new services that went through strategic review or approved via strategic review versus % of those that did not). Tracking this helps you understand your risk with respect to new services. The top risks for the department and for the organization are as follows:

1. The new service does not align with the organization's strategies (or worse, runs counter to those).
2. The new service does not move through a structured review process.
3. The new service does not align with the IT department's strategies.
4. The new service does not conform to current IT standards, including information security standards.

Risk mitigation strategy: Ideally, these new services would start out as project requests that would be reviewed through an IT governance process. Barring that, ensure that 100% of these projects are reviewed at least by an IT leadership team to ensure alignment with business and departmental strategies and objectives. If additional review by subject matter or technical experts is needed, ensure you have a process in place to cause that review to occur. Document all decisions and preserve that documentation for reference. If you have a functional IT governance process in place, you should perform a root cause analysis for each item that comes in without prior review so you can determine how and where your process broke down. With working IT governance in place, you should find that no less than 80% of all new services are reviewed and approved prior to request.

4. Change Management

Change management is one of the most fundamental processes an IT department should have in place. *Change management* is defined as the practice of defining and managing policies, procedures, and standards used to ensure the efficient and effective handling of all hardware and software changes to minimize the impact of changes on the environment. This includes, but is not limited to, updates, application modifications, configuration changes, patches, scripts, and break/fix tasks. Most IT professionals know that a vast majority of incidents are caused by changes—either new services (see preceding section) or changes of any kind. If you don't have change management firmly instituted in your department, this is a significant source of risk and should be among your highest priorities to remediate.

Risk mitigation strategy: First and foremost, your IT team must define a change management process, develop necessary tools (such as a service desk tool) to track those changes, and educate your IT staff on using the process. Finally, you should make the following change management processes a job requirement, and you should monitor and audit results to ensure it is consistently followed. A few resources for developing a change management program are provided in the References section at the end of this chapter.

5. Process Changes

This is closely related to change management, but for non-IT tasks. For example, if you have a process in place to audit userid creation to ensure roles and userids are always correctly created and the audit process changes, you have risk. The risks are that (a) userids won't be correctly created, (b) you open up security holes, or (c) the user cannot access needed information. Another process change risk is that an intentional change is made and it makes things worse instead of better. Any time change is injected, there is the potential for unintended consequences. These are unexpected outcomes that can create significant problems for the organization.

Risk mitigation strategy: First, review your processes and determine how stable they really are. If they're documented and consistently followed, your risk is lower than organizations that have few processes or processes that are rarely followed. Second, treat changes to processes the same way you treat changes to IT systems. Examine what is changing and why, validate the need for change, review for potential consequences, test the new process in as many scenarios as possible, then document the change and monitor the results. If successful, update your process documentation to reflect the new standard. If not successful, revert to the prior process and do a root cause analysis to determine what went wrong. Managing process changes as you do any other change will help reduce your risks in this area.

In this section, we've reviewed a number of organizational risks that IT leaders face on a daily basis. While not exhaustive, it provides a starting point. The mitigation strategies give you a starting point for thinking through how to manage these risks in your department.

People Risk

People are the source of many different types of risks. When looking at people from a risk management perspective, we can categorize these risks as follows:

1. Needed skills and capabilities
2. Skills distribution
3. Teamwork/work styles
4. Human error
5. Bad intentions, bad actions

1. Needed Skills and Capabilities

The biggest risk you face as a healthcare IT leader with respect to people is having the right skills and capabilities you need, today and in the future, to deliver the work expected by the organization. As an IT leader, it is your job to provide a strategic roadmap for your area of responsibility that aligns with the organization's broader goals and objectives. In doing so, one key element is understanding if you have the right people in the right jobs at the right times.

If you're an experienced manager, you know that a team is typically composed of superstars, steady performers, and "sinkers," those whose performance perpetually floats downward without focused managerial attention. Every department needs a few *superstars*. They're typically the ones who come up with elegant, innovative solutions. They solve the hardest problems. They are undaunted by complexity and confusion. The risk of superstar mentality is that the steady, day-to-day, standard work of the department may suffer in the hands of your very talented best. Old advice might have been to coach those superstars so they can do the standard operational work. In a *Harvard Business Review* article in 2011, Marcus Buckingham posed an alternative approach. He said, "Great managers know and value the unique abilities and even the eccentricities of their employees, and they learn how best to integrate them into a coordinated plan. ..." (Buckingham, p. 92). In order to reduce your risk and better ensure continued engagement, transfer routine work to your steady performers (within reason) and continue to leverage the unique skills and talents of your superstars.

The *steady performers* are those you count on to knock out the day-to-day work. They tend to prefer steadiness and don't appear to be interested (or perhaps capable) of tackling the really complex problems. That should be just fine with you—since so much of healthcare IT depends on the day-to-day operational work. Remember our discussion about value? (If not, refer to Chapter 4.) Though operational excellence doesn't move the dial in terms of creating real value, the lack of operational excellence will stop you in your tracks. You need people who are happy chunking through the work each day and delivering steadily on results. If you transfer the day-to-day work away from your superstars, you also need to be careful about messaging and expectations. Otherwise, you'll inadvertently create two classes of employees.

A team that has a good blend of these two types will likely be more successful than a team that has all of one or the other type. That said, your leadership skills will be needed to ensure that the superstars don't get ahead of themselves or don't start acting as if they are better or more valuable than your steady performers. Conversely, you'll need to watch your steady performers to make sure they don't feel slighted or less valued because of the more mundane work they do.

That brings us to *sinkers*, which sounds like a derogatory term, but it really describes the tendency of the weakest members of your team to sink back down to the lowest common denominator. They may barely meet standards and they only excel when challenged directly. They continually sink down toward that line between "meets standards" and "needs improvement." These folks represent several different types of risk to the team and the organization. The issue with sinkers is either *aptitude* or *attitude*. If they lack the skills and abilities to do the job, they either need training or they need to be placed in a job more aligned with their skills. However, the problem often is more linked to attitude. For whatever reason, they have adopted an attitude that allows them to perform to minimal standards. Determine if the issue is aptitude or attitude and address accordingly. Sinkers will not only take up a disproportionate amount of your time; they'll also distract you from real value-added work. Through sloppy, inconsistent, or haphazard work, they put the team and the organization at risk. It's not worth keeping these folks around if coaching and counseling don't fix the issue.

2. Skills Distribution

Once you understand what the near and long term look like with respect to IT demands for your team, you'll need to assess whether you have the skills and capabilities to deliver. The six statements listed here are the usual options for IT:

1. We have the *skills on the team* that we need.
2. We have the *skills in the department* (but not on the team) that we need.
3. We lack the skills we need; we *need to train* someone.
4. We lack the skills we need; we *need to hire* someone.
5. We lack the skills we need; we need a *consultant* to get us up to speed quickly.
6. We lack the skills we need; we need to *outsource* this.

If you have the skills you need, be sure to double-check with some specificity. It's easy to fall into a trap thinking you have the skills because someone was commenting one day about how awesome they are with [insert technology here]. If you can find a more objective way to assess and measure that skill, use it. Sometimes people self-assess really accurately, so if the person has a reputation for always being on target with their skills, discuss in-depth to validate. Sometimes you can rely on a vendor or consultant with that expertise to assess your internal skills. Other times, you can find an online assessment that will validate skill levels. Be creative, but don't just blindly accept statements about qualifications, especially on critical items.

If you lack the skills, training internal staff is usually your best option. It is efficient, it provides professional growth for your team, and it is the least expensive option. If training is not possible, you need to decide on whether you need to add a position (hire) or retain a consultant for a short period of time to fill a gap and transfer knowledge to your team in the process. Finally, you might decide that this need is so far outside your area of expertise that it makes more sense to outsource this function.

As a leader, your job to determine whether or not your team has the skills needed now and in the future and to take proactive steps to address potential gaps. Understanding the various options at your disposal and leveraging them appropriately is key to success. Typically, when assessing the skill gaps and whether to "build or buy" (train or hire), you need to understand what the skill is, how long it will be needed, if it's likely to expand or contract in the future, how hard it is to train or hire this particular skill, what the impact on your team would be for train or hire, and how you will incorporate this into your team going forward. Once you make your decision, document it and save that documentation so you can reflect back on the decision in 3, 6, or 12 months and see if you have room to improve in the future. If you nailed it, it will reinforce the process you used to make the decision. If you missed the mark, you can determine what went wrong and create a plan to avoid those steps in the future.

3. Teamwork/Work Styles

One of the risks you must address as a leader is when there are issues with teamwork. Often this is caused by a mismatch of work styles. One person is bold and she charges ahead with 70% of the needed information; another is more conservative and he holds off taking action until he has 95% of the needed information. They drive each other nuts. Each feels negatively impacted by the other.

As a leader, your job is to find a balance between the two styles (and every style in between) in order to foster collaboration and harmony on the team. No team will get along 100% of the time, but setting guidelines for behavior can help reduce the risk of team dysfunction. Work suffers when teams are not functioning well because they're busy attacking each other or searching for evidence of wrong-doing. Key information may be withheld or doled out. Spirited debates that once surfaced potential problems simply become battlegrounds, and the team fails to generate positive results. Yes, individuals may deliver on their tasks, but overall the team is not functioning as a cohesive unit and is putting the organization at risk as a result.

Addressing these kinds of differences can be challenging, typically because we each have our own style and see the work through that filter. If you're strongly results oriented, you likely value that trait over the more measured person who prefers to analyze data until he or she has formulated an entire plan and is comfortable moving forward. Conversely, if you're a person who likes to talk through results, you're not likely to value someone who prepares a formal report for you to read. Knowing your own biases and preferences is certainly the first step. Beyond that, reinforce the notion that each work style has benefits and strengths that contribute to the whole of the team. Of course, any work style that is too extreme can cause it to move from a strength to a weakness, so moderation is key. Utilizing the various strengths of the team reduces the risk to the organization through viewing things through several different lenses. It becomes a risk when these work styles become barriers to success.

4. Human Error

To quote Albert Einstein, "Anyone who has never made a mistake has never tried anything new." Human error is inevitable, so it's best to plan for it. As a risk, human error is hard to contain because it can happen anytime, anywhere for no apparent reason. However, there are a few key risk mitigation strategies that will reduce both the likelihood and impact of human error occurring in your IT department.

1. *Develop standard work.* All routine work should be standardized (and automated, if possible). When staff perform standardized work, they all do it the same way every time. This standards-based way of approaching routine work helps prevent variation and errors, both of which inject risk into the organization.
2. *Develop processes around change management.* We've discussed the importance of change management earlier. Institute it or reinforce it, as needed.
3. *Remove distractions from the environment.* Errors are much more likely to occur if your staff have an environment that is noisy and full of interruptions. Do what you can to improve the environment, including requiring people to keep noise down or hold lengthy conversations in other locations (conference rooms, break rooms, hallways versus in cubicle, desk or office areas). Help prevent task switching by providing focused time for work. Encourage staff to only check email periodically (instead of constantly) and to turn off instant messaging when performing critical tasks.
4. *Slow down.* Sometimes in our haste to multitask or get a lot of work done before a deadline, milestone, or vacation, we make mistakes. Help your staff to slow down and focus when things get too hectic.

[…more…]

Early in my management career, my team was involved with performing a major upgrade. The enterprise system used by everyone in the company was scheduled for a major upgrade. It required many steps to orchestrate all the moving parts. My lead systems engineer has worked meticulously for months documenting a plan, working with peers to walk through the plan step by step and develop a timeline so detailed it included every step and how long that step should take—even steps that should take "5 seconds" were listed if they were critical steps.

The night of the upgrade came and that same engineer accidentally typed in the wrong command and wiped out a needed backup file. In a panic, he sat at his desk completely incapacitated, unsure of what to do. All he could think about was that he was going to get fired. His manager, aware of the problem, notified me. I asked the manager to have the employee come to my office.

I asked the employee, we'll call Chad, to sit down, take a deep breath, and exhale. I asked him to do that three times. Then, I said, "Listen, Chad, you made a mistake. A big one. We all do it from time to time. You're not known for making mistakes. You're known as the go-to guy when the going gets rough. You are NOT going to lose your job over this, people here don't get fired for making honest mistakes. You are safe. But what I need you to do right now is to clear your mind and approach this as a problem to solve. How can we fix this problem? You're the one who thought through this project so thoroughly, you have deep expertise in this entire process. I trust that you can find a solution. If you need help from anyone, let me know, I'll get them in here or on the phone. Think this over and let me know your plan when you have one."

It was easy to see that Chad was completely overcome with fear. Fear causes people to not think straight. It causes their brains to literally shut down and higher-order thinking is not possible.

As a leader, the most important thing you can do in the midst of an emergency or crisis is to bring calm, rational thought to the situation. In this case, Chad calmed down, walked around for a few minutes processing potential solutions and had the system back up and running about 2 hours later. It pushed the completion of the upgrade by 2 hours, but it was successfully completed thanks to Chad gathering his wits and being able to think without fear.

5. Bad Intentions, Bad Actions

Bad intent and bad action, in contrast to human error, is a choice—a choice to look the other way, to deliver sloppy work, to lie, to misrepresent, to be "maliciously compliant." We have all dealt with employees who have bad intent and take bad actions. This can be a serious organizational risk, to standard IT operations as well as information security. Rather than go into every possible variation of what bad intent can yield, we'll keep it at a high level and simply note that bad intent/actions must be dealt with directly and swiftly. Set expectations on behavior and document those conversations. Ensure you document consistently or work with your HR department to learn your organization's system. Allowing bad behavior to continue unchecked puts your team, your deliverables, and your organization at risk.

Process Risk

Have you ever worked in a blame-filled environment? Every problem turned into a finger-pointing exercise to try to pin the blame on someone? Do you work in a department like that today? It's stressful and it's counterproductive. The best way to change that type of environment is to understand that if people are trained and understand expectations (previous section) and things go wrong, then you have a process problem. A vast majority of problems in IT trace back to process problems.

Standard work is a Lean term (see Chapter 9) that defines work that is done the same way by every person every time. If someone fails to follow the establish standard, it's either a choice (ignoring requirements), a mistake, or possibly another process problem (one process problem causes a downstream problem in a standardized process, for example). Process risk involves these elements: lack of standard processes, processes that yield unintended consequences, and processes that are broken. Lack of process creates enormous risk. Focus on developing, implementing, and managing process in all areas of your department to incrementally reduce risk.

Standardizing processes is fundamental to service excellence, and it ties in with frameworks like ITIL or Information Technology Service Management (ITSM).

Technology Risk

The risks from technology are many, but they fall primarily into these three categories: *architecture*, *features/functions*, and *deployment*. These overlap substantially with process issues, so we'll cover these briefly.

In any project that involves technology, an architectural review should be conducted. This allows the IT infrastructure experts to review the proposed solution before it becomes a commitment or a project. If the architecture of the solution is not aligned with current or desired infrastructure standards, there are two risks. One is that the solution will fail altogether, and the other is that the solution will never reach its full potential. Neither is an acceptable outcome. Reviewing all proposed new technologies in light of architectural and information security standards will reduce or eliminate this risk.

A second common technology risk is that the features and functions of the technology are not suited to the environment. This goes beyond architecture to the functionality that end users will interact with. If an application is difficult to navigate, if the reporting feature is required but poorly developed, if the database is poorly designed and requires constant maintenance, if the product does not perform according to specifications—these can cause significant risk to the organization. Notably, one of the biggest risks is loss of productivity. Not many organizations are willing to rip out a solution that doesn't work well (unless it's very high profile or completely not working). Instead, staff who worked so hard to deploy the solution will plod along and accept that this program, this application, this interface just works like this and there's nothing to be done. The risk of deploying a technology that just doesn't fit often has a slow, deep risk to it that's sometimes hard to spot. Using a review process and leveraging your business systems analysts to develop functional and technical specifications, review solutions against those specifications, and work closely with end users to understand and articulate needs is the best strategy for mitigating this risk.

Sometimes functionality is related to product maturity. Take an application that's been around for 20 years and hasn't been updated. There's certainly a risk to implementing such an application. What about implementing the version of the hardware or software that has been on the market for a while, but is not the latest version? You commit, you deploy, and you find out the newest version has just been released, but you're not eligible for it. On the other hand, take an application that's brand new in the market and the vendor is looking for alpha or beta customers. Depending on where the product falls in its lifecycle, you can have a variety of risks. Your technical analysis should include reviewing these aspects, and as part of your standard work for assessing new solutions, you should include questions that will surface any of these potential risks. It's not to say you should not move forward, but you should do so with a full understanding of the risks and the operational implications of doing so.

Finally, there is deployment risk. This not only has to do with how engaged the end user has been along the way but also how well training has been prepared and delivered, how well tested the product is in a development or test region, how closely the development mirrors production, and how effective the analysis and development of the product has been in aligning with end user needs and organizational requirements. Many projects fail and it's usually after they are deployed that the failure is discovered or acknowledged. To reduce this risk, follow standard project management best practices and make sure you have included, repeatedly and at each step, the voice of the customer.

Financial Risk

Regardless of your current role in IT, you need to be aware of the financial implications of running a healthcare IT department. If you're an application developer or a systems engineer, it's important to understand the financial drivers of your department at a high level so you can be an informed participant. The key financial risks are related to projects, vendors, and contracts. Though ongoing operations pose a financial risk, they typically are related to one of these three aspects.

Of course, the biggest financial risk to your IT team is if you really don't understand the finances of your team, of your department, or of the hospital. If you have only basic financial skills, you can certainly focus on improving them. Often your finance department will provide you with a "budget buddy," someone to help you navigate the financial systems and requirements of the organization. Other organizations embed financial analysts in the department to assist managers with their financial responsibilities. Even if neither of those is true in your organization, most finance departments are more than happy to help educate you about hospital finances and your department's finances in particular. If this is not an area of strength or expertise for you (and for most in IT it is not), make a plan to improve your skills in this area. There's a book called *Financial Intelligence* listed in the References section that is a good primer. However, a quick search of your favorite bookstore will yield plenty of great resources for learning business finance.

Vendor Risk

Two of the most common sources of financial risk in IT are vendors and contracts. Let's start with vendors. In the best case, vendors are trusted business partners who assist in identifying opportunities to improve the business through new or expanded products and services. They behave in a more value-added, consultative mode. In the worst case, vendors are fronted by sales representatives who are pushing the latest offering in hopes of hitting their quarterly sales goal. The financial risk comes from that latter. If you've worked in IT management for any period of time, you've likely had at least one encounter with a less-than-trustworthy IT sales rep. You listen to the pitch, look at a product demo, and try to uncover potential weaknesses and pitfalls. You compare the product to your requirements list, you compare Product A to Product B, relying on sales reps, product demos, and industry research. You may even reach out to existing customers to get their input. All of these steps help reduce the risk that you'll select the wrong product, so these are all good steps to take. None of them remove the risk altogether.

When you have a sales rep who is not informed, not consultative, and not engaged appropriately with your business, you run the risk of being sold the wrong solution. While the ultimate responsibility does fall to IT leadership, there are a few steps you can take in these situations to reduce your risk either immediately or in the long term.

1. *Talk to your sales rep.* Set very clear expectations for the business relationship.
2. *Get a new sales rep.* If you are not pleased with the rep you have, speak to their management and get a new rep.
3. *Find a new company.* This might mean finding a different Value Added Reseller (VAR) for the same product. It might mean finding a different product altogether.

If all else fails and you must do business with this company, you can try to negotiate a no-cost, no-obligation Proof of Concept engagement that allows you to really review and test the product before committing to it. While this takes time and effort on the part of your team, it is an effective financial risk mitigation strategy in this regard.

Contract Risk

Most healthcare organizations have some sort of contracting department or legal review of contracts. That's a good starting point for mitigating financial risk. Remember, though, that even though your legal or contracting department may review the legal aspects such as the boilerplate language, you will need to assess the *operational* aspects of the contract. If you are not well versed in this arena, you should find a mentor—either your manager or a peer—who has experience reading and understanding contracts.

The risks you face if you don't understand the terms of the contract thoroughly can vary widely, but since these are legal documents, you will be required to meet the terms of the agreement. It takes practice to effectively read and understand contracts, so be sure you get help while you're ramping up. That's your best mitigation strategy for dealing with contract risk overall. Here's the best mitigation advice regarding contracts: *If it's not in the contract, it doesn't exist. If it is in the contract, you must abide by it.*

Information Security Risk

Not surprisingly, if you do a search for books on IT risk management, you're most likely to find hundreds of results related to information security. Some would argue the greatest risk in IT these days is information security. From the standpoint of safeguarding patient data and sensitive/confidential information, information security is absolutely the largest area of risk. This chapter on risk management is intended to provide a wide view of risk management so you can identify and develop risk management strategies. Certainly you can (and should) do further research on information security risk management if this is an area of responsibility or interest to you.

Thousands of books have been written about information security risk and it's a rapidly changing landscape. Though it's beyond the scope of this chapter to provide a thorough discussion of information security risk, there are a few key elements that healthcare IT leaders should know and understand.

The risk of users downloading and activating malicious code is probably one of the highest information security risks your organization faces. End-user education programs along with innovative technical controls are your best mitigation strategies for these risks, though none are perfect.

The demand for interfaces between healthcare applications and technologies is enormous and growing each year. The demand for "interconnectedness" is a sound one, but another area that drives significant information technology risk. Data no longer simply resides in the data center. Keeping track of your data and keeping it secure is a large undertaking.

Many medical devices communicate across wired or wireless networks, receive updates from a vendor site on the Internet (i.e., require Internet connectivity), and have operating systems that sometimes can't be patched or run antivirus/antimalware software. Larger systems, such as cardiac or hemodynamic monitoring systems and imaging systems, are largely composed of computer systems, but because they are FDA regulated, they cannot be managed like an IT asset. It's a serious source of risk—if a system is compromised, serious or deadly patient harm can occur. This is a growing area of concern for information security professionals.

Third-party connections and external vendors are another source of operational and information security risk. In the past several years, some of the more high profile data breaches outside of healthcare came from vendor accounts or breaches at vendor sites that allowed access to other systems. Ensuring you tightly manage vendor accounts, vendor connections, VPN tunnels, open firewall ports, etc., will reduce your risk. This is a key element of solid information security management that's been receiving heightened attention in recent years.

This is a very compressed look at information security, and we only touched on some highlights to help you understand the nature of information security risks. Everyone in an organization is responsible for IT security and that includes everyone in IT. As an IT leader, you understand that regardless of your role, information security is part of your job.

Summary

We've covered a lot of ground in this chapter. Risk management is a broad and deep topic, and we've only scratched the surface, hitting on a few highlights along the way. As a healthcare IT leader, you need to be aware of the constantly changing risk landscape so you can identify and mitigate risk to the best of your ability. Having a working understanding of where risks reside and how you might address them (avoid, accept, transfer, mitigate, or sometimes exploit) can help you manage these elements more successfully. To quote the world-renowned Indian economist, Raghuram Rajan, "Not taking risks one doesn't understand is often the best form of risk management."

References

For more on this topic, visit http://susansnedaker.com/leading-hit.

QR7.1

Berman, Karen and Joe Knight with John Case, *Financial Intelligence: A Manager's Guide to Knowing What the Numbers Really Mean*, Boston: Harvard Business School Press, 2006.

Broadbent, Marianne and Ellen S. Kitzis, *The New CIO Leader*, Boston: Harvard Business School Press, 2005.

Buckingham, Marcus, "What Great Managers Do," *HBR's 10 Must Reads: On Managing People*, Boston: Harvard Business Review Press, 2011, pp. 91–110.

Cisco Systems, Inc., *Change Management: Best Practices*, White Paper, 2008, http://www.cisco .com/c/en/us/products/collateral/services/high-availability/white_paper_c11-458050.html, viewed May 29, 2016.

QR7.2

Hernandez, Steven, ISC², *Official (ISC)² Guide to the HCISPP CBK*, Healthcare Information Security and Privacy Practitioner, Boca Raton, FL: CRC Press, 2015.

Herzig, Terrell W., *Information Security in Healthcare: Managing Risk*, Chicago: HIMSS, 2010.

Herzig, Terrell W., Tom Walsh, and Lisa A. Gallagher, *Implementing Information Security in Healthcare: Building a Security Program*, Chicago: HIMSS, 2013.

Hickman, George T. and Detlev H. Smaltz, *The Healthcare Information Technology Planning Fieldbook*, Chicago: HIMSS, 2008.

Wager, Karen A., France Wickham Lee, John P. Glaser, *Health Care Information Systems: A Practical Approach for Health Care Management*, 2nd Ed., San Francisco: Jossey-Bass, 2009.

Chapter 8

Managing, Directing, and Leading

Overview

In this chapter, we're going to look at the similarities and differences among managing, directing, and leading. Though these all have traits in common, there are distinctly different skills needed to progress from managing to directing to leading.

Peter Drucker was a renowned and respected American consultant, educator, and author and has been described as the founder of modern management. One of his often-cited quotes is, "Management is doing things right; leadership is doing the right things." Interestingly, he also said, "Efficiency is doing things right; effectiveness is doing the right things." Therefore, if both statements are correct, then it would follow that management is about efficiency and leadership is about effectiveness.

Let's turn to another very well-respected thought leader in management practices, John Kotter. Kotter is professor emeritus at Harvard Business School, author, lecturer, and consultant. In an article in the *Harvard Business Review* entitled "What Leaders Really Do," he said, "Management is about coping with complexity; it brings order and predictability to a situation. But that is no longer enough—to succeed, companies must be able to adapt to change. Leadership, then, is about learning to cope with rapid change" (Kotter, p. 39).

These two concepts are closely related. Managers deal with complexity every day and their primary function is to ensure things are being done right. Leaders also deal with complexity, but their primary function is to effectively guide the organization through that complexity and rapid change.

Managers' jobs are primarily involved with defining and directing the day-to-day work of the team. That involves managing people, process, technology, and operations. In healthcare IT, directors often have teams of managers as direct reports. What are the skills needed to be a successful director? What skills are different from basic management skills and how can you gain those skills? This chapter will compare and contrast managers' and directors' roles to help you understand what skills, traits, and behaviors are needed for you to progress along your career path. We'll also point out differences between these management (manager, director) functions and leadership. You'll learn traits of effective leaders so you can improve your own leadership skills as well as support, foster, and develop leaders within your organization.

Managing

Managing healthcare IT is one of the most challenging, complex, and engaging management roles you can have these days. Whether you're new to IT management, new to healthcare IT management, or a seasoned healthcare IT manager, you know there is always something new to learn, always a way to do better tomorrow what you struggled with today. That's what's so very enthralling about healthcare IT, and it's why many of us gravitated to this field.

It also is an incredibly challenging role because not only are you responsible for the normal IT manager deliverables, but also you know that at the other end of your technology is a nurse or a doctor or a medical tech who is caring for a patient. You know that your decisions and your actions ultimately can impact patient care. So, it's not just about reviewing a budget or following up on a task; it's about delivering a service that enables patient care. When you keep that first and foremost in your mind, you will stay on track.

Leaving Technical Expertise Behind, Part 1

One of the most challenging changes for new healthcare IT managers, especially those who came up through the technical (application or infrastructure) ranks, is that your technical skills now have to take a backseat to a wide variety of other skills. This is exactly what many technical people strive for when moving into the management ranks. Others seem to hold on to the illusion that they can remain technical and be a manager. Even if you're perfectly prepared to let go of your technical expertise, there can be an adjustment period when you fear you've made the wrong choice as you see your technical expertise slowly fade away. You see your former peers exceed your technical skills with a bit of envy. That's pretty normal, but it's important to focus on your new role as a manager. And, for what it's worth, if you were a great technical person and your skills fade but you ultimately decide management is not for you, you can always re-focus and get back to your former technical level of expertise.

That said, the technical skills and experience you bring with you are part of the value you bring to the organization. Specifically, you can (and should) use your technical skills in these ways:

1. *Reviewing technical solutions proposed by the team.* While you may not know specifics, you can still tell if the path they're heading down makes sense or not. You can determine if someone has done their homework, if their recommendations are technically sound, if their solution is aligned with the architecture and standards of the department.
2. *Working with vendors.* Your technical background gives you credibility when discussing technology, solutions, and problems with vendors. Even if you need your team to give you a brief update, a refresher on this technology, or a reminder of some of the technical facts, you have the ability to understand, retain, and use that knowledge to the benefit of the department and the organization.

3. *Discussing technology with your peers or executives.* At this level of discussion, you should be presenting high-level data, not gritty technical details. As a manager, you should be able to have these discussions at this level with relative ease.

4. *Understanding the work of your team.* Whether you rose up through the ranks of your team (or a similar team) or you moved over from another field (applications to infrastructure, for example), you need to have enough technical expertise to understand, plan, and manage the work of your team. If you are unfamiliar with the specifics of the work of the team, you should make an effort to learn. That may entail enrolling in classes, attending webinars, or shadowing your staff for a few days. Do whatever it takes to understand the work they do.

5. *Ability to assess a situation.* You have sufficient technical knowledge to be able to quickly identify the core issue and not get distracted by the "noise" that surrounds it. Similarly, you can use your technical skills to help you understand the big picture, but you need to be careful not to get bogged down in the details. This can be one of the most difficult aspects of leaving technical expertise behind—especially for people who are very detail-oriented to begin with.

6. *Knowing when to escalate.* If you have a technical background, you'll quickly recognize when to escalate a situation. Having the background gives you insight into the situation to accurately assess severity. This is especially important because when dealing with a situation, your staff may be so heads down in the solution that they can't recognize they're at a critical point.

Effectively Managing Staff

Entire books are written on management and we couldn't possibly condense that down into one section in one chapter of a book. However, in healthcare IT, there are a few aspects of management that are worth highlighting. The list is presented here; explanations are below. If you're a visual person, take a picture of this list on your phone and look at it daily—or print it out and post it near your monitor. It's a quick reminder of what is really important in your role.

1. Create and communicate a vision.
2. Be highly available, responsive, and effective.
3. Create an environment of trust, where it is "safe to fail."
4. Learn to listen.
5. Understand the work style and strengths/weaknesses of everyone on your team.
6. Find out how each person likes to be acknowledged for good work.
7. Be consistent and fair.
8. Address issues quickly.
9. Model the behavior you expect.
10. Have fun.

Now that you have the short list, let's get into some specifics of each of these behaviors.

1. *Create and communicate a vision.* As we discussed in Chapter 2, it's important that your team have a clear understanding of where you're headed. Whether you develop a strategic plan or simply lay out a vision for the department, providing this clear sense of direction is vital for a highly functioning team. It helps the team understand the larger context for the work they're doing and helps them make better decisions about what their priorities should be.

When they're aligned with strategy and vision, you can allow them more latitude to make decisions about their work. Empowering your staff in this manner typically results in a more productive and satisfied team.

2. *Be highly available, responsive, and effective (learn to delegate and mentor).* In terms of managerial impact, it's almost impossible to overstate the power of this one sentence. Your job is to provide guidance to your team, to provide resources to get the job done, and to remove roadblocks preventing them from accomplishing the required work. If you're not available and not responsive, you might as well go home. This is one of the most important aspects to being a successful IT manager. Yes, you may find yourself in back-to-back meetings every day, but you'll need to develop strategies for handling that. Block out times during the week that simply are not available to any but the most urgent meetings. Schedule and consistently have 1:1s with your staff. Let them know they can text you with urgent issues or call if it's really critical. When they have issues, questions, or concerns, respond quickly and effectively. Above all, make sure you are delegating effectively so you are not the bottleneck in the workflow.

This may sound really basic, but not all managers take the view that they are there as a resource for their team. If you're working under the old "command and control" mindset, the one that says "I'm the boss, I don't have to explain myself to my staff," you are not likely to be successful in healthcare IT in the future. The successful manager understands their role is a facilitator to those doing the work—the frontline staff. You set direction, you control the chaos, and you ensure the work gets done correctly. You can only do that if you're available, responsive, and effective.

Being effective also means learning to delegate. You are no longer a frontline employee delivering the work. You are managing the efforts of the team. One of the biggest mistakes new managers make is not delegating effectively. This is especially true when there are big projects or big deadlines looming. New managers will often jump in and help do the work thinking this will help the team. It might help in the short term, but it will be very detrimental in the long term. If you are not sure how to delegate tasks, talk with your manager and ask for assistance. As a general guideline, you can delegate by handing a specific, defined task to an employee with a clear expectation of the desired outcome and the timeline. Keep track of this delegation and follow up. Once you understand the basic process for your team, it will become easier and you'll see how to best parse out tasks based on employee skills and overall workload. Beware of handing all the choice assignments to your top performers—it's a natural bias to do so. Ensure you give stretch assignments to staff and that you spread the workload across the team appropriately.

One additional note on delegation is this: avoid micromanaging. New managers, or insecure managers, will appear to hand off a task but continue to direct it to such a degree that they might as well do it themselves. You might also note that highly competent staff often "flatline" on an assignment if their manager is also doing the work. If you assign a task, it's fine to give parameters or requirements, but then allow the work to be completed. Your job is to indicate what needs to be done; the staff person's job is to decide how it should be done (within reason).

3. *Create an environment of trust, where it is "safe to fail."* That begins with you. Say what you'll do and do what you say. Keeping your word builds trust. If you can't keep your word, renegotiate, but don't just drop things. When your team understands that they can trust what you say, you will build personal and professional credibility and environment of trust. That also means that when there's bad news, you convey as much as you can in as direct, honest, and compassionate way as possible. Finally, trust is built through setting clear expectations and following up on those. When everyone on the team understands what is expected of them and what success looks like, they feel a sense of security and trust with you as their manager and, by extension, to the organization at large.

   Creating a "safe to fail" environment is not the same as tolerating people who make mistakes over and over or coddling low performers. What it means is that when a mistake happens, it should not become a blameful situation. While it may be important to understand who made the mistake, it's vital to create an environment where people are willing to speak up and own their errors. Otherwise, they go underground and remain silent, fearing retribution or reprimand. That only makes problems worse. Examine processes to see what failed and if the process worked but the person failed to use the process, then it's a coaching opportunity. If that same person fails to follow process consistently, then you have a different matter to address.

4. *Learn to listen.* We discussed the importance of listening in Chapter 4, but it's worth repeating here. Listening is the foundation to all successful communication. It means taming your inner dialog and refraining from preparing your response while the other person is speaking. It also means ignoring your smartphone or tablet, closing the lid on your laptop, and otherwise removing distractions.

5. *Understand the work style and strengths/weaknesses of everyone on your team.* Every person on your team has a work style. These can be determined through tools like DiSC® or Myers-Briggs® or similar assessment tools. However, even without a formal assessment, you can pretty much tell which people like calm, orderly work and those who thrive on the ever-changing, issue-of-the-day type of environment. Assigning work and roles that really allow a person to work to their strengths will make that person more effective and happier in their work. Everyone should have a chance to grow and learn and improve upon their weaknesses as well. However, if you assign unpredictable, innovative work to someone who really needs and values stability, you have a mismatch that may well lead to failure. The symptoms are often loss of productivity, loss of accuracy, and loss of job satisfaction. Be sure to figure out work styles and work preferences for each member of your team so you can allow them to expand into their strengths.

6. *Find out how each person likes to be acknowledged for good work.* We often tend to think that others like what we like; nothing could be further from the truth. If you're someone who just loves to have your birthday celebrated in a big, loud, public fashion, don't assume everyone shares that joy. Ask each person about how they like to be acknowledged at work. If they come up short on answers, ask them to think back to a previous manager they may have had who did a great job at making them feel appreciated. Have them describe what that other manager did.

[…more…]

A quick search on the Internet brings up thousands of hits on "acknowledging employee performance," but here are some of my favorites:

a. Say thank you directly, specifically, and sincerely. There's not much worse than a generic thank you. If you're not good at saying thank you, use this formula. "Thank you, [insert name], you did a great job on [insert accomplishment]. In particular, I was really impressed with the way you [insert action]. I really appreciate it. Thanks."
b. Post a thank you note on their door or cubicle touting their performance.
c. Say thank you to them at a team meeting; highlight their performance.
d. Buy them coffee or lunch.
e. Buy bagels or pizza for the whole team and say it's in honor of this person's performance.
f. Let them come in late, leave early, or take a long lunch one day. If it's within the guidelines of your organization, provide them a day-off with pay if the effort required long hours.
g. Create a certificate (it can be serious or contain a bit of humor).
h. Have a story written about them in the company newsletter.
i. Arrange for your manager or a higher level executive to stop in and note their achievement.
j. Come up with something silly that the individual and the team appreciate. For example, take a photo of the person and run it through a photo filter that bends it, distorts it, or adds a hat, glasses, or beard. Enlarge it, add a few words of praise, and post it in a team location for all to see. After a while, you'll have a wall of fame—and you can start fresh each year.

Remember, not everyone likes public acknowledgement, so be sure to select a method that makes the employee comfortable; not a method you would personally prefer.

---

7. *Be consistent and fair.* One of the key dissatisfiers for employees is when they are subject to inconsistent and unfair behavior. If you insist everyone be at work at a certain time, you can't consistently allow one person to come strolling in late day after day. If you need to make an accommodation, then do so consistently. For example, if someone has a child in daycare that doesn't open until 8 am and your team starts at 8 am, if you can make the accommodation, require that person to show up consistently at 8:30, not whatever time they happen to come to work. Though there are times you may need to make special exceptions to meet employee needs. However, hold everyone to the same standard. Watch your personal biases, as well. We are often more lenient with people we like personally. The true test of a leader is if you can treat everyone equally, regardless of your personal opinion of them.

8. *Address issues quickly.* Issues rarely get better with age, so addressing problems with staff quickly and consistently will make your job as a manager easier. It will help employees understand expectations and correct behaviors before they become big problems. Employees become confused when the rules are inconsistently applied (as do we all) or when a behavior is allowed for months and then suddenly becomes a disciplinary action. We'll discuss handling employee issues in the next section.

9. *Model the behavior you expect.* If you expect your team to deliver outstanding customer service, deliver it yourself to your team and your stakeholders. If you expect the team to treat

each other with respect, show respect to your team, your peers, your customers, and your executives. Simple in concept, not always easy in practice.

10. *Have fun*. Healthcare is a serious business and we can lose sight of the fact that we can enjoy our time at work. Yes, we have to pay attention to the details and get it right every time, but that doesn't mean that a bit of good-natured humor can't be used. By using humor appropriately (and sparingly), you can lighten up the mood, break the tension, and help build rapport with your team. It's nice to go home after a long day and have something you can smile about.

Handling Problems

As a manager, you'll have to address problems with people, process, technology, and operations. The latter three elements are usually easier for people to address than issues with people, so we'll focus on people problems in this section. There is no one-size-fits-all answer to personnel issues, but there are some key elements that can be used in troubleshooting and addressing any personnel issue.

1. Attitude versus Aptitude

The first question you'll need to answer for yourself is whether the problem is an *attitude* or an *aptitude* problem. Being late to work, doing sloppy work, being rude to customers or coworkers are all attitude problems and can be addressed as such. Sometimes fixing these issues requires a bit of retraining, such as a refresher course in customer service skills, but most of the time, it simply requires a conversation to reiterate the requirements of the job and your expectations for appropriate behavior. This doesn't have to be a harsh or blameful conversation, but it should be clear and direct. For example, "Chris, this is the third time I've gotten complaints from customers about you. It sounds like you're being rude with them. What's going on?"

If the problem is one of *aptitude*, you might see sloppy work, inaccurate work, or even missed deadlines. Since sloppy work can be the result of a poor attitude, you need to figure out the root cause. If it's aptitude-related, you need to look at the individual's skill set. You may have assigned work to the individual that really is not a strength. Review assignments to determine if this is the case. If the person is struggling with some new aspect of the job that their peers have easily picked up, they may lack needed skills. Additional training, pairing with someone on the team who is strong in this skill, or providing additional time to come up to speed may be warranted, to a point.

Tips: Don't assume your information is correct; always ask and verify before taking corrective action. Sometimes a situation is misconstrued or there's a simple explanation. Also, keep an eye out for repeated variations of the behavior, which can lead you to believe the problem is not recurring when, in fact, it is. Don't accept a "reasonable explanation" for multiple variations of a problem. Understand this is the same problem manifesting in slightly different ways. Take notes in near-real time; keep them in a safe place (a locked file drawer, for example). Add details such as time, date, location, nature of issue; time, date, location of discussion of issue and expectations. Add them to your file so you have solid documentation. It would be great if you never needed the documentation; the goal is always to coach for success. Having specific documentation, though, will help you spot trends and patterns more easily. Printing out email follow-ups and other documentation and placing in a locked file drawer actually makes reviewing issues pretty simple and is highly recommended for ease of managing issues.

If the issue is *aptitude* and it's not resolving with additional training, time, coaching, and focus, it may be best to see if the person can be reassigned to a role more suited to their skills. If they are unable to perform the required tasks of their job, they should not be in that job. While this sounds a bit harsh, it's best for the individual not to require them to accomplish things they are incapable of doing (stress, certain failure), it's best for the team to hold to established standards (fairness, work load), and it's best for the organization to require that each person fulfill the obligations of their role (deriving value). So, rather than seeing it as harsh, you should view it as good for all involved.

2. Clear Expectations in Writing

Regardless of the root cause of the problem, it's important to set very clear expectations in writing. Verbal conversations and coaching are most appropriate when you catch a problem early on. It might be just a casual conversation, the first time or even the second time it occurs. If you think this may be part of a developing pattern, make a quick note for your files. Time, date, and topic are sufficient. If the problem recurs, it's time to document expectations. In most cases, your Human Resources (HR) department will have guidelines, forms, and a required process to follow for formal disciplinary action, so follow your organization's processes. That said, the best documentation is clear, direct, and neutral in language. Neutral language is a bit formal, but it's helpful in removing the anger or frustration you may be feeling from what you write.

Tips: Use neutral language including phrases like "This document is to identify areas for improvement," "We have had previous discussions about [insert topic]," "To date, you have not applied the coaching feedback that has been provided," "This plan establishes a corrective course of action to assist you in successfully addressing these areas," etc. Also, be very clear about the expectations, the timeline for improvement, and the metrics used to measure that improvement. Unfortunately, this will take a fair amount of time, but you can spend the time now managing the situation or you can spend time dealing with this issue and the repercussions of poor performance for months or years. It's certainly true that you'll "pay now or pay more later." For attitude problems, the expectation can be set that the behavior change immediately and not reoccur. For aptitude problems, the expectation can be set over days, weeks, or months to improve the specific skill deficit noted. Always keep in mind the goal is to coach for success; this documentation is to be sure both you and the employee are on the same page.

Unless there is imminent danger or threat, do not address issues when you are angry, frustrated, or exhausted. Take time to think through the issue; talk it over with a trusted colleague, your manager, or an HR representative so you can clarify your thinking and resolve your emotions. Once you reach a more neutral emotional state, you can have an effective conversation with your employee. It takes practice to set aside emotion when having difficult conversations, so you may want to practice alone or role play with a colleague so you feel more comfortable when you have the conversation with the employee.

[…more…]

One of the best pieces of coaching advice I ever received as a manager was when I was preparing for a difficult conversation. A mentor allowed me to talk through the problem then said, "OK, so what is the overall theme here?" I identified a pattern of behavior and my mentor said, "Good, stick with that. If the employee argues or tries to distract you by bringing in extraneous facts, go back to this statement. Write this statement down and memorize it. Use it as often as needed." While that may sound a bit robotic, it was really helpful for addressing very challenging problems. For example, "Ben, this conversation is about your unacceptable interactions with your peers, we're not going to discuss other topics right now." This will help keep you focused on the outcomes and prevent the conversation from getting off track.

Be sure to follow your organization's policies, procedures, and guidelines for all disciplinary actions so you don't compound the problem. If you believe there is a risk of the employee taking retaliatory action, always discuss with your manager and follow their recommendations. If you're not getting the assistance you need from your manager, work with HR so you have assistance in dealing with difficult situations. In some cases, it is best to have the conversation with someone else present in the room—whether it's your manager, a peer, or HR—so there is no question about what was said and done. If you fear for your safety, you have a very serious issue on your hands and you should clearly state to your manager and to HR that you have a safety concern. Unfortunately, that may then involve having a security officer nearby; *always* take appropriate precautions.

3. Management Action Plan for Follow-Up

Once you have documented the situation, the requirements for success, and the timeline and metrics associated with each improvement, you need to create your own plan for following up. It's tempting to simply consider the job done, leave the onus for improvement on the employee, and move on. Yet, your job as a manager requires one more step if you want this time and effort to be successful. You should create your own action plan for following up. Some people work this way naturally, so it might be an obvious next step. For others, though, this detailed monitoring of progress (aka micromanaging) is anything but natural. For those of you who fall into this category, do yourself a favor. Create your follow-up action plan right after you complete the formal documentation. This will help you track next steps and progress in a consistent manner.

Tips: Create a document that contains several columns and rows. In each row, write the behavior or expectation. In the column to the right, note the metric, the timeline, your review frequency, and any notes or comments about your expectations. Figure 8.1 shows an example you might find helpful. Remember, this is only for your eyes and is intended to make it easier for you to follow up consistently. Of course, you may have organizational requirements that define expectations for follow-up. If not, create a plan for yourself so this consumes less of your time and brain cycles than it otherwise would.

Task	Metric	Review freq.	Comments/Notes
Respond to all critical issue emails	4 hours	Daily	
Respond to all normal issue emails	24 hours	Daily	
Response includes timeline commitment	100%	Daily	
Timeline commitment met	100%	Daily	
Communicate any exceptions	100%	Daily	Had discussion regarding how to re-set expectations when you are unable to meet an agreed upon timeline, ensure this is used.
Report daily tasks completed with estimated duration of each	100%	Daily	Addresses concern about lack of productivity and gives better insight into how work is being prioritized.

Figure 8.1   Management follow-up action plan.

Once you have worked through the plan with the employee, there are only a few outcomes that should occur.

1. Successful completion of action plan. The behaviors or problems have been resolved, and there has been a consistent demonstration of success. Action plan ends.
2. Partial completion of action plan. The behaviors or problems have largely been resolved, but there are still issues remaining. Action plan extends with renewed expectations and "last and final" language is included.
3. No completion of action plan. The behaviors or problems have largely not been resolved (i.e., there may be some improvement or no improvement). Next-level disciplinary action is taken. This may involve documenting a last and final warning or termination.

Coaching an employee through issues is challenging, time consuming, and often emotionally draining. Your job as a manager is to assist the employee in achieving success, but it is a partnership where the employee needs to do the bulk of the work. You can only do so much and if the employee is unable or unwilling to make the changes needed to be successful. Sometimes the best outcome for the employee *is* separation from the organization. While that can be a difficult transition, it's in everyone's best interest to ensure each employee is willing and able to do a good job.

Handling employee problems is often the area of a manager role that people struggle with. It's never pleasant nor is it ever easy. However, with practice, you can develop the skills you need to effectively address issues so they don't consume you.

Managing Yourself

Though the notion of managing yourself may seem odd to you, it's key to remember that as a manager (and as you continue up the ranks), your words and actions hold more weight. What you say and do matters more to your staff, whether or not you agree that it should. People are typically title-driven in hierarchical organizations, and they will take their cues from their manager and those above them. So, one of the key elements of success as a healthcare IT leader is to learn to manage yourself. Here's the short list:

1. Model good behavior.
2. Control your emotions.
3. Address negative situations or bad news professionally.
4. Know your limits.
5. Ask for help.
6. Always tell the truth.
7. Listen.

1. *Model good behavior.* We mentioned this in the previous section, but it bears repeating. What you do carries weight. If you fly off the handle, storm around, get worked up, become accusatory, use sharp or harsh language, you have a problem. We all need to let off steam at work, but do so in a professional and appropriate way. Go into your office and close your door. Go for a walk. Grab a glass of water or a cup of coffee and calm down. These blustery behaviors might have worked when you were an analyst or engineer, but they'll earn you a reputation as a volatile manager. You'll become increasingly less effective. If you find yourself reacting, take time to develop a set of quick "go to" fixes for yourself. Count to ten, leave the room for a moment,

remind yourself that your job is to maintain composure and solve problems—whatever it takes for you to be the model of good behavior for your team and your peers.

2. *Control your emotions.* This is closely related to the first item, but it's more specific. Controlling your emotions can be challenging, especially when you're in the middle of a difficult situation over which you feel you have little or no control. For example, when some part of an application suddenly stops working, it's having a seriously negative impact on patient care, you don't know the root cause and your team does not seem to be properly focused on finding the solution, you may feel the pressure building more rapidly than you can handle.

   Remember, *Your first reaction is your emotion, your second reaction is your choice.* It's fine to feel whatever emotion comes up, but pause before you take your next step. Understand you are not your emotions. Acknowledge how you feel, then step back and ask yourself what the best next step is. By controlling your emotions, you'll develop a crucial skill—being calm under fire—which is a trait the best leaders strive to cultivate. And, if your brain is not consumed by emotion, you can maintain higher-order thinking functions, which is how you solve complex problems.

3. *Address negative situations or bad news professionally.* Another common challenge for new managers is finding the balance between telling the truth to your team and finding a way to present information in the best positive light. First, understand that not all details are appropriate for the team to know. Ask yourself, what does the team really need to know? What matters to them? What impacts them?

   For example, imagine a big project was just approved and it's going to disrupt all of the other work underway. You're highly annoyed by the surprise and you also think the project is a mistake. How do you address this with your team? Do you lie and tell them you're completely on board with this decision thinking that doing so will make you "the good soldier?" Do you tell them the truth that you completely disagree with the decision and you think it's foolish and short-sighted? Or, do you tell them that you share their concerns about the timing and nature of the project and that you've set up a meeting to discuss your concerns with your manager? The third option is the most honest and the most helpful. Make no mistake, this takes practice. If this doesn't come naturally to you, remember that you should only offer information that is true, kind, and relevant. Write down what you'll say and edit it until it conveys the right balance. Read it over, memorize it, then set it aside and speak to your team. Having focused yourself on the key aspects and the right words, you'll be able to communicate in a way that is congruent and honest, even in difficult situations.

4. *Know your limits.* Being a new manager can go to your head. Suddenly, you're calling the shots. You may thrive being in control and being in power. That's fine to a point, but when it becomes extreme, that power and influence can go to your head. Keep in mind that the manager's role is to facilitate the work that needs to be done. As such, you need each and every one on your team to actually *do* the work and *deliver* the results. They're far more likely to be successful without you than you without them.

5. *Ask for help.* No one knows everything; don't be afraid to ask for help when you need it. No one will lose respect for you if you simply admit you need help with something, even if it's something you think you *should* know. However, everyone will lose respect for you if you ignorantly plow ahead when it's obvious you don't have a clue.

6. *Always tell the truth.* Not all management books will advise you this bluntly, but it's one of the most important things you can do for your career: always tell the truth. If you build a reputation for always telling the truth, your word will be trusted. Even if you're mistaken, people will more likely give you the benefit of the doubt. Telling the truth doesn't have to be bold and abrasive; it can be mild and measured. If you recall from Chapter 6 on communication, your message involves timing, target, topic, and tone. Don't confuse the message with the delivery system. And here's the best part—when you know inside yourself that you always tell the truth, your actions will be guided by the desire to always be able to tell the truth. Said more directly, you'll behave honestly if you know that you always want to be in a position to tell the truth. It's a great closed-loop, self-correcting system for self-management.

7. *Listen.* To quote management expert Peter Drucker, listening is not a skill, it's a discipline. We typically spend less time listening to the speaker and more time crafting our reply. The reverse should be true. Listening is a powerful tool and Drucker calls it out as the first competence of leadership. As a new manager, you might feel like you need to always have the right answer or the right response so you end up talking more than listening. The more you listen, the more you'll learn. Practice the discipline of listening fully. Close your laptop, put your smartphone away, put files to the side, and intently listen to the person speaking. If you aren't sure if you're a good listener or not, observe your inner dialog when someone is speaking…or if you're brave, ask your friends or trusted colleagues if they feel you're a good listener and be willing to *listen* to their feedback.

Effectively managing yourself will help you become a better person and a better manager for your team. As you develop these traits and skills, you'll find they come more easily and become second nature for you.

Working Effectively with Your Manager

Working effectively with your manager is sometimes called "managing up," but that's not a term we'll use here because it can have negative connotations. Instead, we'll focus on how to be effective in working with your manager. Here's the list we'll discuss next:

1. Do your homework first.
2. Clarify expectations, don't assume.
3. Never allow your manager to walk into an ambush. Communicate effectively, learn when to escalate.
4. Help your manager be successful.
5. Always tell the truth.
6. Be willing to take a stand and disagree, respectfully.

1. *Do your homework first.* Your manager has their own job to do, so lobbing a problem at them is just not acceptable and more importantly, it won't help solve the problem. If you need assistance with something, come prepared with a clear picture of the problem, what solutions you've considered, why you need help, and what the desired outcome might look like. While you may not always have suggestions or solutions to present, the more prepared

you are to have an intelligent and proactive meeting, the better. It's OK to say, "I don't really know what to do here, I'm looking for your ideas or suggestions." Admitting you don't know something is fine, tossing responsibility for solving the problem to your manager is not.

2. *Clarify expectations, don't assume.* Just as with your staff, it's important to have clear expectations. Hopefully, your manager is good at this, but if not, it's your job to ensure you understand what's expected. If your manager gives you an assignment to "look into something," do you know what that means? Does that mean drop everything and begin formal analysis? Does that mean doing an Internet search and becoming familiar with the topic? If you've worked with your manager long enough and you know exactly what those vague statements mean, fine. If not, clarify by asking timing, urgency, context, etc. Help your manager to clarify by asking for these specifics.

3. *Never allow your manager to walk into an ambush, communicate effectively, and learn when to escalate.* This is also known as "avoiding a resume generating event." While it's never good form to passively let someone walk into a problem without warning, it's particularly problematic to let your manager do it. Regardless of what you may think of your manager (highly capable to completely incompetent), allowing them to walk headlong into an ambush will never help you achieve your objectives. This also goes hand in hand with communicating effectively and learning when to escalate. You can develop a sense of when and how to escalate if you understand how your organization works and how your manager operates. If you know there are sensitive issues, if you know there are details your manager has forgotten (or even chosen to ignore), if you are aware of an issue possibly bubbling up, let your manager know. Use a communication style that works for your manager. For example, if you know they only check email four times per day and the issue is time-sensitive, text or call them. Get in front of them, get the information to them, and don't back down until you've done your best to prepare them.

4. *Help your manager be successful.* This concept is sort of the mate to Item #3. Aside from not actively causing (or allowing) your manager to be ambushed, you can and should do what you can to help your manager be successful. This is not the Dilbert® view of the world; this falls under the teamwork umbrella. The more successful your manager is, the better it is for everyone—your patients, your organization, your department, your team, and yes, ultimately, you. What does this typically look like? Provide clear, timely updates. Provide "heads-up" about trends you're seeing in the industry or great suggestions from staff.

   If your manager relies on your timely submission of a weekly status report in order to develop their report, make sure you provide it on time 100% of the time. You'd be surprised how much of a positive impact this can make not only on your relationship with your manager but on your professional reputation as well.

5. *Always tell the truth.* As you can see, this is a recurring theme. Not telling your manager the truth can have ripple effects. It can damage their credibility and professional reputation if they are using false information you have provided. It can also impact your organization, department, and team. Finally, it will definitely impact your relationship with your manager and your professional reputation. Becoming known as a person who always tells the truth goes a long way in building trust and credibility.

[…more…]

In a May 2016 *Harvard Business Review* article entitled "Keep a List of Unethical Things You'll Never Do," author Mark Chussil makes a very compelling case for keeping a hard line of ethics with yourself. The basic point he makes is that most people who seriously violate ethical or legal boundaries do not set out to do so. Instead, they start with small indiscretions (telling a lie, hiding a mistake), and it seems to just expand from there. Chussil's recommendation is to make a list of things you'll never do, but it can start as simply as building the self-discipline to always tell the truth, regardless of how uncomfortable that might make you. As we've discussed, there are many ways to present the truth so it doesn't mean blurting out the first unfiltered thing that comes to mind. "John told me the project was complete, he lied to me" versus "I relied on John's assertion the project was complete, but I didn't follow up to verify the facts." Both are true; certainly the second statement is a more professional statement while still providing facts and accountability. So, to go back to Chussil's recommendation, maybe you should create that list of things you'll never, ever do (Chussil, 2016, QR8.2).

6. *Be willing to take a stand and disagree, respectfully.* As a manager, you are viewed as a leader in the organization. Your manager (usually a director) expects you to have knowledge and to have an informed opinion. It is incumbent upon you to speak up when you disagree. Ensure your manager understands your objections or reservations. Stand firm if you believe you are headed for a serious mistake. It's important to have data when they're available, but it's also important to state your opinion. Be sure to have this conversation in an appropriate setting. Sometimes it might be in a meeting with your manager and your peers, but often it's best to take it offline. Allowing your manager to "save face" is an important success factor as well. For example, you might say, "I understand your perspective, but I'm not sure I agree. My concerns are. …" or "With all due respect, I disagree. I feel very strongly that this course of action has serious risk and I'm not comfortable moving forward with it in this manner. However, I think we can. …" In both cases, you're respectfully disagreeing and either stating your concerns or suggesting an alternative. You may not prevail in every instance, but you will sleep better at night knowing that you spoke up and clearly asserted your viewpoint. If you are confident your manager understands your concerns and directs you to proceed anyway, it is your job to deliver to the best of your ability. You may want to document your concerns for your own records. If things go south later and you're being held accountable, you can help refresh memories that may have faded. However, referring back to Chussil's article, there are some lines you should not cross. If you are being required to cross legal, moral, or ethical boundaries, you should use your organization's established channels for reporting wrongdoing.

Regardless of whether you like and respect your manager, your job is to work within the team and organizational hierarchy to achieve results. A large portion of your success rests upon your relationship with your manager. Working to develop a trusted relationship may be all you can achieve with someone you don't like or respect, but trust is a valuable attribute. If you're fortunate to have a manager who is competent, motivated, and engaged, these six success factors will certainly help you both achieve better results.

Getting to the Next Level

If you've been a manager for a while and you'd like to move into a director role, you'll need to position yourself so that you are the best candidate, whether that's an opening in your area, another area, or at a different healthcare organization. There is no "one-size-fits-all" set of skills and attributes you need to move into a director role, but there are a few things you can do to enhance your candidacy. Here are a few ideas; you can come up with additional ideas and create your own personal action plan to achieve your goals. With that, here's the short list.

1. Volunteer for stretch assignments.
2. Always deliver on your commitments.
3. Develop relationships outside the IT department.
4. Understand the business.
5. Address difficult problems.
6. Find ways to innovate.

1. *Volunteer for stretch assignments.* This is a great way to gain additional experience and show that you're up for new and interesting challenges. Stretch assignments should be a challenge but don't volunteer for the impossible orphan project no one else could push through—unless you're certain that (a) you will succeed where others failed because you have a special skill, talent, or insight or (b) you are granted official immunity should you fail ("No one else could make this work, can you give it a shot? If it doesn't pan out, that's fine, at least we'll know we gave it 100% effort by putting you on this project."). By working in areas outside your normal day-to-day duties, you develop new skills, new perspectives, and new relationships. All of these will serve you well in broadening your horizon. As a frontline manager, it's easy to get pulled into a narrow view of your team and your work. Stretch assignments can pull you up into a broader perspective and help you better understand the organization and your role in it.

2. *Always deliver on your commitments.* If you want to be looked at for a leadership position, keeping your commitments is important. This might sound like a no-brainer, but it's surprising how many people seem to allow commitments to their peers or staff lapse while focusing solely on deliverables for their manager. That may work with your manager for a while, but you'll develop a reputation for pandering to your boss and disrespecting your peers or staff. If you can't keep a commitment, renegotiate it. Just letting it drop or not meeting the commitment is not a professional response. When being considered for a leadership position, questions like consistency and results often come up.

3. *Develop relationships outside the IT department.* As an IT manager, it's pretty easy to stick to your area of expertise and manage it effectively. If you want to be considered for other opportunities, you need to develop working relationships with others across the organization. Regardless of your IT role, it's always helpful to go out and talk with customers, users, and stakeholders. Learning more about their work, their challenges, their opportunities, and their goals can really help you better understand how to deliver the services you provide today. It also can help you understand how the broader IT function interacts with the organization. It also helps you achieve objective #4.

4. *Understand the business.* You don't need to understand absolutely every aspect of the business, but you certainly should understand at a high level what types of patients you serve, how revenues are generated, what kinds of providers you have, how providers are paid, how care units operate, how supplies are managed, how staffing is handled, and more. By developing relationships with others in the organization, you can round out your knowledge of how things work. Having a working knowledge of the overall organization's operations will put you in a strong position for leadership opportunities.

5. *Address difficult problems.* Just as taking on a stretch assignment (objective #1) can help advance your career, so too can taking on difficult problems to solve. If you take on the thing no one wants or no one has done well and you turn it around, you will develop a reputation as someone who solves problems, turns things around, and delivers. That's the gold standard in most organizations. If you develop a reputation as someone who can resolve difficult problems but avoid developing a reputation for "running head first into the flames," you'll be seen as a leader, regardless of your actual title. New opportunities often follow on the heels of these successes.

6. *Find ways to innovate.* As we discussed in previous chapters, we can reduce the time and effort we spend on standard operations and shift those time "savings" toward more innovative work. This holds true not only for your teams but for you as well. Your area of innovation may be a new process or a new form that streamlines something or a new tool that solves a problem everyone sees but no one solves—these are the kinds of innovative opportunities that can build your reputation. Clearly, you can't always find opportunities to innovate, but if you look at your environment, you talk with your counterparts in the organization, and you think critically about what you're seeing, you may find these opportunities. Making substantial improvements in your environment also positions you well for promotion and leadership opportunities.

These are just a few ideas for ways to develop your skills, broaden your perspective, and hone your reputation. These certainly are not the only ways, and in some organizations, some of these ideas might not fly. The key is to understand what the organization values and what your strengths are, and match them up with tasks, assignments, and opportunities to grow.

Manager Summary

As a healthcare IT leader, you are looked to for setting goals, defining performance expectations, and holding your team accountable for results. Using leadership skills discussed throughout this book and the techniques reviewed in this section, you should have a stronger sense of what it takes to become a successful healthcare IT leader. The tools, techniques, tips, and advice in this section are meant to help you begin your path of discovery so you can create a plan for becoming the best manager you can be. Success means having a team that is highly functional, that delivers exceptional results on a consistent basis, that gets along reasonably well, that enjoys the work it does, and that enjoys working for you. That's the goal and it is achievable with focused effort and a desire to learn and grow.

Directing

Directors in healthcare organizations typically manage a team of managers. Sometimes this role is referred to as a senior manager, director, executive director (this can also refer to one who manages directors), associate vice president, or even associate Chief Information Officer (CIO). Regardless of the title used, we'll refer to this role as the director. The key is that most directors do not manage frontline staff directly (though there are exceptions and we'll discuss those); they manage managers. There are some similarities to the skills needed as a manager of frontline staff, but there are distinct differences as well.

Some argue that any director-level role in healthcare is one of the most difficult roles. Perhaps because it is truly a "middle management" role where your hands are no longer directly on the levers that make work happen and you are not in an executive role shaping the strategy. You're expected to deliver results through your management team, and you're expected to take responsibility for the things that go wrong within your area of responsibility. That can be a challenging position to be in, but the director role is also an amazing opportunity to broaden your skills, extend your influence, and really get involved in some of the higher-level discussions of the organization.

In this section, we'll be discussing behaviors, traits, and attitudes that will help you successfully navigate the director role. If you're currently in this role, you should find some great reminders and some helpful tips. If you aspire to this role, this section should provide you with a better sense of what's required to be successful. From there, you can decide if this role is a good fit for you, and you can develop a professional development plan to augment existing skills and learn new ones in preparation for moving into this role in the future.

Leaving Technical Expertise Behind, Part 2

After you've been in a manager role for a while, you accept that you are no longer the go-to-geek, it is no longer appropriate for you to focus extensively on technology. That trend expands dramatically in the director role. A director is typically tasked with overseeing numerous teams, so having an expectation of technical proficiency across all those areas is unrealistic. For example, a director of clinical applications is not going to know (or remember) how to configure the electronic medical record (EMR) flowsheet rows or fix the interface between two applications. The director in that role should have enough technical expertise to understand the answers provided by the team, but time spent maintaining technical proficiency at that level is inappropriate in most organizations.

As a director, you should be spending time reading about industry trends that impact not only your area of responsibility but also the broader healthcare IT and healthcare industry overall. Having awareness of industry trends is crucial in this role.

Effectively Managing Managers

Managing managers is different from managing frontline staff because you are one layer removed from the actual work. In this section, we'll discuss the traits that will help you make the transition from frontline manager to director. These include the following:

1. Ensure the manager has a good command of the basics.
2. Help ensure the manager is delegating effectively.
3. Discuss your expectations regarding how employees are managed.
4. Define your expectations for success.

5. Be available to and engaged with your direct reports.
6. Stand up for your managers.
7. Take calculated risks and allow your direct reports to do the same.
8. Give feedback in small, specific segments.

1. *Ensure the manager has a good command of the basics.* Whether the manager is new to management, new to the role, or new to the organization, you still need to set them up for success by defining the basics. If you're fortunate enough to work in an organization that has a formalized leadership development and onboarding process, you can simply track progress through the program. However, most organizations either have programs that are general leadership and not specific to the role or they have no program at all. If that's the case, then you'll need to ensure the manager understands management basics. You can review the previous section and develop a management review plan or professional development plan for your new manager to fill any gaps and to refresh any skills needed in this role.

   These are all attributes for being a good mentor. Whether your direct reports are new or seasoned, there are things they can learn. They have strengths and weaknesses, and part of your job is to help them grow and develop professionally. Listening and sharing your experience and insights will help them develop professionally and, hopefully, help them avoid some of the pitfalls along the way.

2. *Help ensure the manager is delegating effectively.* Sure signs the manager is not delegating is when their workday keeps getting longer, they start missing deadlines and deliverables you've discussed (their deliverables to you), or they seem exhausted and overwhelmed. Of course, this is assuming that the manager has the staff needed to get the work done. If you've dropped a manager into an understaffed area and it has large, looming deliverables, you've set them up to fail.

   If you are moving up from a manager to a director role, the temptation can be very strong to do the manager's job (micromanage, take over, do familiar tasks that are no longer yours). Avoid this. Take a deep breath. Step back and ask how you can help this new manager learn whatever it is that is needed. Teach, don't take. If you overstep, you will undermine the new manager. There may be times you can pitch in to help, but think carefully if this is the right action at the right time.

3. *Discuss your expectations regarding how employees are managed.* For example, you may expect weekly team meetings, weekly 1:1s with staff, monthly reports, etc. This will provide a management framework for the manager as well as ensure consistency of management across your teams. Discuss how you expect the manager to discuss problems and issues with the team or individual team members. Have them practice with you so you are confident they can handle the situation effectively. If needed, sit in on the first one or two difficult discussions the manager has with staff simply as an observer. While it may seem awkward, you can participate if the manager starts to stumble and you can also observe firsthand how the conversation goes. This is also appropriate to do if you're getting complaints from staff about their manager.

4. *Define your expectations for success.* Your direct reports need consistent and clear communication just as we discussed in the Managing section in working with frontline staff. Outline what success looks like, what traits, behaviors, and deliverables will meet your criteria.

Sometimes defining what success does not look like helps as well. This is also your best control mechanism as a director. Since you will not be engaged with the frontline work of the team, you have less direct evidence of the work the manager is doing. If they're being effective, they are guiding their team to deliver what's expected, removing roadblocks and providing resources. Those are sort of soft deliverables that are best seen through the reflection of the team's work. Nonetheless, you need to ensure the manager is doing that work and being successful. Setting clear guidelines and expectations about both manager activities (coaching, 1:1s, status reports, financials, etc.) as well as team activities (operations, projects, etc.) provides the framework in which you can define and measure success.

5. *Be available to and engaged with your direct reports.* Your role as the director will no doubt pull you in a myriad of directions outside of your IT role. Through that, it's easy to lose sight of the fact that you are first and foremost a manager and your team needs you. They shouldn't be overly dependent on you, and you certainly should not be involved in every decision the manager makes; but you have to manage your team just as they have to manage their team. The same basics apply to you in managing your direct reports, so use all the information presented in the section on Managing and apply it to you and your team.

6. *Stand up for your managers.* Standing up for your staff does not mean you allow them to get away with bad behavior or that you lie or misrepresent on their behalf. What it does mean is that you support them and give them the benefit of the doubt. For example, if a manager makes bad decisions and the team turns on them, you need to find a way to support the manager while assisting in deescalating the situation. It can be tricky to walk that fine line, but you need to preserve your integrity while helping the manager recover.

    The same is true if something the manager does comes under fire from the organization, from your manager, or from the executive team. Standing up for them means responding with something like "Thanks for letting me know. Let me look into it and get back to you." Through this type of response, you are acknowledging the issue and still supporting the manager, especially because you don't know the facts of the situation. You only know what one person reported to you. Contrast that with a more reactive response like, "Well, thanks for letting me know, it sounds like Patty really blew it. I'll talk with her and let her know that's not acceptable."

7. *Take calculated risks and allow your direct reports to do the same.* Healthcare IT is a fast-paced, complex environment in which to work. Taking risks is part of the job. Of course, we're not talking about risking patient safety or regulatory compliance. We're talking about stepping outside your comfort zone and exploring new ways of thinking and operating. Calculated risks are just that: calculated. You've weighed the evidence, there is no clear path forward, so you make the best decision possible in light of the information you have. You've estimated the risk of success versus failure and determined the risk is worth taking.

8. *Give feedback in small, specific segments.* It's easy to fall into the habit of just assuming the managers know how they're doing because things are going well (or not). Providing even the smallest amount of feedback on a routine basis will help them stay focused and continue to meet your expectations. Of course, this holds true with frontline staff, but is very important for your managers as well. If you've made a correction, be sure to reinforce every time you see the right behavior. For example, "That was an excellent email. You provided a thoughtful

analysis—that's exactly what I've been looking for from you. Good job." You're clear and specific and they now know that hit the target. That sense of clarity and small success adds up over time to a manager who is confident they're meeting your expectations.

You may have noticed a lot of recurring themes between the Managing section and Directing section. As stated earlier, in many cases the behaviors are the same; they just have to move up one level because you are no longer engaged with the frontline work of the organization.

Effectively Managing Frontline Staff as Director

In some organizations, directors may be asked (or required) to manage frontline staff, though this is not a typical situation. It can be difficult because it requires a different level of focus and attention. The key to success is to set the same types of expectations that have been discussed throughout this chapter while (perhaps) adjusting downward the levels of proficiency expected. For example, frontline staff typically need more feedback, input, and guidance than managers do. You'll need to adjust your cadence for communication according to the needs of your team. Setting aside office hours so you're available to staff, going to visit staff in their work location, spending time in team meetings, etc., will all help provide staff the input needed to be successful.

If you can identify a leader among your direct reports who can assist with some of the day-to-day management such as monitoring distribution and completion of tasks or documenting work hours (PTO, vacation requests, medical appointments, etc.) or taking notes at team meetings and distributing them, you can utilize these emerging leaders. This process can also help you start to identify those with leadership or management potential. It will also help relieve you of some of the administrative work in managing direct reports. As we'll discuss in the Leading section, leaders tend to rise regardless of the circumstance.

Managing Yourself

Managing yourself and your career as a director includes all the aspects of managing yourself as a manager with a few upgraded skills. Below is the short list and, following that, the longer explanations.

1. Build a strong team.
2. Take calculated risks and learn from them.
3. Know yourself, manage your blind spots.
4. Develop your critical thinking skills.
5. Learn to be resilient.
6. Cultivate an attitude of pragmatic optimism.
7. Ask for, listen to, and act upon feedback.

1. *Build a strong team.* Your success is heavily dependent upon the success of your managers and their teams. If the managers who report to you are not strong managers, the impact will be magnified. Their strengths, or their weaknesses, will be amplified by the team(s) they manage. So, if you have three direct reports who are really in high gear but you have four others who are just complacent or barely making the grade, you will be evaluated on the sum total of those managers and their teams' results. More importantly, it has a huge impact on the team the underperformer manages. Ultimately, this has a negative impact on

the environment and on the care provided to your patients. So, it really does matter if you have a few bad managers. Building a strong team starts with good team selection followed by consistent and clear coaching and mentoring. You don't often get to choose your team, though as openings occur, you can "trade up" and improve the skills of the team in the process. Beyond coaching and training, address poor performance quickly and effectively, just as you coach a frontline manager to do with their staff. Problems don't improve with age.

Knowing that your success and your reputation are so closely related to the success of your direct reports, you also understand that even one underperforming manager can negatively impact you. While your primary motivation should be to develop a strong team for the success of the organization, it's important to understand that their performance points directly back to you, your success, and your overall effectiveness.

2. *Take calculated risks and learn from them.* We discussed encouraging your direct reports to take calculated risks and the same applies to you as well. It's easy as a healthcare IT director to have so many diverse areas of responsibility that you feel all you can do is try to keep your head above water. Having competent direct reports and developing a strong team certainly helps, but you need to move out of your comfort zone from time to time and take calculated risks. That usually means committing to a course of action when the picture is still murky and not likely to clear up anytime soon; it means taking action on imperfect or incomplete data if your experience and expertise tell you it's a smart move. Challenge yourself and then review results. Be brutally honest with yourself about what worked and what didn't and learn from those experiences.

3. *Know yourself, manage your blind spots.* As you rise in the management ranks, you tend to develop stronger management skills, but you also tend to accommodate your blind spots. For example, if you always hire very analytical people, but you continually struggle with your team meeting deadlines, you likely pick up the slack yourself (or you have some other compensating mechanism). However, as you grow as a director, you need to evaluate your blind spots and determine if you need to take some other action. Using the previous example, you may choose to hire someone less analytical or you may choose to challenge your analytical managers to become more action-oriented. Knowing yourself and your responses to your environment is a powerful self-development tool. Addressing areas of weakness and blind spots is a mature and professional action to take in furthering your career.

4. *Develop your critical thinking skills.* Most of the day in healthcare IT involves responding to new or changing information and assisting your team in making decisions. It can be challenging to stop long enough to think more critically about a situation. For example, your CIO calls you up and says, "I heard from Vendor X there is a major security update coming out on Tuesday, what are you doing about it?" A rookie might say, "I will investigate and we'll schedule the update for Tuesday" in hopes of pleasing their boss. A more seasoned professional might say, "This is the first I've heard of it, I'll contact our Vendor X technical representative and first understand why the normal communication channel didn't surface this, then I'll have the team look at the update and determine criticality and impact. I'll report back as soon as I know more." You're not *reacting*, you're *responding*. That's a key difference. In responding, you are taking in new information and processing it, using critical thinking skills. As you progress in your career, this skill accounts for more and more of your job and your success will hinge on your ability to hone this skill.

[…more…]

Critical thinking skills are often taught or reinforced in college courses. However, many people are not exposed to this discipline and may need assistance in learning critical thinking skills. Critical thinking skills can be learned and developed. According to two experts in the field, Richard Paul and Michael Scriven, critical thinking can be defined as the intellectually disciplined process of actively and skillfully conceptualizing, applying, analyzing, synthesizing, and/or evaluating information gathered from, or generated by, observation, experience, reflection, reasoning, or communication, as a guide to belief and action. (Paul, "Paul-Elder Critical Thinking Framework," *n.d.*, QR8.3 and QR8.4)

---

5. *Learn to be resilient.* Resilience is defined as being able to come back to original form after being bent, stretched, or compressed. It is defined as elasticity. So, to use an old Japanese saying (in rough translation), "Seven times down, eight times up." Of course, this is much easier said than done. At the end of the day, your team looks to you and what you say and signals back to them your view of the world. If you think your organization is completely dysfunctional and you've pretty much given up on making sense of things, you're probably short on resilience. That negative attitude will show in what you say and what you do. If, on the other hand, you have learned to be resilient, you may allow the problems to roll off you. If you can face adversity with a sense of calm, knowing that you can handle just about anything that comes at you, you will signal the same to your team. And, resilience helps you maintain an even keel and achieve your objectives more readily. There are many excellent books on learning to be more resilient; one is listed in the References section to get you started.

6. *Cultivate an attitude of pragmatic optimism.* This is really a corollary to becoming more resilient. You might be surprised to know you can change your attitude and you can cultivate a more optimistic one if you naturally see the negative side of every situation. Pragmatic optimism is marked by a realistic view of the situation (pragmatism) combined with confidence that a positive outcome can (and will) occur (optimism). Optimism without a realistic view of things is often naïve and can create risk in healthcare IT ("let's not test, I'm pretty sure everything will be OK"). Pessimism, on the other hand, is not only difficult to be around; it is like the anchor on a boat. It pulls you down and prevents you from moving forward. As a healthcare IT director, you need to be sure you are energizing your team to achieve the difficult work of the organization. Having a realistic but positive view of the likely outcomes is an engaging way to align your team with your vision.

7. *Ask for, listen to, and act upon feedback.* In order to be effective, you have to be willing to learn and grow. That starts with asking for feedback from your team, your managers, and your supervisor. It means really listening to the feedback provided and being willing to take action to improve based on that feedback.

Working Effectively with Your Manager

As a director, you are probably reporting to a Senior/Executive Director, Associate Chief Information Officer, or the Chief Information Officer directly. Regardless of the title of your manager, your interactions with your manager will determine your overall success. In this section, we'll look at a few elements that are distinctly different from the manager/director reporting relationship discussed in the Managing section.

Different Perspectives

An executive in a healthcare organization develops a different perspective of the business over time. They become less engaged with the details of the work and more engaged with the bigger picture. They address strategic issues and work with their peers to ensure the organization is moving in the right direction. This is important to understand because, as a director, your perspective is the link between strategy and operations. The director role is the place where the strategic initiatives are translated into the operational work of the company.

If you understand this key difference in perspectives, you will be able to more successfully work with your manager. For example, if you need their assistance on a problem, they will need high-level information that is actionable rather than blow-by-blow technical detail. You'll need to determine what outcome you need, in advance of the conversation, so you can prepare information appropriately. Often you'll only have a slice of time with your executive, so you should distill issues so they are clear and concise.

For example, suppose there is an issue with some technical detail of the EMR application. The application team raised this concern with their manager, who in turn raised it with you. It requires an executive decision as to whether you should stay the course with Risk A or change course and incur Risk B. How do you present this to your manager, the CIO? Though every manager is different and you should adapt to their style, you'll typically find that you need to sum up the situation and make a recommendation. You should also have enough of the details at the ready to answer most questions that will arise.

Some managers want all the details, some don't want any. Some want details if the first phase of the conversation isn't clear to them. So, you can prepare for conversations with your manager by developing the high-level details, then creating a summary. Provide the summary data first and detail if needed. Whenever possible, come ready with a recommendation or solution as well. This will make the best use of your time and executive's time. It will present actionable data and provide information in a format that could be shared with other executives if the situation warrants it.

Different Deliverables

Do you know what your manager's deliverables are? If you're in a director role at your organization, you may want to take a moment during your next one-on-one meeting and ask. You might be surprised by what you find out. As previously stated, your role is to engage the organizational gears to cause work to happen; your manager's job is different. They are tasked with coordinating the overall activities of the IT department to align skills, capabilities, and resources with strategic direction. It's less about engaging in the work of the organization and more about making sure the IT function is delivering on all fronts. Healthcare IT keeps expanding as requirements for interoperability grow. Healthcare information exchanges, meaningful use, accountable care organizations, HIPAA, and other external IT drivers continue to expand as well. These are things you may be responsible for as a director, but your executive is responsible for ensuring all those bases are covered on behalf of the organization.

If you don't know exactly what your manager does, it would be beneficial for you to spend a bit of time learning more. This will help you not only understand what your manager's priorities and pressure points are, but also broaden your skills should you want to pursue this next-level position in the future.

Directing Summary

A director in healthcare IT is responsible for connecting strategy to operations. As such, the role is literally and figuratively in the middle of things. This position has enormous potential to transform the organization. The director role is where strategy becomes tactical—ideas into action. It's where strong managers can be developed who engage staff and foster a positive, productive environment. Managing managers requires strong basic management skills as well as an understanding of how managing managers is different from managing frontline staff. As a director, you are expected to be able to behave and respond in a professional manner, to be a role model for your managers, and to set the tone for expectations across all your teams through your managers. Whatever your weaknesses as a manager, they will be amplified as a director. It's important to develop self-awareness and to work on growing professionally and personally so you can reduce your weaknesses and extend your strengths. You'll need to build relationships outside of IT to not only ensure your success but also expand your awareness of the operations of the business and the IT implications. Finally, you'll need to understand what drives your manager, what pressures and deliverables they are responsible for, and how to be effective in this middle layer of the organization.

Leading

As Peter Drucker points out, *managing is doing things right, leading is doing the right things.* That is an excellent summarization of the difference between managers and leaders. In this section, we're going to discuss leadership, which spans all levels of the organization.

In many ways, management is a set of skills, leadership is a set of behaviors. What are leadership behaviors? You've probably spotted them. These are the people who step up to fill a void, who calm people down when things go wrong, who inspire others to action when things get tough. As a manager or director, you may or may not be a leader. While your organization expects you to be a leader, you may be busy doing management tasks and completely ignoring leadership behaviors. They are not mutually exclusive, and in your role, it is important to develop leadership skills.

Traits of a Good Leader

The personal styles of good leaders vary, but traits are fairly consistent. Daniel Goleman, who popularized the concept of emotional intelligence, believes that the traits are self-awareness, self-regulation, motivation, empathy, and social skills. In contrast (though not in contradiction), Harvard's John P. Kotter states that management is about handling complexity and leadership is about handling change. Managing and leading are essentially two sides of the same coin. At a high level, management is concerned with control and organization; leadership is concerned with vision. You can't be an effective manager without vision, and you can't be an effective leader without control and organization. It's clear, though, that the concrete skills and mechanics of being a manager are certainly easier to define, study, and master than leadership skills and traits.

In this section, we'll highlight a few of the more critical leadership skills, but it is by no means comprehensive or exhaustive. If this is an area you're ready to focus on for your professional development, there are many excellent resources available to you for further research.

[...more...]

As we'll discuss in the following sections, leaders are not always in management roles. Leadership can be exhibited by frontline staff, and leadership can be absent in executives. In my experience, *leaders always rise*. If you're wondering if someone has leadership potential, create a gap and see what happens. If they don't rise, they may not be ready, willing, or able to lead, and that's also helpful information about an individual. This is a great example of taking a calculated risk, which we've discussed throughout this chapter. Find a safe area in which you can allow a gap to exist and see if someone rises to fill that gap. Chances are good you will identify your leaders in this way. Leaders rise to fill gaps, to address problems and complexity. They differentiate themselves from their peers not by posturing and public announcements but by stepping up and addressing a need. Though leadership skills can be taught and honed, it starts with a leadership mindset that, if not present, can be more difficult to develop. If you'd like to identify your leaders, give them a bit of space and an opportunity to rise up and you will spot them. From there, you can help hone their skills through education, training, and mentoring. Not everyone is suited for leadership and there are always plenty of people on your teams who are quite to content contributing without being in leadership roles. That's fine. The key is to recognize and foster those leaders that are on your teams.

Sets Vision and Tone

We've discussed providing the vision of the organization as both a manager and as a director. The vision you have for your team sets the tone for the work. However, you don't need to be a manager (we'll use the word *manager* for any level of management for simplicity) to set vision and tone. In many cases, when the manager fails to set the vision or tone, someone on the team will rise up to fill the gap. They'll rally the team to achieve a difficult objective or cajole the team into resolving a problem or take the initiative to escalate an issue, whatever it takes.

This is important to know as a manager, because the underlying message is, either lead your team or someone else will. The caveat is that if your organization is dysfunctional or the manager is inept, leaders may not rise; they may wisely wait in the wings. This is really unfortunate when it occurs because it means that things are running suboptimally; the team is failing to reach its full potential as a team and as individuals.

Motivates and Mobilizes Others

Motivating others to achieve results is a hallmark trait of leadership. As a manager, you can require staff to complete tasks and resolve issues. As a leader, you can motivate them to want to do their job to the best of their ability. We all have worked with people who go the extra step in everything they do and people who do the bare minimum just to check the box to mark a task complete. Sometimes the difference is the personalities of the individuals, as we discussed earlier, but sometimes it's about leadership. Even moderate performers can achieve better results when leadership actively motivates and mobilizes.

If you've worked in the workforce for any length of time, you've probably seen an example of someone who was not the manager rising up to motivate the team to achieve a goal. They rally the team and address the naysayers all without the formal title or organizational authority to do so. These are your team's natural leaders, and they should be encouraged to grow their leadership skills.

Leads from the Front

Leading from the front doesn't mean doing the frontline work. It does mean being in front of the team, in front of the issue, in front of the problem, and helping guide the way. If you think of rescue efforts you've seen on television or in the movies, someone has to forge the dangerous path out of the emergency and get everyone to safety. That means taking the lead and showing the way. In healthcare IT, that often means figuring out the complexities of healthcare IT and developing the framework for the path forward rather than dropping a complex problem on the team and leaving them to sort it out in a vacuum. While empowering all levels of employees is vital for optimal results, just lobbing problems is not empowering. As a manager at any level, you can't just drop a complex, cross-team problem on one of your staff with the expectation they'll just figure it out. This is especially problematic when a manager does this in order to avoid taking responsibility for solving a problem. For example, if your CIO comes to you with a complex problem that falls entirely in your area of responsibility, it's your job to own it. That doesn't mean you have to solve the problem yourself, just the opposite. The people doing the work are best suited to finding the solution. However, you cannot absolve yourself of responsibility through delegation either.

A leader will pose the problem to the team, will help facilitate discussion and problem solving, and will ultimately own the results, whether good or bad. A leader takes responsibility for the problem, but gives credit to the team for solving the problem.

Adapts to Complexity

Healthcare IT is a rapidly changing and complex environment. That's the reason so many IT professionals love their work in healthcare. However, the rapid pace of change, when not managed effectively, can create chaos, inject risk, and wear down even the most enthusiastic employee. A leader's job is to sort out this environment so that complexity is reduced. To quote Peter Drucker, "There is nothing quite so useless, as doing with great efficiency, something that should not be done at all." This is really the essence of leadership in healthcare IT. Managers will typically stay focused on the day-to-day work of their teams and delivering on their commitments. However, someone (the healthcare IT leader) needs to have their eye on the ever-changing environment and decide when it's time to change, flex, adapt, expand, or cancel a line of work.

Adapting to complexity means dealing with often imperfect or incomplete data and making smart decisions that will set the course for the team. It also means not being overwhelmed by the complexity of the situation and finding a clear path forward.

Focuses on Results

Managers focus on deliverables, leaders focus on results. The best leaders set the course and get out of the way. When they attempt to also manage the deliverables, results are often muddled. It's like having two (or more) people trying to drive a car. One person has their foot on the gas, the other on the brake; one is trying to course correct to the left, the other to the right. Once direction is set, the leader needs to focus on achieving the result by actively defining what success looks like and by providing helpful feedback along the way. To use the car analogy again, it's like the manager is driving the car and the leader is in the passenger seat as the navigator saying, "How are you doing on gas? After this next gas station, it's 245 miles to the next one." It's keeping the big picture in focus and ensuring the tools and resources are available to achieve success. It is not the leader in the passenger seat saying, "Accelerate just a bit more to get over this hill and move to the left lane in 100 feet." That's micromanaging, not leadership.

Is Solution-Oriented

Managers tend to be problem-oriented. They are good at identifying and defining problems. If they're also leaders, they will move toward being solution-oriented. For example, the leader will bring a problem to their manager with proposed solutions and a recommendation about those solutions. That solution orientation is key to leadership because it moves the conversation from stasis (problem) to action (solution) after assessing options. Being solution-oriented means you're not willing to allow a problem to persist beyond a reasonable timeframe. As a healthcare IT leader, you'll need to hone your ability to move from problem to potential solution to recommendation to calculated risk.

Innovates

The last trait we'll discuss (though there are many others) is innovation. A leader in healthcare IT needs to innovate. That doesn't mean blowing up existing structures and starting from scratch, though it can. Innovation really means being willing to challenge the status quo, being willing to ask *why*, and being willing to look at problems with a fresh perspective. Earlier in this book, we discussed innovation as being that part of IT effort that can be expanded (or created) when operations are optimized and project work is well managed. That level of innovation is a desirable goal, but in the interim you can innovate within your area of responsibility. Innovation at the operational or project level is what helps drive exponential gains and allows you to take on truly valuable, higher-order work as an IT department. Innovation doesn't just happen in big bursts of huge, impactful projects. Innovation can happen in all aspects of the work. Leaders look for ways to innovate, to fundamentally change (for the better) the outcomes of the department for the benefit of the organization, and ultimately, the patients it cares for.

Leading Summary

Leadership is a skill that can be honed and developed, but it starts with a mindset. Once you decide you want to be a strong leader, you can develop the necessary skills over time. Though some people are natural leaders, anyone can master the skills to become an effective leader with time, effort, and focus. Leadership happens at all levels of the organization and should be fostered. Throughout this book, we've identified leadership traits, so this short section is just a brief recap of some of the more critical elements. As with other topics, we've provided some resources in the References section at the end of the chapter to help get you started on delving into this topic more deeply.

Summary

Though we ended this chapter talking about leadership, all of the traits and skills discussed in the chapter are elements of leadership. To be successful as a manager, director, or healthcare IT executive, you need to develop very solid management skills and expand them to be broader and deeper as you progress in your career.

No one does all of these things all the time with success. In fact, it's rare that anyone does all these things all the time. This chapter is intended to be your playbook, something you can refer back to when you get lost or stuck or disheartened. You can pick one thing and focus on it for a while. You can read the chapter and develop your own professional growth plan and work your way through it. You can research aspects of management and leadership that are your weaknesses.

The intent is to provide you a roadmap with markers along the way so you can incorporate these elements into your work.

As healthcare IT continues to move to center stage of almost every healthcare organization in the world, the demands and the complexity will only continue to increase. Arming yourself with strong management and leadership skills will help you better navigate this environment and help you achieve extraordinary results. Your organization is counting on you to do so.

References

For more on this topic, visit http://susansnedaker.com/leading-hit.

QR8.1

Benjamin, Susan F., *Perfect Phrases for Dealing with Difficult People*, New York: The McGraw-Hill Companies, Inc., 2008.

Bradberry, Travis and Jean Greaves, *Leadership 2.0*, San Diego, CA: TalentSmart, 2012.

Broadbent, Marianne and Ellen S. Kitzis, *The New CIO Leader*, Boston: Harvard Business School Press, 2005.

Bruce, Anne, *Perfect Phrases for Documenting Employee Performance Issues*, New York: The McGraw-Hill Companies, Inc., 2005.

Burger, Edward B. and Michael Starbird, *Five Elements of Effective Thinking*, Princeton, NJ: Princeton University Press, 2012.

Chussil, Mark, "Keep a List of Unethical Things You'll Never Do," *Harvard Business Review*, May 30, 2016, https://hbr.org/2016/05/keep-a-list-of-unethical-things-youll-never-do, viewed May 31, 2016.

QR8.2

Drucker, Peter F., *"The Effective Executive:" The Definitive Guide to Getting the Right Things Done*, New York: HarperCollins Publishers, 2006.

Greitens, Eric, *Resilience: Hard-Won Wisdom for Living a Better Life*, New York: Houghton Mifflin Harcourt Publishing Company, 2016.

HBR's 10 Must Reads, *On Leadership*, Boston: Harvard Business Review Press, 2011.

HBR's 10 Must Reads, *On Managing People*, Boston: Harvard Business Review Press, 2011.

HBR's 10 Must Reads, *On Communication*, Boston: Harvard Business Review Press, 2013.

Holtsnider, Bill and Brian D. Jaffe, *IT Manager's Handbook: Getting Your New Job Done*, San Francisco: Morgan Kaufman Publishers, 2001.

Kallet, Michael, *Think Smarter: Critical Thinking to Improve Problem-Solving and Decision-Making Skills*, Hoboken, NJ: John Wiley & Sons, Inc., 2014.

Kotter, John P., "What Leaders Really Do," *On Leadership*, Boston: Harvard Business Review Press, 2011, pp. 37–55.

Paul, Richard and Linda Elder, "Paul-Elder Critical Thinking Framework," http://louisville.edu/ideastoaction/about/criticalthinking/framework, viewed July 1, 2016.

QR8.3

Paul, Richard and Linda Elder, "The Miniature Guide to Critical Thinking: Concepts and Tools," The Foundation for Critical Thinking, 2006. http://www.criticalthinking.org/files/Concepts_Tools.pdf, viewed July 1, 2016.

QR8.4

Poole, Laura, *Perfect Phrases for Coaching Employee Performance*, New York: The McGraw-Hill Companies, Inc., 2013.

Runion, Meryl and Wendy Mack, *Perfect Phrases for Leadership Development*, New York: The McGraw-Hill Companies, Inc., 2011.

Wager, Karen A., Frances Wickham Lee and John P. Glaser, *Health Care Information Systems: A Practical Approach for Health Care Management*, 2nd Ed. San Francisco: Jossey-Bass, 2009.

Chapter 9

Lean in Healthcare IT

Overview

Healthcare has become increasingly complex and leaders are actively looking for ways to improve how care is provided. With the shift from a volume to value-based payment model and the increasing pressures on healthcare organizations to reduce costs and improve outcomes, many healthcare leaders have turned to process improvement methodologies. There are numerous quality or process frameworks that have been used (and are still in use) such as total quality management (TQM) and Six Sigma. However, in the past decade, Lean has been gaining traction in healthcare. Lean in healthcare today is fundamentally based on the Toyota Production System (TPS) used in automobile manufacturing. Seeing parallels in healthcare workflows, early healthcare Lean champions began experimenting with adapting Lean principles and tools to healthcare. Today, there is a growing interest and deployment of Lean in healthcare.

In IT, there are also other frameworks used such as Information Technology Infrastructure Library (ITIL), Information Technology Service Management (ITSM), Capabilities Maturity Model (CMM), National Institute of Standards and Technology (NIST), and International Standards Organization (ISO), to name a few. Many healthcare IT leaders are now trying to understand how to leverage these frameworks and Lean in a useful way.

In this chapter, we'll discuss Lean at a high level and how it relates to these IT frameworks. We'll also look at current initiatives in healthcare and how Lean is being applied. This chapter will not make you an expert in Lean in healthcare, not even close. For that, there are many great resources including a few to get you started in the References section. However, this will serve as a basic introduction to some of the current thinking in Lean and how IT leaders are working with this in healthcare today.

Lean Basics

According to author Ron Bercaw in *Lean Leadership for Healthcare: Approaches to Lean Transformation*, the cornerstone of success in Lean in healthcare is leadership. Since this book is focused on healthcare IT leadership, we're going to discuss Lean leadership in this context. However, before we can discuss Lean leadership, it's important to understand some of the fundamental concepts in Lean. According to Bercaw, there are two core concepts: *continuous improvement* (CI) and *respect for all people*. Under CI, Bercaw states that in most transactions, 95% are waste and only 5% add value. Value is always defined from the customer's perspective, and there can only be one customer in a transaction. *Value*, according to Bercaw (and other Lean experts) is defined as "any action for which the customer is willing to pay" (Bercaw, p. 2). That means, by definition, *waste* (non-value) is that for which the customer is not willing to pay. With that in mind, let's look at a very typical healthcare experience, a visit to a primary care physician office.

Customer's Perspective

We all have had the experience of making an appointment by phone or online, showing up for the visit, presenting insurance information, perhaps filling out some forms. We sit in the waiting room browsing through dog-eared, magazines until we're called into an exam room. There, a medical assistant takes our vitals and gathers initial information about the reason for our visit. The doctor comes in, assesses our information, makes a diagnosis, and recommends treatment. That might be a prescription, a diagnostic test (blood, image, etc.), or some other action. We leave via the checkout desk where we receive copies of paperwork or perhaps schedule a follow-up visit.

That visit can be viewed as a single patient transaction. From the patient standpoint, where is the value? Seeing the physician and getting a diagnosis or treatment plan. That's it. The rest of the experience is not valuable to you as the patient or customer. Even though things like insurance forms or making sure the exam room is clean and ready for the next patient are necessary parts of the process, they do not add value to you directly and therefore you would consider them waste.

When we boil down transactions to their essence this way, we can develop a better understanding of the elements of value. Once we understand what actually adds value, we can make a choice in our CI efforts: increase value or decrease waste.

Value-to-Waste Ratio

With this very binary view of all transactions, it becomes pretty clear that the vast majority of most transactions are *waste*. As mentioned earlier, according to Bercaw, 5% of transactions are value-add (Bercaw, p. 4). Given this lopsided equation, it seems clear that there is ample opportunity to reduce waste pretty easily. If you think of any recent transaction you've had—whether at your doctor's office, your bank, or your local restaurant—you probably noticed inefficiencies. You may have even found yourself commenting that, "if they just did [*insert activity*], things would run much more smoothly!" This is truly the essence of Lean thinking—because in these cases, you *are* the customer and you have identified activities that are meaningless, unproductive, or wasteful (time, motion, money, etc.) from your perspective.

Seven Wastes

We've seen several types of waste in our physician office example. When we look at the world around us, we see examples of waste everywhere. Lean experts typically define seven types of waste. We'll run through these briefly.

1. Overproduction

Overproduction is pretty straight-forward—making too much or making too much too soon. In the physical world, it's fairly easy to spot. A bakery that bakes too much bread for the day's demand has day-old bread on sale the next day. A hardware store buys too many seasonal items and puts them on sale at the end to clear them out. A surgical nurse opens too many supplies; they are unused during the procedure and must be thrown away.

Spotting overproduction in IT is not quite as simple because it typically does not involve physical things. In IT, what exactly do we produce for our customers and how can we overproduce? One example is implementing a new software application that has 50 new features and we deploy them all. All but four key features go unused. Another example is that we produce 12 different reports daily but only three are actually used. Given this view of IT overproduction, you may begin to view your work through a different lens.

2. Waiting

Virtually all healthcare organizations have rooms simply designated for waiting. There are waiting rooms in emergency departments, in surgery lobbies, in physician offices, in imaging and lab offices—they're everywhere. Though there are some very brave (and disciplined) Lean healthcare organizations who have been designing their workflows and buildings without waiting areas, they are the exception. It seems everywhere we go in healthcare and beyond; there is the waste of waiting.

In healthcare IT, how does the waste of waiting manifest? Again, from the customer perspective, they have to wait for an upgrade to fix a bug in the system; they have to wait for a slow application to respond; they have to wait on hold for someone at the Help Desk; they have to wait for a computer to be repaired. Granted, some of these aspects of waiting do not mean they are idle. For example, when there are 14 computers at a nursing station and 1 is down, they might be waiting for it to be repaired, but they are not literally sitting there waiting. Still, these are aspects of waste.

3. Overprocessing

The waste of overprocessing is the waste of providing more value than the customer wants or needs. A great example is one we pointed out earlier—generating multiple reports that are seldom or never used. Similarly, in IT, we've all known people who worked on something to such a level of detail that they really over-engineered the solution. They accounted for every possible contingency, even if that event was unlikely to ever occur.

Overprocessing means wasting time, money, and effort on making something far better than it needs to be to meet the need. In IT, when we overprocess, we see delays, a rising backlog of work, needless rework, cost overruns, and frustrated customers.

4. Inventory

Inventory is not only physical assets like bandages and syringes; it's also people waiting to be treated (excess inventory of people), too many staff (or not enough), or numerous reports that have overlapping data (excess inventory of data). Too much inventory can cause congestion, delays, excess cost, expiration of inventory, or duplication of inventory ("I can't find it in this mess, so I'll just buy more."). On the other hand, running out of needed inventory causes delays, errors, and perhaps omissions. If a pharmacy runs out of a medication, the patient that needs it experiences a delay; perhaps a substitute medication may be ordered, but it possibly has some unpleasant side effects or maybe the medication simply doesn't get administered until it comes back into stock. This is inventory-related waste.

In healthcare IT, the physical assets such as PCs or network cables are inventory and can certainly cause delays if you don't have them on hand when needed. If you have poorly organized inventory, you may not know you have 50 network cables on hand because you can't find them, so you order some more. What about on the EMR or application side of IT? What constitutes inventory waste? It might be three different ways to enter the same patient data that causes duplication of that data in the EMR (data are inventory). It might be that reports are generated that are never used. It might be that there are four different applications that do basically the same thing. The shortage or excess of inventory is a source of waste.

5. Motion

If you've ever eaten at a restaurant that was poorly designed, you've certainly noticed servers walking from one place to another to yet another and back again just to do simple tasks like pick up spare silverware or fill a glass of water. You can see how it delays service, creates errors, and makes the server's job that much more difficult. The same is true in healthcare. Bercaw uses an example of an organization that studied how much nurses walked in a given day just to get something. They estimated that 53% of the nurse's day was spent walking from one place to another (Bercaw, p. 10). So, at least half their day is spent *not* caring for patients. If they had 500 nurses and could save 25% of their time, that means they could free up an additional 250,000 hours each year that could be dedicated to patient care.

What sort of motion is considered waste in IT? The big one that immediately comes to mind is the number of mouse clicks. If it takes 14 clicks to access basic information, there's a good chance that about 10 of those clicks are waste. Though we've all been conditioned by big online retailers who have championed quick, easy shopping with a few mouse clicks, it's also demonstrated that many processes can be streamlined to reduce clicks. Other examples of wasted motion in IT? Multiple logins for different applications, inefficient electronic workflows that require going back and forth among screens, and poorly placed computers and printers on nursing units or in physician offices are all examples of motion waste.

6. Defects

Defects are errors that reach the customer. If your mortgage company fails to apply your latest payment to your balance, your account will be flagged as delinquent and additional interest and penalties will be charged. However, if that all happens on the backend and the error is corrected before you ever see it, then it's an error and not a defect. If you receive a notice saying you're delinquent when you know your payment was processed, then it's a defect. It causes rework and review that do not add value.

We clearly know what defects are in IT because software bugs, errors in software configuration, errors in analysis, design, development, and deployment of applications, reports, etc., do hit the end user and do have a negative impact. In some cases, these defects are annoying and make it harder to use a system. In other cases, though, these errors can be quite serious and create serious patient safety issues.

7. Transportation

Waste in transportation can take several different forms. If you've been moving inventory from one place to another, that adds no value to the customer and is considered waste. Similarly, if you have the patient walk from one place to another throughout their encounter (registration, check-in, lab, x-ray, exam room, checkout), that's transportation waste if the layout is not efficient for the patient. Buildings are sometimes designed around the delivery of care without considering the patient flow, which creates transportation waste.

[…more…]

An example of transportation waste came to light when a hospital looked at its workflow related to medication pumps. Pumps were always believed to be in short supply. Every year, nursing unit requested capital funding to purchase more, though the data suggested there were more than enough to meet the needs of the hospital.

After a team investigated, they found that pumps were being piled up in dirty equipment rooms on each unit, and a person from central supply would periodically come around with a large cart and gather them up. That person would cart them across the entire hospital (often with some falling off the pile, hitting the floor and breaking) to bring them to a centralized cleaning location. The analysis team estimated the number of miles each pump traveled each year in the hospital and were astounded at the number.

They worked with clinical staff and central supply staff to redesign the workflow. Instead of carting around pumps, there was a designated area in each unit where dirty equipment was cleaned and then placed in clean storage. This ensured that the proper number of pumps (par level/inventory) remained on each unit to meet nursing needs. It reduced the transportation of the pumps. Only pumps that needed to be repaired were removed from the unit and they were replaced on a one-for-one basis.

The hospital saw reduction in pump breakage, increase in the availability of pumps when needed, and an overall improvement in nurse confidence that the pumps would always be available when needed. This is a great example of removing the transportation waste, which in turn reduced patients waiting for medication, nurses wasted motion looking for pumps, and cost associated with repairs and purchasing additional pumps that were ultimately not needed.

Transportation waste in IT usually is less physical. It refers to transactions and handoffs. Think of how many tickets come into your Service Desk and how many are placed in queues. Each time that ticket moves to another queue without adding value, we have waste. You might think that may not matter, but look at it from the customer's viewpoint. They call for status and are told, "we assigned it to the desktop team, but they determined it was a network issue. However, the network team discovered it's a problem with the application, so it's waiting for an analyst to take a look at it." None of those steps added value for the customer. Many times IT processes are developed to meet a need, but they don't evolve as the need changes. If you look at your IT processes where handoffs occur, you will no doubt find numerous opportunities to reduce IT transportation waste.

We've provided brief IT examples of each of the types of waste, but it would be worth your time to give some thought to how these types of waste manifest in your IT department. If 95% of activities are waste from a customer perspective, there's plenty of opportunity to reduce and remove waste across the IT function.

We'll discuss Lean tools later in this chapter, but right now, let's turn our attention to IT frameworks so we can then tie Lean and these IT frameworks together.

ITIL and ITSM Basics

As mentioned at the beginning of this chapter, the Information Technology Infrastructure Library (ITIL) and Information Technology Service Management (ITSM) are frameworks used to manage the IT function. IT Service Management is how you design and manage services you deliver to your customers. ITIL is a framework of processes for delivering the service.

ITSM relates to Lean because ITSM is often described as a means of delivering *value* to your customers, not simply managing technology. ITSM is essentially a way of designing and organizing service delivery. ITIL is a set of practices or procedures used to define, deliver, and manage IT services.

The ITIL elements are defined as *service strategy*, *service design*, *service transition*, *service operation*, and *continuous service improvement*, as depicted in Figure 9.1. Though the ITIL elements are often depicted in a linear fashion, continuous improvement (CI) impacts each of the elements and is shown in this diagram as being at the center of all activities.

1. *Service strategy*—This involves developing a strategic view of IT service delivery taking into consideration market and organizational drivers. This is where needs, demands, capabilities, and priorities are determined.
2. *Service design*—This aspect relates directly to the design of services that provide value to customers. This may include technical architecture, service solutions, and tools, to name three elements. Service design takes the requirements from the service strategy phase and develops specific solutions around those requirements. The result of service design is a service catalog, which is exactly what it sounds like—a list of services the IT department provides based on service strategy.

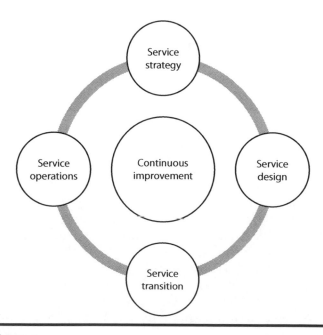

Figure 9.1   ITIL elements.

3. *Service transition*—Service transition is the phase where the design becomes operational. It includes processes such as knowledge management, service asset and configuration management, change management, release and deployment management, and more. Organizations that use a standard process for implementing services typically see better project estimates for time, cost, or effort; a higher percentage of successful changes; reduction in delays and rework due to standardization and improved communications with end users. This ties in closely to the Lean concept of *standard work*, discussed later in this chapter.

4. *Service operation*—The primary function of service operation is to ensure that the services designed and implemented meet service levels. The key benefits are maintaining end-user satisfaction and confidence in the IT department through meeting agreed-upon expectations and through minimizing outages. Striving to standardize (and automate) operations leads to efficiencies including less downtime, fewer errors, more consistent service delivery, and ultimately, a reduction in the overall percentage of time IT spends on these operations. This ties in with the concepts of eliminating waste and CI in Lean.

5. *Continual service improvement*—In ITIL, this phase is related to the iterative process of reviewing strategy; ensuring design is still aligned with needs as strategy and organizational needs shift over time; reviewing service transition and identifying processes that didn't work as expected or are not working as efficiently as possible; reviewing service operations and finding opportunities to improve the way service is delivered (can service levels be delivered with less effort or greater consistency, for example). Of course, there is a direct connection to Lean.

ITIL is not the only framework for managing IT services. There are several other popular ones including COBIT, NIST, and ISO. As with all frameworks, there are proponents and detractors of each. If your organization is using one of these frameworks, you can take the elements of the framework and tie them to Lean, as the connection is about delivering service, reducing risk, and increasing quality through standardization.

Two common criticisms of ITIL are that it does not directly address IT architecture nor does it directly address the business applications that run on the IT infrastructure. As with all frameworks, ITIL can be helpful in providing an organized structure for looking at and managing IT infrastructure. If it is taken to an extreme, it can become just another over-engineered process that becomes a roadblock, rather than a facilitator, to success. In other words, *overproduction* and *overprocessing* create waste.

Lean and ITIL Intersect

Clearly, Lean and ITIL have a few things in common. Words that are used in both areas are value, waste, efficiency, errors, consistency, process, predictability, and standardization—to name just a few. So how exactly do Lean and ITIL intersect? Figure 9.2 depicts the relationship between Lean and ITIL. Some have said that ITIL is a set of processes to manage IT services, and Lean is a method of improving those processes.

ITIL includes continuous process improvement and each of the phases of ITIL includes numerous processes. Lean is focused on reducing waste and increasing value for the customer through process improvement. In short, Lean can be used to improve the processes implemented under

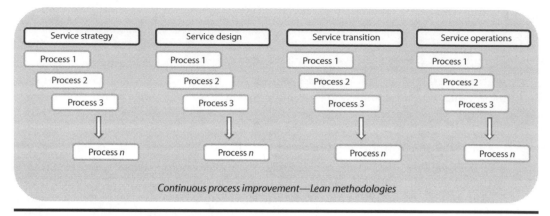

Figure 9.2   Lean and ITIL.

the ITIL framework. In fact, Lean is a great approach to improving processes in the Continuous Process Improvement area of ITIL.

Clearly, you can implement ITIL without implementing Lean, though if you follow the ITIL framework, you'll need some method for conducting continuous process improvement. You can certainly implement Lean without using ITIL. However, if you work in an IT department that has implemented ITIL and your hospital is focusing on implementing Lean, you can weave these together effectively.

Lean Management System

Before we jump into Lean leadership, it's important to note that in order for Lean to be successful in an organization, it must be implemented via a Lean management system. Just like with any other type of business transformation, Lean requires that leaders demonstrate a standard set of skills and behaviors that help sustain Lean activities. Figure 9.3 represents the activities of Lean leadership at three levels of the organization. For more on this topic, see *Lean IT* (Bell and Orzen, 2011, p. 243).

In essence, executives need to deploy strategy via Lean management (more on that later). Directors need to practice the discipline of using Lean management system tools and techniques, such as *value stream mapping* and *A3 thinking*, to tie strategy to operations in order to create and sustain transformation. (These tools are discussed briefly later as well.) Managers need to understand the strategic direction, the chosen course of action and then consistently drive frontline

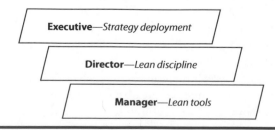

Figure 9.3   Lean leadership focus.

activity to meet those objectives. Frontline managers typically use Lean tools with their teams in order to create change by adding value and/or reducing waste. While this may be an overly simplistic notion of these three tiers of Lean management, it helps depict where the focus is at each level.

In most deployments, the Lean management system is composed of these six fundamental skills/behaviors:

1. Lean leadership
2. Strategy deployment
3. Leader standard work
4. Daily accountability
5. Visual controls
6. Discipline

Together, these elements create a management system that supports and sustains Lean in your organization. We'll briefly review each of these elements and tie them back to healthcare IT leadership. For those of you familiar with Lean, you may notice there are a few gaps as we go through this topic. This chapter is not intended to be exhaustive on the topic of Lean or Lean management. It is intended to tie in Lean leadership with healthcare IT leadership and provide a few insights into implementing Lean in healthcare IT. Of course, there is a vast amount of authoritative information available on Lean and Lean management systems, especially in healthcare. You should seek additional training, mentoring, and coaching in Lean if this is a path you're interested in pursuing. The References section contains several great starting points.

1. Lean Leadership

Lean leadership is a mindset and a set of skills and behaviors. At its core is respect for the individual and an understanding that those who are doing the work are best suited to improving it. According to Bercaw, "Senior leadership actions and behaviors are the single largest factor for delivering a successful Lean transformation" (Bercaw, p. 168). That makes sense when we remember that senior leadership behavior drives organizational culture. In this case, senior leadership truly adopting Lean leadership behaviors (versus just towing the line) is the only way Lean transformation is sustained.

It takes time, focus, and consistent effort to make any kind of change. Organizations and people have a natural tendency to slide backward to old habits until new ones are firmly entrenched. In fact, one hallmark of Lean is creating *countermeasures* to remove or reduce the possibility of sliding backward. Once new habits become ingrained, they can be monitored to ensure they don't revert to old ways. When that happens, new change initiatives can move to the area of focus for active improvement. Perhaps one of the biggest shifts for some healthcare IT leaders is that in Lean, the manager or director is not the source for all the answers ("just go do this"). Instead, they are active collaborators in steering the team to the solution ("what happened when you tried this?", "what if we tried that?").

Lean leaders set the vision (or context), they create and sustain the culture of empowered and engaged staff, they lead by example, they challenge the status quo, and they strive for CI. If you already manage your teams in ways aligned with these Lean leadership principles, you might be wondering what the big deal is. While there are additional tools and techniques that are part of Lean leadership, your natural style may already be very empowering for your team. In that case, the transformation for you and your leadership style will likely be more of an evolution than a total change in your approach.

2. Strategy Deployment

Part of both Lean leadership and Lean Leader Standard Work (discussed in the next section) is *strategy deployment*. We used this term earlier in the book when discussing how IT leaders translate organizational strategy into IT operations, but we mentioned there was a specific use of the phrase in Lean. *Strategy deployment*, in Lean terms, is the set of management activities required to plan, implement, and review the core business objectives. It operates at two levels. According to Bercaw, "first, at the strategic planning level, and, second, at the daily management level on the more routine or fundamental aspects of the business operation" (Bercaw, p. 29). The practices we're discussing with respect to Lean management are all part of deploying and managing strategy. There are seven steps and three phases, according to Bercaw, and they tie back to an organization's "True North" objectives. Check the References section at the end of this chapter for more on strategy deployment in healthcare (specifically, Bercaw, 2013).

[…more…]

One criticism about Lean in healthcare, especially in IT, is that it requires a lot of "extra" work on the part of teams and managers, that it is redundant or that the required activities, themselves, are *waste*. That seems to be a fair criticism in some cases because of the way Lean is introduced and rolled out in an organization. When compliance with organizational-wide "solutions" is required, the one-size-fits-all approach will not fit some segments of the organization. As you read about Lean IT in this chapter and in other resources, you should begin to see a pattern emerge. The key is to standardize, automate, reduce variation, reduce waste, and increase value from the customer's perspective. In healthcare IT, this is how many departments already operate to a large degree (though perhaps not focusing enough on the *customer's* perception of value or not using standard Lean tools).

Lean in *healthcare* and *healthcare IT* are not at odds with one another; they are well aligned. But what works out on a nursing unit may not be at all suited to the IT department. The key is to avoid implementing anything with your teams that doesn't make sense and add value. Though some Lean tools and activities can seem counterintuitive at first (and must be tested for a while before being modified or discarded), many aspects are very much in tune with current IT trends. We look to standardize and automate anything that is repeatable to reduce workload, avoid errors, reduce risk, and streamline operations. The less time we spend on these routine tasks, the more time we can spend on activities that actually add value to the customer. (This refers back to optimizing operations so there is more time for innovation, discussed in Chapter 4.) That's essentially a Lean mindset.

If we take it to the next level and examine the steps in the automation, we may find unnecessary steps that can be eliminated. More importantly, we can then examine the result to ensure it adds value to the customer. Automating user provisioning is a good example. User provisioning includes the activities involved with user accounts including creating, modifying, disabling, and deleting user accounts and their access to IT resources. Automating this process reduces human work effort, reduces errors, reduces security risks, ensures standards are always upheld, and can be audited and monitored. Once automated, there may be an opportunity to improve your organization's overall approach to user provisioning further. This is the essence of Lean and ITIL's continuous service improvement.

Your job as a Lean leader is to support and sustain these efforts and to keep visible the improvements that are being worked on. This is done through leadership tools discussed next.

3. Leader Standard Work

Leader Standard Work (LSW) is a set of daily behaviors leaders undertake to ensure they adhere to consistent behaviors. Typically LSW is in the form of a checklist that is used daily by leaders to check on various aspects of operations. If you look online for templates of LSW checklists, you'll find wide variation. That's because Lean is rarely prescriptive. Instead, it provides frameworks and tools, and leaders need to experiment with them to develop a system that works for them (or adopt organization-wide standards that have been set through a collaborative discussion). The key is standardization, consistency, and focus on the things that actually drive value or reduce waste. Unlike some other systems you may have used, in Lean, if the task or the report or the checklist isn't generating the result you expect, you should modify it. Small, rapid change is one of the hallmarks of Lean, and if your LSW is not working as expected, you should revise it.

Let's look at what one section of LSW could look like in IT. On the infrastructure side, your desktop manager may walk a section of the hospital each morning with the desktop analyst responsible for that area. The checklist might include things like those listed in Figure 9.4. The manager of Clinical Engineering may do the same with Biomedical Equipment Techs (BMETs) inspecting medical equipment, checking for Preventive Maintenance (PM) stickers, and ensuring broken equipment is tagged and removed from the unit. This is work that happens every day like clockwork. It drives consistency and standardization, and it ensures the manager is both visible in the clinical areas and is aware of the circumstances of the clinical areas. The sum total of this is called *going to gemba* or *going to the place the work is done.*

Let's look at LSW on the application side. It might be the manager of clinical or business systems holds a daily morning huddle reviewing the priorities of the day and reviewing any critical issues from the prior day. It might be a 10-minute stand-up meeting every day to align staff with the work needed. For a manager in a Project Management Office, it might be to review key tasks for the day for each project managed by a project manager.

Sometimes daily huddles are impractical in IT because teams work various hours or at different locations. For example, a system team may have staff rotate schedules to patch servers during the night, leaving a partial team in the morning. In that case, the manager needs to be creative and think about ways to organize work and ensure consistency and standardization. Though Lean often emphasizes the use of solutions that do not involve technology (such as paper, whiteboards, etc.), in IT, it sometimes makes sense to use electronic systems to which all staff have continuous access. In this case, it might be a message board or a team website used to update each other on key work being done, or by using webinars/teleconferences to connect.

Daily checklist for patient care units
a. All PCs are working.
b. All printers are working.
c. All cabling is properly managed and tidy.
d. All UPS units are functional and installed correctly (i.e., correct power in/out, not sitting directly on the floor, etc.).
e. Unit manager and unit clerk check in.

Figure 9.4 Daily checklist for desktop manager example.

As a leader, you may want to require that each team member post an update at the end of each shift. However, an approach more aligned with Lean would be to discuss with the team the information *they* need to be effective. As the manager, you can certainly add in your requirements or suggestions as well. Discuss the access to information, the cadence of updates, and any recent communication problems that need to be solved. You can guide the team through questions or suggestions in order to ensure they remain aligned with the objective (versus letting them go off on their own and end up off course). Ask the team to come up with a solution that they can standardize on. In this way, you have defined the *requirement* and they are defining the *solution*. When staff solve the problem in a manner suitable to them that also meets your requirements, they are more likely to comply with their new standard. This drives leadership objectives for standardization and accountability.

Now, let's go up one level to a director or executive version of LSW. Figure 9.5 shows an example of how an LSW template might be formatted, and Figure 9.6 shows that same form with sample data.

LSW similarly defines work you do as a leader the same way every time. This might be how you participate in morning huddles, how you reconcile your budget variances each month, or how you prepare and review contracts for signing. It might be even more simplistic. You might choose to make a list, similar to the one shown in Figure 9.6, of tasks you do daily, weekly, monthly, and even quarterly. For example, you may have to prepare a quarterly report to the executive team or Board of Directors on the status of a strategic project. You can add standard work elements to your weekly or monthly sections so you always remember to do that work. This framework can be modified to suit your needs.

Whatever you do on a regular basis that can be standardized and documented is suitable for LSW. As with frontline staff, the more effectively you document your LSW, the less "brain power" you need to devote to remembering work you need to do consistently. While it lacks the step-by-step procedure or specificity that frontline standard work might provide, it nonetheless creates a standardized set of leadership tasks to work with. Figure 9.6 shows an example with this form

Leader Standard Work							
Name				**Week of**			
/	**Daily**		**Interruptions**		/	**Weekly**	
						Mon	
						Tue	
						Wed	
						Thur	
						Fri	
			Improvements			**Monthly/Quarterly**	

Figure 9.5 LSW example.

Leader Standard Work						
Name			**Week of**			
Daily			**Interruptions**		**Weekly**	
8 am	Morning huddle		Mon	Unapproved project requested	Mon	Payroll
8:15 am	Daily task review		Tue	Research invoicing errors	Tue	Executive roundtable, 1:1 JD
8:30 am	Daily walks (customer visits)		Fri	Vendor caused ERP app outage	Wed	Clinical committees, 1:1 SL
			Fri	Problem with timekeeping app	Thur	Team meeting, 1:1 FZ, 1:1 BR
9 am	*Review PI projects*			surfaced during Fri gemba walk	Fri	1:1 CM, 1:1 VK
					Fri	Project status huddles
			Improvements (PI Projects)		**Monthly/Quarterly**	
				Improve ERP login process	2nd Tue.	Budget variance review and report
					4th/mo.	Prepare quarterly executive report
3 pm	Manager check in			*Improve timekeeping app*		
				scheduling process		
5 pm	Daily wrap up			*Monitor XYZ app response time*		

Figure 9.6   LSW with sample data.

partially filled out to give you a more concrete idea of what this might look like. This example might be something used by an application manager.

Though many of the items are updates, there is also a section for monitoring the improvements that are being worked on (shown in *italics*). One of the key tasks for a leader is to monitor progress of the process improvement projects (or Lean initiatives) underway and to ensure they remain on track. Another purpose for this tool is to keep an eye on prior improvements to ensure they don't slip back into old patterns. In this example, "Monitor XYZ app response time" is a reminder for the leader to ensure the response time for this application, a previous process improvement projects, remains as expected.

You should use your LSW form to remind you of daily/weekly tasks and to keep visible the current improvement efforts underway. With easy visibility to this information, you can more easily monitor activities and keep things on track.

Here are a couple of tips: don't overthink this and do go back and review periodically (you can add a task in your monthly column for reviewing your documents). This way, you can see patterns in the interrupters, see if you're maintaining discipline and holding yourself accountable, and see where you may have an opportunity to modify your work or your template. If you're really bad at establishing new habits, set reminders in your electronic calendar or even alarms on your phone to keep you on track.

Other common elements in LSW are responding to urgent issues, noting interrupters and emergencies (to look for patterns or root cause), daily or weekly tasks such as payroll, budget management, procurement, inventory management, task and incident (new versus break/fix) tickets, etc.

As you can see, there is no single solution that works in all areas. The key for LSW is to develop a process that works for you and the way your team operates. It drives you to behave in a consistent and standardized way. It provides a crucial link to the team and to your manager, which improves communication of key elements of the work. We'll review additional Standard Work examples later in this chapter when we discuss Lean tools.

4. Daily Accountability

In Lean, everyone needs to be held accountable, but as a leader, you have to hold yourself accountable for developing Lean leadership behaviors. In your IT department, this means ensuring you, your managers, and their staff are all trained and held to standards that have been developed, defined, and documented. This can be challenging, especially when Lean is newly implemented. Often there is a vagueness about what managers and leaders are expected to do and from that lack of clarity comes confusion. Confusion leads either to waste or to maintaining the current system, even if it's horribly broken or dysfunctional.

Most Lean experts would agree that you need to start small and build on your gains. Going "big bang" in many cases can simply cause disruption and further confusion. For example, defining standard work is a great place to start. Standard work for one task can be developed and tested. Then, the team can be trained on how to develop and use standard work more generally. From there, you can develop more standard work. Ultimately, this should free up time and resources to do more value-added work. Once you reach that, your team will likely come on board quickly. In IT, the fastest, most sustainable path to Lean value is through standardization, then through automation. Of course, standardization can (and should) entail reviewing the work or the workflow and optimizing it before deeming it to be the standard. By starting with something relatively small and tangible, the entire team can learn the mechanics of the process, see and understand the value of the process, and adopt it from a positive ("this makes sense") perspective rather than a negative ("because I said so") perspective.

5. Visual Controls/Visual Management

Of all the Lean tools and methods used, visual controls seem to be the one that often makes IT people crazy. Most IT people really dislike using paper or even a whiteboard to track anything. This seems to be one of the most challenging "cultural" aspects of Lean and IT. For example, one IT manager complained that she had 47 projects underway and she would spend more time writing them on her board than she would overseeing the work. Clearly, there are two problems here, the first being that she has 47 active projects and the second being that writing all this on a whiteboard may truly be a waste of time. Based on her view of the world, writing these 47 projects on the board does not add value to the project and therefore does not add value to the customer. On the other hand, how can she know and communicate project status at a glance? Her solution was to track her projects in a spreadsheet, print on paper the names of the projects in large type, and attach to her whiteboard. She would then have the project manager write the current task in progress with a status (red if it was not on track, green if it was) and an explanatory note, if needed. An overall project status was also indicated (red or green). In this way, daily work could be monitored more efficiently. The manager could talk about any of the projects on her whiteboard with her team, her peers, or her manager, but no one spent hours just transcribing onto a whiteboard (which would be waste).

Let's get back to the elements of visual management. The purpose is to have always visible the work that is being done to make improvements. The purpose of visual management, more specifically, is

1. To verify that the work is being done (tracking)
2. To track expected versus actual
3. To ensure that deviations (or "misses") are clearly visible and documented
4. To ensure deviation is responded to appropriately
5. To provide an easy-to-use system to spot problems and track actions quickly

One organization that implemented visual management found that certain improvement projects were in the red week after week. While it's good to visually track these issues, it's also important to determine how long something can be in the red before another action is taken. One of the traps you can fall into is to believe you're "doing" because you're "tracking," which is not the same. However, having these data visible for staff, managers, and executives alike can help align efforts and drive accountability and discipline, all key Lean leadership traits.

If you're faced with a challenge where your organization has mandated the use of a particular tool and it doesn't make sense for you, think about what problem you're trying to solve. In the case of the manager with 47 projects, the problem she needed to solve was *project status visibility at a glance*. There are many ways the IT manager could have solved this problem; the one she chose worked for her and her team. If her solution was questioned, she could easily explain the choice by describing the problem and the solution.

Of course, having 47 projects for this one manager also seems like a problem (it may not be, depending on how projects and her IT manager roles are defined). However, by making these projects visible, it provides the opportunity for her director, vice president, CIO, or even CEO to see the workload and determine if a change is needed. (Healthcare is notorious for not wanting to "deselect" IT projects, but this too is part of Lean.)

While visual management often is applied to process improvement initiatives, it can be used for monitoring just about anything. One manager used it to track the various statuses of contracts he was working on because any given time, he seemed to have three or four contracts that were up for renewal, due for review, up for termination or replacement, etc. Representing this on his visual management board helped him track these more effectively, and he added to his LSW a weekly item to update these data.

Tracking status is one purpose of the visual management system, but keep in mind that (to paraphrase Edwards Deming), "without data, it's just your opinion." What data are you using to determine whether things are on track or not? What data will indicate whether your improvement projects are achieving the desired objectives? Recall the example earlier about automating user provisioning? In that case, data were pretty simple. The manager tracked:

a. How many userid requests were made each week
b. How many userids were created each week (for organizational reasons, it wasn't always a simple one-to-one ratio)
c. How many userid problem calls the Service Desk received historically (12 months back, by month)
d. How many userid calls came in daily and weekly
e. Reduction in total duration from request to provisioning

Through tracking these data, the manager discovered that some calls to the Help Desk were being incorrectly coded as userid issues when, in fact, the user had forgotten their password. The team created a new category to peel these issues out, reran their data, and began tracking against the "clean" data. All of these metrics were tracked in a spreadsheet (for ease of calculation and tracking). Daily results were written for the day prior on the board, and weekly results were printed for display on the team board. The solution hits all the requirements of visual management. The information was visual, the process was being tracked, variations from expectations were seen daily, and the team corrected several problems along the way. Since the team worked three shifts and there was no common time all were present, the board helped them see daily and weekly stats and trends, helping them remain visible to the team.

Your visual management will vary depending on your role in the organization, but the common theme is to make visible the key initiatives, metrics, and improvements that are your focus. There are plenty of examples of visual management boards available if you do a quick online search. If your organization does not have a requisite standard, start with something that works for you and take it from there.

In Lean, visual management is typically tied to improvements your team is working on related to strategic goals (sometimes called "True North"). However, making any helpful data visual to improve your ability to manage is certainly acceptable.

6. Discipline

If you've worked in a healthcare organization that lacked discipline, you may cringe at the mention of this. Organizational discipline is a big topic and one we're not going to tackle here. So, let's narrow our focus to the discipline needed to be an effective Lean IT leader. As an IT leader, you need to be consistent in using good work habits, in supporting and re-enforcing the use of standards and processes, and most importantly, in creating a culture of accountability. *You* must be consistent in order to drive these behaviors throughout your span of control and influence.

Even that may sound like a tall order, especially if you work in a healthcare IT environment that is chaotic or overloaded on most days. As with all improvements, you can focus on making one small change and making it stick before taking on the next improvement. In fact, you can practice your Lean skills on yourself by tracking your discipline as a process improvement project itself. Sound trivial? Maybe, but if discipline is not your strong suit, this may be an effective way to change your own behavior in a mindful and consistent way.

If you work in an organization that lacks discipline, it can be challenging and you may have to focus only on areas within your control. Though it may not be your responsibility to address issues outside your department, you can still wield influence in areas outside your control. For example, if your project management process includes a step that requires the operational or clinical owner to describe the resulting change and new standard work that will be required on their part to sustain the change, you can help foster discipline by assisting them in completing this step (if needed). In some cases, the pressure to get a project underway is so strong that you may be tempted to just move on and allow this key step to be skipped "in the interest of time" or "in the interest of being a good business partner." However, we also know this will result in delays, defects, or rework later on, so you're just kicking the problem down the road. *Discipline* in this case probably entails working with your operational or clinical counterpart to review the requirement for this step, working through it with them, or escalating to your manager for assistance if this step is not being completed and is holding up the project.

It's relatively easy to define Lean leadership discipline for your own work and to require it of yourself; it's much more challenging if there is a lack of discipline elsewhere. While you may not be able to completely counteract this problem, with visual controls and with engaged leaders in your organization, you can begin to connect the dots and make small CIs. If you work in an environment where that's just not the case, then focus on instilling discipline in your work and that of your team since we are primarily looking at Lean leadership behaviors that you as a healthcare IT leader can work on. If you're fortunate to work in an organization with good discipline, you can appreciate how this reduces effort and improves outcomes.

Finally, it's important to remember that *practice doesn't make perfect, perfect practice makes perfect*. Developing the discipline to practice perfectly will serve you well in all your endeavors.

We've looked at Lean management system elements very briefly. There are a number of excellent books for further study. Now, let's turn our attention to Lean tools.

Lean Tools

It bears repeating that this chapter contains just a small sampling of information about Lean, and you should use this chapter as a jumping-off point to learn more about Lean in healthcare, particularly the use of Lean tools. As such, we're not going to go into much detail on Lean tools. To paraphrase Lean author Ron Bercaw, "if you want to build a house, you don't start by sawing lumber." To extend this analogy, if you want to build a house, you need a building site, an architectural plan, a builder, and so forth (Lean management system). All that has to happen long before the carpenter begins using a saw or the electrician begins using a drill (Lean tools). And, using the right tool for the right job is also key. It's not helpful if the carpenter needs to saw lumber but only has a hammer. Tools are helpful when deployed at the right time in the right way. That almost always means that Lean management systems should precede the broad deployment of Lean tools. Of course, some Lean tools can be used in any context. For example, we'll discuss 5S, a method of cleaning up your physical environment and keeping it clean.

Lean tools are used at all levels of the organization in different ways just as there are different types of saws suitable for different types of cutting. It's still called a saw whether it's a jigsaw, rip saw, circular saw, or miter saw, but they have distinctly different uses. Lean tools are similar. An A3 (one of the tools discussed in this section) works the same whether being used by an executive or a frontline staff person, but the A3 itself may be very different. The key is to learn about the Lean tools, learn what the appropriate uses are for each of these tools and start with one, get comfortable with it, and add it to your Lean management system. Focusing on all at once will guarantee a lack of focus and therefore lack of success. Start small and build your toolkit just as you would with any other skillset. These commonly used Lean tools are listed here and described in this section.

1. A3/Plan–Do–Check–Act (PDCA)
2. Value stream mapping
3. Continuous improvement (in Japanese, *kaizen*)
4. Standard work
5. Maintaining an orderly workplace (5S, visual workplace)

1. A3/Plan–Do–Check–Act

The A3 document derives from the reference to a commonly used paper size outside of the United States, which is roughly 11 × 17 inches. It is a single sheet of paper used to define and summarize a problem using specific sections (scope, analysis, findings, etc.) or as a project proposal template. The A3 form helps focus thought and facilitates the use of the scientific method often referred to as PDSA (plan, do, *study*, act) or PDCA (plan, do, *check*, act) or even "the four-step method." It is the iterative process used in Lean and is particularly suited for solving problems whose solutions are not evident. Figure 9.7 shows the elements typically used in developing an A3. The boxes for information are quite small in the example; normally you might lay this out in landscape mode on an 11 × 17 piece of paper. That way, you could modify the sizes of the boxes to fit your needs. The

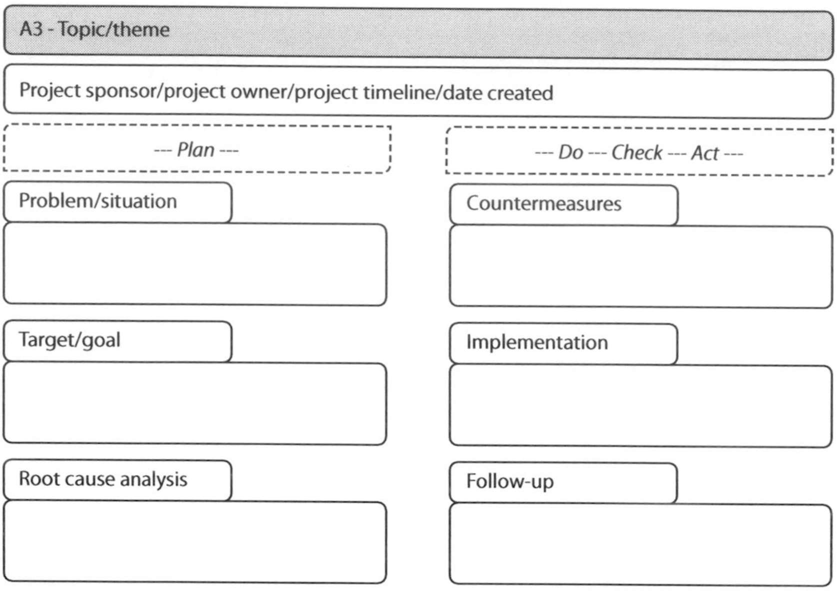

Figure 9.7   A3 elements.

dotted boxes in this example serve only to point out the PDCA cycle within the A3 context. The elements on the left are part of "plan"; the elements on the right are elements of "do, check, act."

An A3 helps focus thinking for solving problems. According to Kim Barnas, author of *Beyond Heroes: A Lean Management System for Healthcare,* "The A3 includes a problem statement, business context, possible root causes, counter-measures, results of experiments and next steps in sections labeled Plan, Do, Study, and Act. The standard form notes the project owner, timelines, and sponsors of the project" (Barnas, p. 187). As you can see from the A3 elements, this format can easily be used for project proposals as well. It's an excellent way to document all the required data for solving complex problems and can (and should) be posted on the visual management board. Is the A3 the right tool for solving all problems? No, it's not. You need the right tool for the job and the A3 is not the cure-all.

For example, if you have a process in the IT department that requires a task to flow back and forth among four different teams and your team decides it's very inefficient and should be changed, do you need an A3? Do you need a PDCA cycle? It depends. Does the team have strong confidence it knows what the root cause is (because it's pretty self-evident) or is the problem still murky and undefined? If the former, then an A3 may not be helpful (may not be the right tool for the task). It might be that a simple map will highlight the problem and the team may then make a recommendation as to how to improve the process. Once that's documented, then the PDCA comes into play as the change is made and results are monitored.

[…more…]

One of the criticisms IT people sometimes make regarding Lean is that using the tools takes more time than solving the problem would. In those cases, it's often a case of the *wrong* tool being deployed. If the tool is not helping to solve the problem or add clarity and instead is only adding perceived busywork, then it's likely not the right tool. Keep this in mind, especially as you begin learning and deploying Lean tools. For example, an A3 is intended to solve problems permanently and is useful with difficult, complex, or persistent problems. On the other hand, if you've deployed a new application and your team discovered you now have three "information handoffs," which they deem to be waste, then a process map or VSM may be the more appropriate (effective, efficient) tool. If so, map out the process, decide on the change, and test it. If you force the use of the wrong tool, you will drive Lean transformation backward. However, also beware of those who will say a tool is not working simply to hijack the process and avoid change. As a leader, your job is to monitor progress and help steer the team to the right tools in the right way at the right time in order to achieve CI. The team will climb on board once the awkwardness of using a new tool subsides if the value of the tool is experienced. Your team should receive value from the process as well.

2. Value Stream Mapping (versus Process Mapping)

Let's define the difference between value stream mapping and process mapping, an activity you may be familiar with from your IT work. These are two different processes, though they are often confused. *A value stream map* (VSM) is a Lean tool that documents all the steps required to deliver value to a customer. It includes work flow and information flow; it identifies steps as value-added (for the customer) or waste. It ends with the customer's request being delivered.

Value stream mapping (VSM) is exactly that—a visual map of a process that provides a detailed, end-to-end view of a process or procedure, each input/output, and each decision point.

The act of creating a VSM can be very powerful when it brings together the stakeholders in the defined process. The level of understanding about things outside one's area of focus increases exponentially, and it tends to help "connect the dots" for all. A great example is doing a VSM of an Emergency Department visit. That crosses all teams in one way or another—including nursing, physicians, care techs, supply chain, IT, biomed, infection control, facilities, security, and more. Driving an understanding of the ED *patient* flow, along with the associated information flows, increases awareness of all involved and contributes not only in solving the problem at hand. It also educates participants about areas outside their own. At its most basic, a VSM defines each step to deliver a product or service to a customer. It identifies the value-added steps and the waste steps. It typically also identifies the wait time or lag time between steps. VSM can include many more data points; we've just provided the simplified view of VSM.

Contrast that to a *process map*, which is the method of documenting all steps in a particular process. Essentially, it is a visual diagram of a workflow.

In your role, you may have used process maps for a variety of purposes, and they can be helpful in documenting and improving IT processes. VSMs are developed from the perspective of the customer and therefore serve a different purpose in Lean IT. If you're interested in learning more, please see the References section at the end of this chapter.

3. Continuous Improvement (in Japanese, Kaizen)

In reading about Lean and Lean in healthcare, you'll come upon the Japanese word *kaizen* (pronounced kye-zen). Translated, it means *good change*, which we typically refer to as *continuous improvement*. CI is a mindset that does not accept the status quo, especially when things are not working optimally. In Lean books, you'll read about all kinds of kaizen activities: kaizen blitz, kaizen events, kaizen projects, etc. Essentially, a CI event can be small and fast (minutes) or slower and longer (days or weeks). The mindset behind CI is to look for opportunities for improvement and use the best method for addressing it. For example, if your development team is working on an interface and spots a problem, they might pause on the spot, discuss the problem, pose a solution, try the solution, and (if successful) implement the solution. That might take 5 minutes and it's done.

Other problems are more complex or are outside the control or scope of the team. For example, perhaps setting up prescription printers to print from the EMR is a complex process due to business and clinical rules and some inefficiencies in the IT department. You might need to facilitate a kaizen event that gathers the clinical build team, the server team, the desktop team, and the information security team. You may also need a representative from pharmacy and a representative or two from nursing, though it depends on the nature of the problem you're trying to solve. If it's "just" an internal workflow issue, an IT team is appropriate. Some Lean practitioners would suggest adding outsiders for a "beginner's mind" perspective, though that's not always needed and you don't want to add a cast of players who are not vital to the process. You may schedule a 1–2 hour meeting to map the process to identify waste, spot opportunities to remove steps, reduce complexity, increase standardization, apply automation, etc. Larger still are CI projects that may tap an even broader group of organizational resources to solve a particularly challenging or complex problem. All are great examples of CI, and they also demonstrate that it's the process of identifying and solving problems (or developing hypotheses to test) that is the hallmark of a CI or kaizen event.

4. Standard Work

We've discussed standard work as part of your Lean leadership management system, but it's also a specific tool that can be used effectively in many different ways at all levels of the organization. For frontline staff, documenting the work you expect to be completed the same way every day or every week can help drive consistency and reduce waste by preventing everyone from doing it their own way. If you're familiar with project management, you can create a work breakdown structure (WBS) for your standard work.

For example, if you have a documented way of submitting a change request so that standard information is always collected, if the review is always completed in the same manner, and if the change control documentation is consistently updated according to this process, you're much less likely to have unexpected problems from changes. Documenting the change management process at a detailed level is an example of standard work. Another example is applying server operating system patches or updating antivirus signature software or building new desktop computers so that they are done the same way, 100% of the time. Standard work reduces or eliminates variation, which can cause many kinds of waste.

If you're interested in creating standard work, you should begin with understanding if your organization already has a standard work template that you can start with. If not, you can find plenty of online resources showing examples of standard work templates that you can modify to suit your needs. Keys to good standard work documents include header data with the following:

1. The standard work is named (so standard work documents can be easily identified).
2. The author or approver is listed along with date created and/or revised.
3. The scope (does this apply to the whole IT department or just the business systems team?).

The body of the document should contain the specific details, or the breakdown of the work, including:

1. Each step, clearly defined
2. A brief reason for the step (why this step matters)
3. A note regarding the proper execution of the step (to ensure correct execution of the step and to eliminate variation)

Once completed, you should be able to give the document to anyone with the technical skills to accomplish the task, and they should be able to do that task exactly the same way every time. As important, everyone who has to do this task is trained in the standard work, and everyone does it the same way every time. Imagine if you no longer had to worry about whether staff were documenting changes or applying patches or building computers consistently? Once you implement this, you can monitor results. If the steps need to change, modify and test again. Once it's deemed to be efficient and accurate, monitor results (so you and your team don't stray from standard) and move on to another task to be standardized. Continue until all routine and repeated work is documented as standard work.

This may take a while, but the gains your team will experience along the way will be worth it. At first, they may complain that they know how to patch a server. Having standard work then allows them to focus on more difficult, challenging, or interesting problems. It also provides the perfect document for training new staff. No longer will knowledge transfer be random or subjective. Instead, it's standardized, documented, and available for anyone coming in the door to instantly master.

5. Maintaining an Orderly Workplace (5S, Visual Workplace)

Last but not least, this tool also applies equally but differently at the staff and leadership levels. Staff who work in a disorganized area are less productive and more stressed than those who don't. If you've ever watched a cooking show on TV, you'll likely have heard the French term, *mise en place*, (it sounds like "me's on plahs"), which roughly translated means *the arrangement* or *the placement*. It's used to indicate that a chef must set up (arrange) their station in an orderly fashion to ensure that all needed tools and ingredients are on hand and organized before cooking begins. If you've ever started making something at home only to discover halfway through that you're missing a key ingredient, you understand the value of *mise en place*.

This relates directly to Lean. Creating and maintaining an orderly workplace enables you to be productive instead of wasting time searching through a tall pile of unfiled papers to locate needed information, for example. It also pertains to your data center, your network closets, your software code, your application documentation, your EMR flowsheet rows, your reports, and your shared network folders, to name a few.

The process of organizing the workspace is often referred to as 5S. The five "S"s are as follows:

1. *Sort*. Decide what's needed, what's not.
2. *Straighten*. Organize the space—file documents, arrange equipment, etc.
3. *Shine*. Now that you've removed excess items and organized them, you can clean the space and maintain that cleanliness with periodic review and upkeep.
4. *Standardize*. Develop standard work such as putting things away at the end of each shift, to maintain standards.
5. *Sustain*. Ensure that the workspace remains tidy.

You might believe this is only applicable to nursing units or supply closets or warehouses. However, it can be easily applied to the data center, the cabling in a data closet, a training classroom, or your desk. In addition, it can be used to keep electronic workplaces tidy as well—periodically deleting unused files on network shares, obsolete electronic documents, or cleaning up code versions no longer needed.

Next Steps

If you're new to Lean or struggling to make sense of Lean in your IT department, there is hope. Though there are many ways to approach this, we'll provide one sample method that has worked so you can understand how to approach your own Lean journey. Feel free to kick the tires, try it, modify it, or throw it out entirely. The key is to develop your understanding of Lean leadership and Lean tools so you can successfully transform your IT department into a highly functional, value-added department.

1. Develop Your Own Plan

First, map out the Leadership management system elements and the Lean tools according to how you see them fitting into your current role. Essentially, you'll perform a gap analysis and develop your own action plan. This is one of the most powerful steps you can take. Use this document (in whatever format you've selected) as a living, breathing document. Think of it as putting yourself on an action plan where you are defining requirements, what success looks like, and what behaviors will drive that success. Make sure you also prioritize and identify what you will do first. If you attack five things at once, you'll likely fail. Create a timeline so you know how long you're going to commit to learning. Implement and master one element before moving that to "monitoring" status and tackling the next item. Figure 9.8 shows an example to get you started.

Make sure you review and update this document weekly, just as you might if you were on an action plan. Hold yourself accountable and develop discipline. You can do this without ever using the word *Lean* with your team.

2. Start Small, Experiment Frequently

By now, you recognize this is a recurring theme. It is a fact that most humans have trouble sustaining positive change. Unfortunately, we're masters at sustaining negative change like not exercising or not eating well. In order to make positive, meaningful, and lasting change, you need to break down that change into small bites. To paraphrase advice from a behavioral modification coach, break change down into "laughably small change." For example, start with just writing your To Do list each morning when you arrive at work. Sound silly? It's the beginning of standard work.

Item	Description	Start	Est. End	Self-Coaching Notes	Checkpoint
Lean LMS	Understand elements of Lean Leadership Management System	1-Feb	1-Mar	Create notes on each of the key elements	7-Feb
Lean LMS	Develop draft of LMS system for self	15-Feb	1-Mar	First draft of personal LMS approach	21-Feb
Lean LSW	Understand Leader Standard Work and develop draft	1-Mar	15-Mar	Develop first draft of LSW and begin experimenting	7-Mar
Lean Tools	Understand Lean tools	15-Mar	22-Mar	Map Lean tools to existing problems	20-Mar
Lean Tools	Teach Lean tools (1–2)	23-Mar	1-Apr	Engage team in learning top 1 or 2 tools	27-Mar
Lean Tools	Pilot Lean tools (1–2 tools, 1–2 problems)	2-Apr	30-Apr	Develop first pilot process improvement using tools	12-Apr

Figure 9.8   Lean leadership personal action plan example.

Once that becomes a habit, you can tackle another change. If starting the day with your To Do list doesn't work and you choose to start the day with a team huddle, make the change immediately and monitor results. Don't sit and ponder this type of change; just do it and see what happens. These types of small changes and continuous refinements will lead you to the solution that works for you and your team. Be methodical in your approach and disciplined in your behavior as you make changes and monitor the results. Change one thing at a time (basic IT troubleshooting advice still holds true here); see what works. Then continue on.

3. Tackle Small Add-Ons Sequentially

With the pressure to deliver results and the desire to implement Lean, you may be tempted to deploy five tools at once. That might be a mistake. On the other hand, you may experiment with one tool in one circumstance and another tool in a different scenario. For example, maybe your data center is a mess and you decide to have the team try using 5S to clean it up and sustain a clean, orderly environment. In another case, though, you may have an application that users are calling in about on a daily basis because a recent change significantly increased the time it takes to do a simple but daily task. You may choose to do an A3, a value stream map or a process map to tackle that problem.

As you master the Lean management system and thoughtfully deploy tools, you can monitor results and adjust accordingly. Again, this goes back to your master plan created in Step 1, which allows you to track successes and determine the best next step. It goes back to making small CIs.

4. Align with Organizational Initiatives

If there is tremendous organizational or executive pressure for you to quickly implement Lean in your area, one of the most effective things you can do is sit down with your manager (or whomever they designate) to review your action plan (Step 1). This can have two powerful effects. First, it shows your commitment to the process and demonstrates that you've given this topic serious thought. Second, it provides a roadmap for you to follow or for your organization's Lean leadership to weigh in on. Perhaps you've slightly misunderstood the use of a tool or you don't quite lock onto the elements of Lean leadership the way your organization expects. This document can provide the opening for an honest dialog so you can fine-tune your plan and proceed.

Finally, your Lean initiatives in IT can't live in a vacuum. Once you get a handle on your own world, you need to extend your awareness and participate in organizational events. Not only will your "outsider" perspective lend fresh eyes to a non-IT problem or process, but you'll learn a lot about how your organization works and where its challenges lie. As an IT leader, this perspective is crucial to your overall success, and participating in organizational initiatives is an excellent way to gain that knowledge and further hone your leadership skills. The reverse is also true. Look for appropriate opportunities to involve people from the rest of the organization IT-centric kaizen events. You'll gain fresh perspectives and build new relationships that are crucial for long-term success.

Summary

This chapter on Lean leadership ties together many of the concepts in the book regarding leadership. We started by discussing Lean and ITIL to demonstrate how process improvement can be applied to IT frameworks. We also discussed Lean leadership and Lean tools to give you an initial glimpse into how Lean can be applied to IT in healthcare. Leadership in Lean is the key to success. As a healthcare IT leader, you may have been asked to implement Lean in your area but weren't sure where to start or how you could reconcile some of the seeming conflicts between Lean in your organization and the work of IT. Hopefully, this chapter gives you a running start, some ideas worth considering, and a jumping-off point for further exploration.

For Lean to be successful, it needs to be actively championed by leadership and adopted across the entire organization. That can be a long and slow process. Organizations that have undertaken this journey have had varying degrees of success. Adopting Lean is no guarantee of success nor does it mean your organization won't ever make errors or slide backward. That said, adopting a methodology like Lean that drives standardization and reduces variability will absolutely improve quality over time.

At minimum, we are being compelled to find ways to reduce waste and streamline operations. Using Lean in conjunction with your existing IT frameworks can help you deliver those results. At the end of it all, we are being called upon to examine our areas of responsibility and deliver more value and, ultimately, improve patient care.

References

For more on this topic, visit http://susansnedaker.com/leading-hit.

QR9.1

Barnas, Kim with Emily Adams, *Beyond Heroes: A Lean Management System for Healthcare*, Appleton, WI: ThedaCare Center for Healthcare Value, 2014.

Bell, Steven C. and Michael A. Orzen, *Lean IT: Enabling and Sustaining Your Lean Transformation*, Boca Raton, FL: CRC Press, 2011.

Bercaw, Ronald G., *Lean Leadership for Healthcare: Approaches to Lean Transformation*, Boca Raton, FL: CRC Press, 2013.

Chalice, Robert, *Improving Healthcare Using Toyota Lean Production Methods*, 2nd Edition, American Society for Quality, Milwaukee, WI: Quality Press, 2007.

Charron, Rich, H. James Harrington, Frank Voehl and Hal Wiggin, *The Lean Management Systems Book*, Boca Raton, FL: CRC Press, 2014.

Damelio, Robert, *The Basics of Process Mapping*, 2nd Edition, Boca Raton, FL: CRC Press, 2011.

Kenney, Charles, *Transforming Health Care: Virginia Mason Medical Center's Pursuit of the Perfect Patient Experience*, Boca Raton, FL: CRC Press, 2011.

Madison, Daniel J., *Process Mapping, Process Improvement, and Process Management: A Practical Guide to Enhancing Work and Information Flow*, Chico, CA: Paton Press LLC, 2005.

Rother, Mike and John Shook, *Learning to See: Value-Stream Mapping to Create Value and Eliminate Muda*, Version 1.4, Cambridge, MA: Lean Enterprise Institute, 2009.

Toussaint, John, MD with Emily Adams, *Management on the Mend: The Healthcare Executive Guide to System Transformation*, Appleton, WI: ThedaCare Center for Healthcare Value, 2015.

Toussaint, John, MD and Roger A. Gerard with Emily Adams, *On the Mend: Revolutionizing Healthcare to Save Lives and Transform the Industry*, Cambridge, MA: Lean Enterprise Institute, Inc., 2010.

Chapter 10

Fast Forward

Overview

The chapters of this book have provided a roadmap toward becoming a better healthcare IT leader. We've focused on the fundamentals of healthcare IT leadership to provide actionable information for you. In this last chapter of the book, we're going to look at the current state of healthcare IT—the drivers and demands—that we are all dealing with. These are topics you may recognize as initiatives in your own organization or things you've read about in industry news. As you progress in your healthcare IT leadership role, these topics will certainly impact your environment, the work you do, and the capabilities you must develop. Five high-level categories of initiatives impacting healthcare IT today fall broadly under *optimize*, *engage*, *innovate*, *analyze*, and *transform*. We'll look at current trends through this framework.

Optimize

We've discussed optimization from several viewpoints throughout this book, especially in Chapter 4. It's a solid base for everything else you do. This includes streamlining operations, improving service delivery processes, and working to reduce costs related to applications and infrastructure by fully leveraging existing assets. We'll review some of the current trends in operational optimization. In addition, we'll discuss one specific aspect of optimization, which is a very active topic of discussion in healthcare IT today: electronic medical record (EMR) optimization. In recent years, the U.S. government, along with numerous other authoritative sources, have cited concerns about patient safety related to the user of the EMR. With that, let's look at operations briefly.

Operational Optimization

Cost optimization is always a topic for healthcare IT leaders, and as we look to the future with vastly different payment and reimbursement systems for physicians, hospitals, and other providers, we know we need to be partners in this transformation.

1. Consolidate, Update, Standardize Technology

The most fundamental thing you can do as an IT leader is to review your own areas of responsibility and drive out waste and reduce cost. The goal isn't to shrink your budget or reduce your staff; the goal is to optimize the use of the financial resources for which you are responsible. We've discussed looking at applications for redundancy, overlaps, or gaps; replacing expensive-to-maintain applications or equipment for more efficient ones; reducing costs through standardization and optimization. We discussed ways to improve operations through Lean improvements. These methods have become standard work for leaders in healthcare IT.

2. Improve Software License and Access Management

The current trends are moving software to the cloud and software as a service (SaaS). Though there are still many companies that sell software licenses with annual maintenance fees, many are shifting to annual subscriptions. This shift can mask cost increases and can also lead to slowly increasing operational costs that go almost unnoticed. To counter these potential increases, consider software that helps you manage licenses and user access. By provisioning only what is required and licensed, and by rescinding unused software or access, you keep costs down, avoid potential penalties, and improve your overall security stance.

3. Improve Procurement and Contracting

Depending on how your organization runs, you may be responsible for procuring hardware and software. That means working with vendors, getting quotes, reading contracts and statements of work, understanding the legal and operational implications of the documents, and negotiating the best deal possible for your organization. While every company deals with this function differently, you should actively work to improve your skills in all these areas so you know you're getting the best deal for your organization.

4. Review and Update Your Information Security Strategies

Information security technologies and teams are core capabilities in today's environment. Your security strategies are also part of your risk management and insurance policies. Reviewing your security strategies along with other operations will ensure you don't have unneeded overlap or any gaps. Many security tools overlap with network, systems, or access management tools, so working across the IT teams can potentially yield optimized capabilities and reduced costs. Working with your risk management group, your organization may be able to adjust insurance premiums based on the security tools in place.

5. Develop Technology Roadmaps

Roadmaps help you understand what you have today and where you should be headed tomorrow. This is where optimization and innovation can intersect. Real-time communications is a great example. How many different systems do you have in place today? Analog phones, digital phones, Voice-over-Internet Protocol (VoIP) phones, cell phones, pagers, wireless voice badges, and secure text are several that come immediately to mind. Do they integrate with each other? Do they overlap? Is there confusion about how, when, and where various technologies should be used? What do your end users need? What do they say about the current solutions? Compile these data and develop a high-level technology roadmap to address these current and emerging needs in a holistic manner. You may find savings or efficiencies from doing so; you may improve service levels or end-user communications. Optimally, you may find opportunities to innovate.

Finally, begin measuring IT value through business outcomes. For example, don't just report out the costs of a project; report out the benefits realized by the project. When the conversation shifts from cost to value, you can more effectively articulate the worth you and your team are bringing to the organization.

Fine-tuning your IT costs and operations is a great first step. Now, let's look at EMR optimization.

Patient Safety and the Electronic Health/Medical Record (EHR/EMR)

A May 2016 report from the U.S. Department of Health and Human Services Office of the National Coordinator for Health Information Technology titled "Goals and Priorities for Health Care Organizations to Improve Safety Using Health IT" lays the foundation of the problem quite well.

> Over the past decade, the adoption and use of health information technology (health IT) increased at unprecedented rates. Due in large part to the Centers for Medicare & Medicaid Services (CMS) Electronic Health Records (EHR) Incentive Programs (1) and the provisions of Meaningful Use (MU) (2), the vast majority of both physician practices (over 478,000, or 72% of eligible professionals) and hospitals (over 4,800, or 99% of eligible hospitals) have now adopted certified EHR technologies (3). At the same time, health IT vendors have expanded many other aspects of health IT functionality, enabling advanced decision support, telehealth, and data warehousing, which provide the foundation for quality assessment, research, and predictive analytics.
>
> A substantial body of evidence now supports the claim that health IT improves the quality and safety of health care (4), but that health IT has not yet reached its full potential. A host of residual and emerging challenges limit the impact of health IT, including issues of usability, interoperability, and unintended consequences generally. (Graber, 2016, p. 1, original footnotes omitted, QR10.7)

The document goes on to recommend six categories of activities that healthcare organizations should undertake to improve patient safety with respect to the EMR. The recommendations in this report are compiled from several different industry sources including the Office of the National Coordinator (ONC) and The Joint Commission (TJC). They include

1. Leadership
2. Culture and engagement
3. Planning and readiness
4. Installation
5. Training and proficiency support
6. Upgrades and conversions

As you can see, these activities are less about the technology, per se, and more about the *people* and *processes* surrounding the technology.

[...more...]

There is growing focus on how EMRs contribute to (or detract from) patient safety. A March 2015 Sentinel Event Alert from the Joint Commission focused on this. Though certified EMRs are developed using the User Centered Design framework, what happens after the EMR is deployed is another story. People in IT designing screens and workflows, configuring, and building out the EMR may have little if any experience in optimizing the user experience. Reducing complexity, streamlining the electronic workflow, and simplifying/standardizing data within the EMR are key areas of focus. This problem is partly the result of lack of strong IT governance—both when EMRs were being deployed (learning curve) and as part of ongoing operations (lack of process). Effective IT governance (Chapter 3) can help avoid or counter some of these problems. Lean or process improvement initiatives (Chapter 9) can be used to remediate the current state and improve the EMR going forward. For more on The Joint Commission Sentinel Alert #54, see the References section at the end of this chapter (The Joint Commission, 2015, QR10.23).

A May 2016 blog post by Kristen Lee titled "MGH physician weighs in on avoiding EHR errors" echoes these fundamentals. The physician, Dhruv Khullar, is a resident at Massachusetts General Hospital in Boston. He discussed this topic during a panel discussion at the Health Datapalooza conference in Washington, DC. He discussed recent research findings as well as his own experience as a doctor using the EMR. According to the article, "One study found that only 5% of cases accurately list a patient's medication in his or her EHR while another study found that 50% of medications listed are inaccurate, Khullar said. Furthermore, another study found that 60% of doctor's daily notes have at least one error. Khullar explained that these EHR errors are happening because of the way EHRs are set up and how they allow physicians to enter patient information" (Lee, 2016, QR10.11).

Khullar makes several recommendations regarding how physicians interact with the EMR and how EMRs should function. While these may reflect the view of one physician, they provide insight into the problem healthcare EMR use is facing today.

1. *Only capture what is most important.* Copy/paste and "note bloat" is creating massive amounts of useless data.
2. *Make the art of story gathering and storytelling mandatory.* Distilling and communicating the important information must be a priority.
3. *Encourage more patients to read their medical records.* If physicians knew patients would be reviewing their medical records, the data might be entered in a more succinct or useful fashion. Also, patients who read their medical records can correct errors or inaccuracies and more fully engage in their own care and health.
4. *EHRs should be like scrolling through an iPhone.* Make EHRs something people *want* to engage with. As a healthcare IT leader, you are not responsible for what and how a physician documents, but you can influence other factors.

If your area of responsibility includes clinical applications in any manner, you may be asked to lead or participate in EMR improvement efforts. There is a growing body of research available on recommendations for improving the EMR to improve patient safety. This is one of the next frontiers in healthcare and healthcare IT and one that would be worth additional research on your part. Even if this area does not directly impact your work, it's important to be aware of emerging trends in healthcare IT so you can be a more effective leader in your organization.

EMR Usability and Optimization

Beyond (or including) patient safety, EMR usability and optimization is one of the biggest topics in healthcare IT these days for several reasons. A recent statistic indicated that medical error was estimated to be the third leading cause of death in the United States (Makary, 2016, QR10.12). That's a pretty alarming statistic. Most would argue that many of these errors are preventable. In fact, that was what the big push to implement EMRs was originally all about—reducing errors, improving quality and outcomes of care. So what happened?

Many EMR systems were implemented five or ten years ago under very different circumstances. Organizations weren't really sure what a post-EMR world would look like. Most took a big plunge into the unknown as they did their best to automate clinical operations. As regulatory and reimbursement requirements have changed, so too has the EMR. However, in many organizations, the evolution of the EMR has been a bit more haphazard than thoughtful. Requests for change or optimization were often simply accepted and implemented. Frequently, there was no real thought given to an application roadmap. Ironically, we often had a better vision for our supply chain management software than for our EMR. One of the reasons for this is the diversity of users of the EMR (versus supply chain management, for example). Given the complex needs of the organization, it's understandable that a unified approach to optimization was often lacking. That's not to say that there weren't consolidated initiatives that bundled things together as a project to improve use of the EMR. Those happened in every organization that implemented an EMR. Yet, many healthcare organizations today find themselves at a new level of maturity. We need to better understand what the EMR is intended to do, how it is impacting workflows, how it is impacted by caregiver workflows, the limitations of the software, and the ever-increasing requests for interconnections and interfaces.

[…more…]

The Evolution of the EMR

By Renee Paul, MBA, RN, CNOR, Experienced Perioperative Services Leader

As I think about EMRs and how it's impacted how we deliver patient care, it brings mixed feelings. I think as much as it has brought some standardization with documentation, it has created a patient chart that is often incomplete. To some degree, we have created a healthcare mentality of "click-it" charting and often we are failing to document the important information. One of the challenges with the current state of EMRs is that there are so many gaps in the documentation that it creates records that don't clearly reflect the care of the patient.

For example, a friend received a copy of her medical records from a provider and it was the first time I saw a medical record printed out from an EMR. Though I'm an experienced surgical nurse, it felt like I needed special training just to decipher the flow of care. I think it's much more complicated to follow in printed format, which is something I don't think many people pay attention to. However, I can say, the printed record at least was legible.

One of the challenges I've had with an EMR is during trauma cases, emergency cases or cases "gone wrong." It hasn't increased efficiencies when you have emergent needs during a surgical case. For instance, the need for blood products *stat* to OR. It is not always an easy process to place orders in EMR for blood products or x-ray, etc., to come to OR. As a matter of fact, whenever a trauma case comes into OR, I've had to put an additional nurse in the room to manage the documentation.

As an experienced perioperative leader, my thought is around the return on investment (ROI) and whether or not hospitals realize that they can implement a great EMR system, but we still need to add resources/employees in some situations. The EMR is a tool to assist, but it's a tool that sometimes requires a dedicated resource.

On the flip side are really short surgical cases that are done within 30 minutes. The nurses tend to "pre-document" the things that are standardized in order to be ahead of the game. Often times, they complain that the surgeon is done and they still haven't completed the documentation of their cases. I have personally worked those cases to get a better idea of the frustration and I completely understand it. However, as the leader, I wouldn't tolerate "pre-documentation" for obvious reasons, but mostly because it's dangerous. We haven't been able to fine-tune EMR to be adaptable/flexible for the large variations in its use. I think that's what adds to the inefficiencies with EMR, at least from a surgical perspective.

This doesn't make me think that the EMR is a failure. It's just not finished. There are still too many work-arounds used that increase risk of medication errors and other patient safety concerns. Management and leadership need to do a better job with nursing staff and education to retrain people on proper EMR documentation. When EMRs are implemented, nurses are shown how to document, but because the EMR is always changing and evolving, I don't think we give enough thought to how nurses need to be continuously updated on the proper use of the EMR as it evolves.

With all of that being said, I think that the EMR is still in its early stages. I also think we're in the early stages of understanding how well healthcare providers work within EMR. It doesn't paint a complete picture yet, and if it does, it takes a lot more time to do it. Not bad for Phase 1, but our work is just beginning.

Paul's comments are quite insightful, especially to those in IT who don't often get a chance to hear directly from clinical leaders at such a detailed level. Yet Paul's comments and perspective are echoed throughout all areas of healthcare. The EMR is a good start, but there are still problems to be addressed. If we reflect back on the material in Chapter 9 on Lean and process improvement, we can see how these two topics connect and why many healthcare organizations are looking to Lean to help improve all aspects of operations, including the EMR.

It's no wonder, then, that many EMR implementations are being scrutinized with a fresh perspective. Many organizations are initiating some sort of EMR improvement program. Some organizations are coming to the conclusion that the EMR application they selected five or ten years ago does not meet the future needs of the organization and they are opting to replace the EMR application. That's an enormous undertaking that is disruptive on several fronts. Other organizations are looking at their EMR software and deciding it is the system they want but it has gotten off-course. Inconsistent build, too many clicks, inability to locate critical data quickly, and too much unstructured data (such as "notes" or "comments" fields) are wreaking havoc on many organizations. The proliferation of Internet-connected devices (usually referred to as the Internet of Things or IoT) is also pushing healthcare IT organizations to look at the EMR and other medical data in a new light.

So, where does that leave all of us in healthcare IT? The two major trends underway are EMR *optimization* and *replacement*. These are elements to consider.

1. *Strategic alignment for EMR projects*—All projects related to EMR expansion and optimization should be part of a larger strategic plan. This may be outside your span of control, but you can help the organization focus on this by frequently asking how a project aligns with strategy.

2. *Process improvement before implementation*—As tempting as it is to simply build or configure new software, test, train, and deploy it, you won't ever get to an optimized state if you do that. To the extent possible, you should work with your clinical counterparts to really look at the way the organization wants the work to be done and optimize your processes before building out your software.

3. *Usability studies and improvements*—Some EMR vendors are becoming quite savvy about usability beyond the basic requirements. Newer web-based EMR systems look and feel more like an online shopping site than an EMR, and that can be a good thing. One of the things online shopping has taught us is the value of streamlining and simplicity. Great online sites work to minimize clicks to encourage the customer to shop more effectively, driving up revenue per transaction. EMR vendors need to use the same perspective, to drive the value (of medical data) up per transaction. Reducing clicks, better organizing screens, reducing duplication, etc., are all aspects of optimization beyond just the workflow. EMR vendors with forward-thinking IT departments are taking a hard look at this.

4. *Patient centric view*—It's easy to think about physicians, nurses, pharmacists, respiratory therapists, patient care technicians, etc., when building out the EMR. How often do we stop and think about it from the patient's perspective? Innovative organizations are doing exactly that. If we look at a physician office visit, an imaging (x-ray, CT, MRI, etc.) appointment, a hospital admission, or an emergency department visit from the patient perspective, it looks very different than the traditional view. We need to incorporate this into our improvement efforts.

5. *Data and analytics*—This is a small paragraph for an enormous topic. All the electronic data captured in all the EMRs pose a massive opportunity to better understand drivers of healthcare outcomes. It goes far beyond the canned or customized reports or clinical decision support (a variety of tools to enhance decision-making in the clinical workflow). Developing a data warehouse and building a business intelligence capability certainly relates directly to data in the EMR, but it goes far beyond it as well to include other organizational data (supply chain, financial, other clinical systems, etc.). Where and how we store data in the EMR, how we define data fields, what questions we ask, how we correlate data, how we interpret the data, and finally, how we act upon those data are areas of serious effort in just about every healthcare organization today. Your role may not be in the business intelligence, data warehousing, or analytics area of your IT department (or that function may exist outside of IT altogether, in the Quality department, for instance), but you should be aware of this topic because along with EMR optimization, it is the next major frontier for healthcare organizations.

6. *Security*—Everything in healthcare IT today is vulnerable to attack, from viruses to ransomware to end-user errors and beyond. Application owners, business and process analysts, security engineers, and end users must work together effectively. Ensuring business needs are met while maintaining necessary technical and process security controls is the "new normal" for healthcare organizations.

7. *Interoperability*—Though the number of clinical systems has proliferated, including EMRs, they remain silos of information. There is an increasing drive to develop interoperability between systems. This is intended to drive more seamless and integrated patient data, but ultimately improve care. The challenges have been many, most notably that the major EMR vendors are competitors in this space. However, the field has shifted and it's clear that interoperability among organizations, EMRs, imaging systems, and other clinical systems is a requirement going forward. Though much of the work in this space will be outside your control as a healthcare IT leader, it's a topic you should be locked in on. Your interface teams may already be at work on these initiatives, especially if you've been involved with a local or regional healthcare information exchange (HIE) initiative.

The topic of optimizing and streamlining the EMR has gained traction in recent years and will continue to be a major focus for organizations for the foreseeable future. Today, nearly all organizations have an EMR, and most are now turning their efforts toward optimizing the system to help improve patient outcomes. That was the promise when everyone began this journey—and we all have a vested interest to see that enormous investment pay off. For more on this topic, see the References section at the end of the chapter.

Engage

Engagement is certainly a buzzword right now. More specifically, *patient engagement* seems to be the center of the target in healthcare at the moment. There are two key drivers. First, consumers are more informed (and misinformed) about healthcare due to the proliferation and availability of health and medical information on the Internet. In addition, the more engaged patients are in their own health, the better the outcomes achieved. These two factors are driving providers and patients into more active partnership, often through the use of technology. One of the unique challenges to healthcare is that the target audience for healthcare is everyone. Unlike many other kinds of businesses that target specific age or income demographics, healthcare is pervasive and what works for a 23-year-old female in an urban location doesn't work at all for a 92-year-old male in a rural setting, for example. For that reason, patient engagement, while focused heavily on the use of technology, cannot solely be about technology. As a healthcare IT leader, your focus will be on the use of technology in patient engagement, and that's our focus in this section.

There are a number of other current and emerging trends in this field—and there will no doubt be more when you read this book. Here are a few that are hot topics right now.

Unified Patient Portal

One of the early patient engagement tools was patient portals, providing limited access to the patient's medical data in the EMR. These are still widely promoted by healthcare organizations, in particular because there are requirements for engagement tied to Meaningful Use. If we look at it from a patient perspective, however, the portal solution still falls short. If you have a primary care provider with one EMR and a hospital stay with a different EMR and a specialist with yet another EMR, you may have three different patient portals with three different logins with three different types of data in three different formats. Better, but still not optimal. This is a rapidly evolving field, especially as requirements to share data through health information exchanges increase.

There are new companies moving into this space who are promoting the patient side of the experience. Companies like these are attempting to consolidate the patient's medical data, regardless of provider. That makes sense from the perspective of a person who sees different providers in different locations or providers in different networks of care. Think of an 88-year-old man who moves from New York to Georgia to be closer to his son. The son has assumed a caregiver role and has no idea if his father brought all of his medical record paperwork with him. He's trying to sort through decades of documents and photocopies and a few x-rays as well. If a consolidated portal for his father existed, all his data would be accessible in one place from all points of care. This is the objective of a number of startups focused on the patient side of the equation.

However, there are also organizations that provide a range of services from primary care to acute care (hospital) to lab and imaging services, for example, that are trying to as least consolidate the data they have into a patient portal. In some cases, health information exchanges can be (or will be) tapped to pull additional data from other sources. So, the goal of a unified patient record is starting to coalesce, albeit in sometimes halting, incomplete steps.

As a healthcare IT leader, this may be something that falls within your span of control or influence. Understanding what solutions your organization has in place today along with what your patient population would find most helpful and valuable is a good starting point. If this does not directly impact your work, it may sometime soon. Whether you're called upon to create the web portal, secure the data on the portal, develop the interfaces, or define the data sources, you may have a role to play in designing, developing, and delivering a unified patient portal for your organization.

Secure Messaging

Most of us use text messaging on our smartphones daily. It's become a widely used communication tool and tends to follow demographic lines. Those under the age of about 25 right now think of email as "old school"—something their parents or grandparents use. Texting has gained wide acceptance and it's beginning to infiltrate provider–patient communication channels. Some innovative physician practices enable texting between a provider and a patient. Some online providers allow patients to upload photos for diagnosis. For example, a photo of a rash, a mole, or an infection might tell the provider as much about the condition as an office visit would. The ability of patients to communicate medical data via secure channels to their provider is growing.

How does this affect you in your IT department? The answer depends largely on what sort of organization you work in. However, you should certainly be looking at your patient population and their communication needs with respect to your organization. Work with your providers to understand how they interact with patients, how they would like to interact with patients, and how patients have indicated they would like to interact. From there, you can develop a strategy for moving from the static patient portal-type communication to a more flexible and timely communication model that meets patient and provider needs.

Social Media

The use of social media has gained traction in healthcare in recent years and has been used by some organizations in very innovative ways. At a high level, social media can help drive healthcare literacy, which can improve outcomes. It can also promote provider–patient communication outside of the secure one-to-one methods like phone calls, emails, or texts. A very common example is when someone leaves a physician or nurse practitioner appointment with a diagnosis. Patient education typically comes right at the end of the visit, with someone going over next steps, care instructions, etc. However, that information is often quickly forgotten or misconstrued for a variety of reasons. The same holds true when a patient is discharged from the hospital with a packet of discharge instructions, follow-up care recommendations, etc. It can be overwhelming and, as a result, ignored. Failure to fill prescriptions or make follow-up care appointments accounts for a large number of hospital readmissions. The World Health Organization data suggest that medication adherence in developed countries is only about 50%. Often failure to adhere is tied to confusion or misunderstanding.

Many healthcare organizations have begun using their social media sites to provide some of this information so that a patient can refer back to these data when they are ready to use it. For example, general messages about filling prescriptions or information on post-cardiac care that applies to all patients might be an appropriate use of social media.

Social media has also been very effective in building communities. For example, people with diabetes or heart disease can connect via a provider's or organization's social media presence to connect with others who are going through the same medical challenges or even those who are "simply" working on prevention and wellness. By providing the opportunity for people to connect with others in similar situations, healthcare organizations can facilitate a sense of community, a source for support, and an outlet for accurate and helpful information for patient care.

The use of Twitter is also gaining popularity in healthcare. In fact, a project called the Healthcare Hashtag Project was started to make Twitter useful for providers and patients. A list of current healthcare hashtags can be found at http://www.symplur.com/healthcare-hashtags/ (Symplur, n.d. QR10.22), and you can see topics by category and those that are trending. This is a great example of how patients can connect via Twitter to discuss an incredibly diverse set of healthcare topics.

Many healthcare IT departments are beginning to partner with their communications departments to augment web presence and to develop social media sites. Though the ongoing maintenance of social media accounts typically requires a dedicated resource (typically not an IT resource), there certainly is an opportunity for IT leaders to help facilitate and foster the use of social media for patient engagement.

Wearables and Patient-Generated Data

Probably one of the most pervasive examples of wearables in healthcare are fitness trackers or step counters. As technology advanced and the devices became more sophisticated, a tracker could fit in your pocket or on your wrist and transmit data wirelessly to your smartphone app or your computer. The device can track your steps, your aerobic efforts, your sleep time, and more. Fitness trackers and a wide variety of apps are available on smartphone platforms as well. Healthcare organizations and developers alike are creating new apps and application programming interfaces (APIs) to enable these data connections.

While much of these data are currently for personal use, meaning they don't connect to your physician's EMR for example, the data are becoming more interconnected. Mobile cardiac monitoring devices, for example, can send heart rhythms wirelessly to a cloud-based server, which can then interface with your doctor's EMR. There are an increasing number of mobile monitoring technologies, from fitness trackers to smart scales to cardiac monitors and more, which can be monitored in near-real-time and results can be stored for later viewing and/or analysis.

How does this impact healthcare? Consider the patient who has surgery on a foot or ankle and part of the postsurgical rehabilitation includes walking. Using a fitness tracker to track actual steps taken can help both the patient and the provider see real data and progress over time. Perhaps the recommendation is to walk 2,000 steps per day for the first three days, then increase to 4,000 steps by the seventh day, etc. The fitness tracker provides data versus the patient's perception that they met the minimum daily requirement.

As an IT leader, how does all of this intersect with your world? As personal devices, wearables, and patient-generated data all become more commonplace, it will be our job to help connect the dots. This really means starting with your patient's perspective to understand what would add value for them. It means talking with your providers about how they see these technologies improving their ability to provide patient care. And then it means finding time, resources, and capabilities to develop innovative programs that meet patient, provider, and organizational needs. It's certainly a tall order for most healthcare IT organizations today, but as the climate shifts, we expect to see more organizational focus on driving better outcomes through these methods.

Though we've only brushed the surface of this emerging field, the key takeaway is that this is one of the most rapidly evolving fields in healthcare IT today. Regardless of your specific role in IT, it will be important for you to understand how patient engagement is evolving and how the consumerization of healthcare is impacting healthcare delivery and the relationship between a patient and a provider. Reading industry blogs, subscribing to email newsletters, and keeping your eye on healthcare IT websites such as HIMSS.org are all great ways to stay abreast of growing and emerging trends. If this is an area of responsibility for you in healthcare IT, you might find the book *Engage!: Transforming Healthcare through Digital Patient Engagement* a helpful resource. Details are provided in the References section at the end of this chapter.

Analyze

The vast amount of data being collected in all types of electronic systems used in and around healthcare create a huge opportunity to analyze those data to improve healthcare delivery and patient outcomes. From population health to reducing hospital-acquired infections, data can be utilized to transform healthcare. Of course, data need to be turned into actionable information through the intelligent application of critical thinking and analytics tools. As with most other topics in this book, big data, business intelligence, and data analytics are fields of study on their own.

Big Data, Business Intelligence, Data Analytics

It seems you can't read a healthcare blog, newsletter, website, or journal these days without coming across *big data*. However, data are just data unless they inform. Data need to become actionable intelligence. In this section, we'll discuss big data, business intelligence, and data analytics briefly then turn our attention to how these data are being used to innovate, transforming care delivery.

Since these terms are tossed about a lot these days, let's start by defining each. *Big data* has been defined in many different ways and there is no single, definitive definition. However, it's generally accepted to mean very large sets of data whose size presents challenges in the manipulation and management of those data. Wikipedia's definition is often referred to in online articles and it defines big data this way:

> *Big data* is a term for data sets that are so large or complex that traditional data processing applications are inadequate. Challenges include analysis, capture, data curation, search, sharing, storage, transfer, visualization, querying, updating and information privacy. (Wikipedia, *n.d.*)

Business intelligence (BI) is the practice of using the data to deliver intelligent, actionable information to the organization. Gartner, Inc. defines business intelligence as follows: "*Business intelligence (BI)* is an umbrella term that includes the applications, infrastructure and tools, and best practices that enable access to and analysis of information to improve and optimize decisions and performance" (Gartner, 2016, QR10.6). Typically, business intelligence provides dashboards and high-level views of data from a historical perspective.

In contrast, the term *data analytics* (DA) is often used to describe predictive data rather than historical data. Of course, more broadly, data analytics is defined as manipulating data to provide actionable intelligence. According to a recent article in Healthcare IT News,

> Hospital analytics teams are on the verge of a formidable challenge: evolving their skillsets as fast as data is growing and relevant technologies are coming into play.
>
> "The skills your team is going to need in three years are not the skills they have today," said John Showalter, MD, chief healthcare information officer at the University of Mississippi Medical Center. "They're going to need to be trained."
>
> And that training is going to be complex because there are only a few people who can really master analytics well, according to Sriram Vishwanath, a professor of engineering and computer science at the University of Texas, Austin, even if many claim they can. (Sullivan, 2016, QR10.21)

Analytics and manipulating big data to create actionable intelligence, not only predictive data that can help in managing population health but historical data that can help drive business strategy, is a complex set of skills that many healthcare organizations are struggling to define and acquire. In some cases, reporting teams are being relabeled as business intelligence teams, simply putting a new title on an old function. Reporting and business intelligence are certainly tightly interconnected, but they are not the same thing. Reporting teams will need to hire or train to develop the business intelligence capability.

Use of Big Data

A paper entitled "Health Big Data Recommendations" published in August 2015 by The Privacy and Security Workgroup (PSWG) of the Health Information Technology Policy Committee (HITPC) stated

> The collection, analysis, and use of large volumes of electronic information will be a driver in the U.S. economy for the foreseeable future. Through the proliferation of software applications and mobile devices, the amount of health-related information is growing exponentially...

> Many see the application of big data analytics in healthcare as an opportunity to improve the health of both individuals and their communities. These benefits include safer treatments, the ability to target communities and individuals with tailored interventions, and the ability to respond to the spread of diseases more rapidly. (Privacy and Security Workgroup, p. 3, QR10.18)

This aptly sums up the current environment with respect to the collection and use of patient data. While the report is specifically concerned with security and privacy of the data, it also points to potentially groundbreaking use of the data to improve population and patient health. Specifically, it references the Federal Trade Commission Internet of Things Report and Big Data Workshop, the Precision Medicine Initiative, 21st Century Cures, the Federal Health IT Strategic Plan and the Shared Nationwide Interoperability Roadmap, Patient-Centered Outcomes Research, and the Secretary's Advisory Committee on Humane Research Protections. Clearly, big data have captured everyone's attention. The topics in the preceding list certainly run the gamut and exemplify the depth and breadth of the discussion on big data today.

Though the U.S. government is certainly deeply involved in this conversation, many healthcare organizations are attempting to utilize their own data to improve care for their target populations and patients.

Building Business Intelligence Capabilities

As noted by Sriram Vishwanath of the University of Texas in Austin, Texas, the skills needed to successfully create a business intelligence or data analytics function are relatively high-end skills that are not widely available. Many healthcare organizations work through their quality department's analysts to define data needs and have IT analysts develop the data sets for their use. Although just about every healthcare organization is engaged in analyzing data in some respect, most are at the very beginning stages or the low end of implementation. This is due, in part, to the specialized skills needed to effectively drive business intelligence and analytics. The takeaway is that unless you work in a large, well-funded healthcare organization or one that is dedicated to data and research, you may find it challenging to make real progress with BI. Of course, as with any quickly evolving field, there are a growing number of vendors in this space providing BI and DA consulting services to assist healthcare organizations.

If this is your area of responsibility as a healthcare IT leader and you do not have an educational or experiential background in this field, you would do well to start with getting educated about this topic and then finding resources to assist. As John Showalter, MD stated, the skills your team has today are not the skills you'll need in three years. You can develop a plan for your organization for addressing the skills gap you face. That may involve hiring, training, and outsourcing in some combination so that you can meet the growing demand in this area. An excellent starter resource on building a business intelligence capability in your healthcare organization is a book edited by Cynthia McKinney, Ray Hess, and Michael Whitecar entitled *Implementing Business Intelligence in Your Healthcare Organization*; details are included in the References section at the end of the chapter.

Population Health Management

One of the common targets of big data is population health management, which is defined as improving the outcomes of groups of the entire population. Clearly, when looking at data in order to predict healthcare needs and trends, large data sets have to be analyzed and acted upon. According to Gregg Malkary, managing director of the Spyglass Consulting Group,

> The majority of health institutions have population health initiatives, with many focusing on ways to support chronic health patients recently released from the hospital, Malkary says. With the transition into pay-for-performance care, institutions are recognizing the need to reduce readmissions and increase patient engagement. (Davis, 2015, QR10.5)

This is a large and rapidly evolving field that will continue to demand skills, expertise, and focus from healthcare IT departments in the near and long term.

Innovate

Big data, of course, are one of the sources or inputs for innovation. When an organization has data that suggest a direct relationship between Action A and Action B, it can take steps to influence or change the outcome. For example, on the clinical side, data suggest a direct correlation between the length of time a central line is in a patient and likelihood of infection. Those data for an organization might show, for example, that removing the central line eight hours earlier reduces infection rates by 63%. That's the kind of data that drives incremental change, which is much needed. However, suppose a someone found a new way that showed promise of eliminating central line infections altogether? That would potentially change the dynamics from incremental to exponential improvement. That's the objective in healthcare right now, and everyone is seeking new ways to innovate in order to transform and improve care.

Innovation Leaders

We've discussed big data as part of innovation, but what else are organizations doing to lead the way in innovation? Healthcare organizations that undertake innovation and transformation deliver better healthcare. It's not about innovation for the sake of being different or even for a competitive advantage in the marketplace, per se. It's about driving a result that is exponentially better for patient outcomes and patient care, from which comes success and competitive advantage.

This list of innovators is long and growing, so hopefully if you work for an innovative organization that is not listed here, you won't take offense. Several of the organizations that often top any list of innovation are Mayo Clinic, Cleveland Clinic, University of Pittsburgh Medical Center, Boston Children's Hospital, Brigham and Women's Hospital, and Intermountain Healthcare. As we discussed in Chapter 2, organizations like these seem to create the future—in part because they spend time and resources looking at current needs and future trends to determine the most strategic, value-added path forward. And though it does take time and resources to do so, it begins with a mindset. In addition to these industry leaders, we've highlighted a few called out in a January 2016 article on innovation. We've divided it into two main types: healthcare-business partnership and internal innovation. If you want to read the full list, see the listing in the References section (Becker's Hospital Review, 2016, QR10.2).

Healthcare–Business Partnerships

Many organizations are partnering with technology startups or private sector businesses to develop new solutions for healthcare that run the gamut from patient-centric to technology-focused innovation and everything in between.

At Baystate Health in Springfield, Massachusetts, CIO Joel Vengco helped develop a technology innovation partnership that fostered collaboration between technology startups and healthcare. The goal was to accelerate adoption of new technologies. At Children's Hospital of Los Angeles, a consortium was created to accelerate technology advances focused on pediatric care. Cleveland Clinic has been working on innovation since 2000 and has worked with over 70 companies to bring innovative products to market. Detroit Medical Center's Children's Hospital of Michigan has been responsible for driving significant innovation in pediatric medicine in Michigan. Ochsner Health System in New Orleans, Louisiana, launched a technology and innovation accelerator in 2015 to foster closer relationships among technology developers, innovators, and clinicians to improve patient-centered care. Last, but by no means least, is the University of Pittsburgh Medical Center's innovation center headed by the respected healthcare thought leader, Dr. Rasu Shrestha, Chief Innovation Officer at UPMC. Through their Technology Development Center (TDC), formed more than 18 years ago, UPMC, Dr. Strestha, and his team are working on innovations with vendors including GE Healthcare, Nuance, Microsoft, and Optum.

Internal Initiatives

In addition to business partnerships and technology accelerator programs, there is also tremendous focus on internal initiatives to foster innovation and transformation, including those listed here.

Brigham and Women's in Boston launched a program in 2013 with the purpose of inspiring clinicians, scientists, and employees to assist in taking ideas through the development process to production. The organization also hosts hackathons, codeathons, and idea labs. The Henry Ford Health System, based in Detroit, Michigan, established an innovation institute in 2011. Among other accomplishments, it designed a new "Model G" gown for patients that prioritized comfort and privacy for the patient while still providing the needed clinical functions. Huntington Memorial Hospital, located in Pasadena, California, opened the Institute for Nursing Excellence and Innovation as a way to not only train and educate nurses, but to drive clinical innovation and advances in nursing practice as well. The Presbyterian Rust Medical Center located in Rio Rancho, New Mexico, just outside of Albuquerque, developed an Innovation Lab to bring healthcare workers and consumers together to develop better care approaches with the goal of improving patient outcomes. Finally, Riverside Methodist in Columbus, Ohio, uses human patient simulators along with medical education technology to simulate the patient experience throughout a variety of clinical settings with the objective of improving training of clinical staff and thereby improving the patient experience.

As you can see, there are many organizations who have initiatives underway to develop innovative approaches to patient care and to transform healthcare. As you'll read just a bit later in this chapter, one of the key success factors in developing a center for innovation is vision and leadership. Though time, money, and staff are also key to success, a lot can be done with limited resources, as evidenced by some of the organizations mentioned here. As a healthcare IT leader, you can develop an innovative approach and mindset without having a large team or a special budget. Learning about what other organizations and your peers are doing can be a great jumping off point for technology innovation.

Getting Started

In an article by Zuckerman in Becker's Hospital Review, in 2012, author Alan Zuckerman presented five steps an organization can take to position itself to begin innovating (Zuckerman, 2012, QR10.26).

1. *Rally senior leaders.* Beyond the case for change, clarify the importance of individual and organizational innovation as a critical element of success in the future.
2. *Reexamine and begin to modify your organization's culture to be more risk-bearing.* Recognize and reward innovation, encourage experiments and pilots, and create a nonpunitive environment.
3. *Make innovation a theme of day-to-day operations.* Building on #2, support, highlight, emphasize, and celebrate innovation in daily operations.
4. *Consider structural changes to support innovation.* For large organizations, a chief innovation officer would be a symbolic and substantive commitment to progress; for any organization, an ad hoc committee or subcommittee of a board or senior management group could be charged with keeping innovation visible and moving forward.
5. *Start now.* Don't study and discuss innovation *ad infinitum*; accelerate implementation of small- (and larger-) scale innovations and demand that all senior leaders visibly support such changes.

Since this article was published in 2012, there has been an increasing emphasis on innovation in healthcare. The Healthcare Information and Management Systems Society (HIMSS) launched an innovation initiative, HX360, at HIMSS15 as a joint partnership with HIMSS and AVIA. At HIMSS16, the focus was on addressing four key challenges facing healthcare providers: (1) patient as a consumer, (2) chronic care/behavioral health, (3) long-term/post-acute care, and (4) operations 2.0. The exhibits featured technology startup companies as well as exhibits showing the innovative application (or integration) of healthcare technology.

One Last Note on Innovation

One of the last places you might be looking in for healthcare innovation is from some of your IT teams, but that would be a mistake. Many of your teams interact with your customers on a daily basis. Think of your Service Desk staff, who talk with customers 24/7. Think of your applications team analysts who work with customers daily or weekly. Think of your network team who interacts with customers periodically or your Telcom team who works directly with customers. All of these teams work directly with customers, so they are in an ideal position to spot opportunities to innovate. They know what their customers' pain points are, they know what works and what doesn't. If you foster an attitude of innovation, you may begin to see staff pointing out opportunities to make their customers' work easier, faster, or more efficient. IT leaders certainly understand the value of these customer interactions and see them as the potential source for innovation and inspiration.

Transform

There's a lot of talk about *transforming* healthcare these days, so let's begin by defining what that means. Of course, to *transform* is to change something in composition, structure, or condition, usually for the better. So, *transforming healthcare* is a phrase used to indicate that we need to make substantial, positive changes to the composition, structure, or condition of healthcare delivery.

So, what's the difference between innovation and transformation? Innovation is doing something new or in a new way. Transformation is often created by changing beliefs and behaviors, by approaching a problem or situation from a fundamentally different point of view. Transformation involves changing organizational culture (behaviors and beliefs). It requires transformative leadership. And yes, it often involves technology as well.

A look at some recent headlines will make this really clear.

- *Cedars Sinai launches virtual reality pilots to curb patient pain without drugs* (Monegain, "Cedars," 2016, QR10.13).
- *Intermountain surgeons save patient's kidney with 3D printing during dicey operation* (Monegain, "Intermountain," 2016, QR10.15).
- *Cornell to develop FeverPhone with $2.3 million from NIH* (Monegain, "Cornell," 2016, QR10.14).

These are projects that have the potential to transform the way healthcare is delivered. These almost sound like plots for new science fiction movies. They're not hoping to make an incremental improvement; they're striving to radically transform the field. These are incredibly exciting developments and they all involve technology. Clearly this rate of transformation will accelerate as technology continues to advance.

You might be thinking that is all well and good, but your IT department is swamped, your organization's leadership or direction seems to be shifting, and you're not sure how this even applies to you. Transformation is as much a mindset as an activity. If you begin there, you can certainly apply much of this information to your department and your role.

Every organization has its focus and its constraints; innovation and transformation may be topics you only read about or participate in at professional conferences. That's OK. Every great innovation started with an idea. You may not work in an organization that is ready, able, or willing to experiment with new technology, but that doesn't mean you can't stay informed and think about the possibilities. Learning about what others are doing may just spark creative ideas that you can incorporate in your own organization.

Summary

The future of healthcare IT promises to be dynamic. Deploying EMRs took a massive portion of organization's time and IT resources for the past decade or so. As we emerge from that phase, we look to the future to see how IT can contribute to improving patient outcomes and delivering better care. Through optimizing EMR and related applications, we can improve safety, reduce complexity, and hopefully make EMRs the efficient, care-enabling tools they were intended to be. Through a variety of technologies, healthcare organizations are reaching out to engage with and educate patients to improve the health of entire populations. Through innovation and transformation, we all strive to find better, faster, more effective, and less expensive ways to provide exceptional patient care. This is why we are healthcare IT leaders—because we know that what we do matters.

In this final chapter of the book, we looked toward the future to understand the trends and topics that are facing healthcare IT leaders. Using the skills, traits, and behaviors discussed throughout this book, you should be well equipped to take on these challenges. While we've continually described best practices and the ideal state, there is no single person or team or organization that does everything right all the time. Each of us will hopefully get it right more often than we get it wrong. Each of us will continue to be challenged and tested and honed through these dynamic times. Each of us can strive to become the best healthcare IT leaders we can and thereby truly make a difference as IT leaders of tomorrow.

References

For more on this topic, visit http://susansnedaker.com/leading-hit.

QR10.1

Association for Executives in Healthcare Information Security (AEHIS), http://aehis.org.
Association for Executives in Healthcare Information Applications (AEHIA), http://aehia.org.
Association for Executives in Healthcare Information Technology (AEHIT), http://aehit.org.

Becker's Hospital Review, "40 hospitals with innovation centers," January 29, 2016. http://www.beckershospitalreview.com/healthcare-information-technology/40-hospitals-with-innovation-centers.html.

QR10.2

Bell, James, III and Jon Mertz, "Hashtags and Health Literacy: How Social Media Transforms Engagement," February 24, 2015. http://www.himss.org/hashtags-and-health-literacy-how-social-media-transforms-engagement.

QR10.3

Belliveau, Jacqueline, "How a Proactive Approach Improves Healthcare Cybersecurity," June 6, 2016. http://healthitsecurity.com/news/how-a-proactive-approach-improves-healthcare-cybersecurity.

QR10.4

Bergeron, Bryan, ed., *Developing a Data Warehouse for the Healthcare Enterprise: Lessons from the Trenches*, 2nd Ed. Chicago: HIMSS, 2013.
College for Healthcare Information Management Executives (CHIME), https://chimecentral.org/.

Davis, Jessica, "Big data 'long way' from being harnessed for population health," November 18, 2015. http://www.healthcareitnews.com/news/big-data-long-way-being-harnessed, viewed June 20, 2016.

QR10.5

Dodd, John C., *Healthcare IT Transformation: Bridging Innovation, Integration, Interoperability, and Analytics*. Boca Raton, FL: CRC Press, 2016.

Garets, David and Claire McCarthy Garets, eds., *The Journey Never Ends: Technology's Role in Helping Perfect Health Care Outcomes*. Boca Raton, FL: CRC Press, 2016.

Gartner, Inc., http://www.gartner.com/it-glossary/business-intelligence-bi/, viewed June 16, 2016.

QR10.6

Graber, Mark L., Robert Bailey, and Doug Johnston, "Goals and Priorities for Health Care Organizations to Improve Safety Using Health IT," U.S. Department of Health and Human Services Office of the National Coordinator for Health Information Technology, May 2016. https://www.healthit.gov/sites/default/files/task_9_report.pdf, viewed June 30, 2016.

QR10.7

Health IT Analytics, http://healthitanalytics.com/.

QR10.8

Health IT Interoperability, http://healthitinteroperability.com/.

QR10.9

Healthcare Information and Management Systems Society (HIMSS), http://www.himss.org.

Healthcare Information and Management Systems Society, "What Is Patient Engagement?" Continually updated. http://www.himss.org/library/patient-engagement-toolkit, viewed July 1, 2016.

QR10.10

Institute for Health Technology Transformation (iHIT2), http://ihealthtran.com/.
Krohn, Rick and David Metcalf, eds., *mHealth: From Smartphones to Smart Systems*. Chicago: HIMSS, 2012.

Lee, Kristin, "MGH physician weighs in on avoiding EHR errors," TechTarget, May 2016. http://searchhealthit.techtarget.com/tip/MGH-physician-weighs-in-on-avoiding-EHR-errors, viewed July 1, 2016.

QR10.11

Makary, Martin and Michael Daniel, "Medical error—The third leading cause of death in the US," *BMJ* 2016; 353 doi: http://www.bmj.com/content/353/bmj.i2139 (Published May 3, 2016).

QR10.12

McKinney, Cynthia, Ray Hess, and Michael Whitecar, eds. *Implementing Business Intelligence in Your Healthcare Organization*. Chicago: HIMSS, 2012.

Monegain, Bernie, "Cedars Sinai launches virtual reality pilots to curb patient pain without drugs" June 27, 2016, http://www.healthcareitnews.com/news/cedars-sinai-launches -virtual-reality-pilots-curb-patient-pain-without-drugs, viewed July 1, 2016.

QR10.13

Monegain, Bernie, "Cornell to develop FeverPhone with $2.3 million from NIH," June 24, 2016, http://www.healthcareitnews.com/news/cornell-develop-feverphone-23-million-nih.

QR10.14

Monegain, Bernie, "Intermountain surgeons save patient's kidney with 3D printing during dicey operation," June 24, 2016, http://www.healthcareitnews.com/news/intermountain -surgeons-save-patients-kidney-3d-printing-during-dicey-operation, viewed July 1, 2016.

QR10.15

Office of the National Coordinator of Health Information Technology, "Health Information Technology Patient Safety Action & Surveillance Plan." Washington, DC: The Office of the National Coordinator, July 2, 2013. https://www.healthit.gov/sites/default/files /safety_plan_master.pdf, viewed June 28, 2016.

QR10.16

Office of the National Coordinator of Health Information Technology, "Nationwide Interoperability Roadmap." Washington, DC: The Office of the National Coordinator, *n.d.* https://www.healthit.gov/sites/default/files/shared_nationwide_interoperability_road map.pdf.

QR10.17

Oldenburg, Jan, Dave Chase, Kate T. Christensen, and Brad Tritle, *Engage!: Transforming Healthcare Through Digital Patient Engagement*. Chicago: HIMSS, 2013.

Privacy and Security Workgroup (PSWG) of the Health Information Technology Policy Committee (HITPC), *Health Big Data Recommendations: HITPC Privacy and Security Workshop*, Washington, DC: Privacy and Security Workgroup, August 2015. https:// www.healthit.gov/sites/faca/files/HITPC_Health_Big_Data_Report_FINAL.pdf, viewed July 1, 2016.

QR10.18

Snell, Elizabeth, "Most Healthcare Data Breaches from Unauthorized Access," HealthITSecurity, June 1, 2016. http://healthitsecurity.com/news/most-2016-healthcare -data-breaches-from-unauthorized-access, viewed June 30, 2016.

QR10.19

Snell, Elizabeth, "Preparing Against Current Healthcare Cybersecurity Threats," HealthITSecurity, June 16, 2016. http://healthitsecurity.com/news/preparing-against -current-healthcare-cybersecurity-threats, viewed June 27, 2016.

QR10.20

Sullivan, Tom, "Data scientists, execs share advice for assembling a big data analytics team," June 16, 2016. http://www.healthcareitnews.com/news/data-scientists-execs-share -advice-assembling-big-data-analytics-team, viewed July 1, 2016.

QR10.21

Symplur, "Healthcare Hashtags." Continually updated. http://www.symplur.com/healthcare -hashtags/.

QR10.22

The Joint Commission, "Sentinel Event Alert 54: Safe use of health information technology," March 31, 2015, https://www.jointcommission.org/sea_issue_54/, viewed June 29, 2016.

QR10.23

U.S. Department of Health and Human Services, Agency for Healthcare Research and Quality, "Transforming Healthcare Quality through Health IT," Washington, DC: Agency for Healthcare Research and Quality, Continually updated. https://healthit .ahrq.gov/ahrq-funded-projects/transforming-healthcare-quality-through-health-it, viewed July 1, 2016.

QR10.24

Van Alstin and Chad Michael, "Welcome to the Innovation Suite," Health Management Technology, June 2016, Vol. 37, No. 4, pp. 8–11. Also online http://www.healthmgt tech.com/welcome-innovation-suite, viewed July 2, 2016.

QR10.25

Wikipedia, https://en.wikipedia.org/wiki/Big_data, viewed July 2, 2016.

Zuckerman, Alan M., "Innovation in Healthcare Leadership: The Time Is Now," July 20, 2012. http://www.beckershospitalreview.com/hospital-management-administration/innovation -in-healthcare-leadership-the-time-is-now.html, viewed July 1, 2016.

QR10.26

Index

Page numbers followed by f and t indicate figures and tables, respectively.